THE RULE OF RULES

Larry Alexander and Emily Sherwin

THE RULE OF RULES

Morality, Rules, and the Dilemmas of Law

DUKE UNIVERSITY PRESS
DURHAM AND LONDON
2001

Printed in the United States
of America on acid-free paper ♾
Designed by Rebecca Giménez
Typeset in Monotype Garamond
by Tseng Information Systems
Library of Congress Cataloging-
in-Publication Data appear on the
last printed page of this book.

CONTENTS

ACKNOWLEDGMENTS

This book owes far too much to far too many people for us to acknowledge and thank them adequately. Several chapters benefited from having been presented in at least nascent form at workshops and colloquia. Parts of chapters 1, 2, and 4 were presented at the Symposium on Formalism Revisited held at the University of Chicago Law School. Chapter 4 was presented in some form at the Conference on Legal Reasoning and the Work of Frederick Schauer held at Quinnipiac College of Law, at the Columbia University Legal Theory Workshop, at the Cornell Law School Faculty Workshop, and at the fourth annual Analytic Legal Philosophy Conference in Philadelphia. Chapter 5 was presented at the Conference on Legal Interpretation, Judicial Power, and Democracy in Melbourne, Australia. Chapter 6 was presented at the Faculty Colloquium at the University of Pennsylvania Law School, and at the Conference on Law and Logic at Notre Dame Law School. And chapter 8 was presented at the University of California at Berkeley Legal Theory Workshop.

In addition to the helpful comments and criticisms we received from those attending these presentations, we received ongoing counsel from several people whom we wish to thank by name: our colleagues at the University of San Diego Heidi Hurd, Michael Moore, and Maimon Schwarzschild, and our colleagues in the profession Kevin Clermont, Kent Greenawalt, Leo Katz, Ken Kress (who coauthored a predecessor to chapter 8), and Fred Schauer. And we received beneficial advice and encouragement from numerous other colleagues at U.S.D. and from our dean, Dan Rodriguez. Finally, Roanne Shamsky and Pat Gillis contributed their excellent stenographic assistance.

We dedicate this book to Elaine Alexander, Larry's wife, and to Thomas and Lillian Sherwin, Emily's parents.

INTRODUCTION

In this book we hope to throw some light on many of the jurisprudential debates over the nature of law, legal systems, and legal institutions. Our approach to these matters will not be a direct one, however. We shall offer neither a semantic account of law nor an analysis of the "concept" of law. Rather, the prism through which we wish to refract standard jurisprudential issues is that of authoritative posited rules—rules that are humanly created to settle controversies and questions about what one ought to do.

Our jurisprudential strategy is simple. The key to understanding what is at stake in various jurisprudential controversies is to understand the reasons for authoritative rules, the form those rules must take to serve their purposes, and the moral and practical dilemmas rules create. An understanding of rules will show where legal positivism is correct and also where natural law theory is correct. It will clarify the nature and dilemmas of constitutionalism, the debates over legal interpretation, and the paradox of practical authority. It will provide the means for evaluating claims about the nature of legal reasoning—claims about legal principles, analogical reasoning, and precedent-following—as well as claims about the determinacy and objectivity of legal reasoning. And it will expose the limitations of any answers to questions about how to individuate and identify particular legal systems and about whether a legal system is continuous with or represents a radical break from a prior legal system.

The plan of this book is as follows. Part I—"The Circumstances of Law"—consists of the first three chapters, which set forth the predicament to which authoritative rules are a response, the form those rules must take to deal with that predicament, and the hierarchical structure of a system of authoritative rules.

In chapter 1, we introduce what we term the circumstances of law: there is disagreement and uncertainty regarding what is to be done, and it is realized that the costs of failing to settle this disagreement and uncertainty authoritatively are greater than the costs of settling it erroneously in particular cases. The costs of unresolved disagreement and uncertainty are lack of coordination, inefficient decision-making, and lack of expertise (moral error). "Authoritatively" here means that the settlement supplants the presettlement reasons as the reason for acting in the way the settlement dictates.

The first step might be acceptance by the community of the rule "Let Lex decide." When Lex decides "Drive fifty-five," we now have two rules. The first, based on our acceptance, is "Let Lex decide." The second, posited by Lex, is "Drive fifty-five."

In a close-knit primitive community, this method of settling what ought to be done might be workable up to a point. But there are problems: Lex may die or become incapacitated. Or Lex may be distant from the location where the decision must be made and thus unavailable for consultation within the necessary time frame.

It is therefore necessary that the community have general rules regarding who authoritatively settles matters requiring settlement, general rules of conduct that settle what is to be done when Lex cannot be consulted, and (perhaps) rules for interpreting Lex's rules when there is uncertainty or disagreement over their meaning. Together, these rules perform a function that is essential to a successful community: the function of *moral settlement.*

We should clarify immediately that, although we refer to the function of rules as one of *moral* settlement and describe the costs and benefits of rule-making as *moral* costs, we do not assume or rely on any particular theory of morality. We find it unnecessary to adopt a position on the content of morality because we believe that the observations we make about the nature, role, and importance of rules are pertinent to all or nearly all moral theories. Within a moral theory that treats welfare as a moral concern, the costs that rule-making seeks to avert will always be moral costs. Within a deontological theory in which welfare is not always a moral concern, Lex may sometimes be establishing rules in those domains in which welfare *is* a moral concern, in which case the costs averted will again be of moral concern. When, however, Lex's task is to settle doubts about the meaning of deontological constraints, or how best to comply with those constraints, the costs averted will either be cashed out in terms of mistaken transgressions of deontological rights—clearly moral costs[1]—or in terms of welfare sacrifices necessary to reduce the number of mistaken transgressions of deontological rights. These latter welfare sacrifices are, we believe, also properly deemed moral costs, given that we doubt that any deontologist would argue for welfare sacrifices sufficient to reduce mistaken transgressions to zero. If that is correct, then mistaken transgressions of deontological rights and welfare are morally comparable and tradeable at some rate.

We conclude chapter 1 by comparing and contrasting our account of the circumstances of law with the account given by H. L. A. Hart in *The Concept of Law*.[2]

In chapter 2, we discuss what rules must be like to settle disagreements and uncertainties over what is to be done. The central requirement is that rules be opaque to the moral considerations that they are to make determinate. In other words, to settle moral disputes, rules must not require recourse to disputed moral notions. The rules do their moral work (of settling what morality requires) by supplanting the unsettled moral considerations with more determinate ones. A rule can determine what ought to be done partially or fully, depending upon how many of the moral disputes covered by the rule it settles.

Now if some moral notions are quite determinate within the community, rules can refer to these and still do their work of moral settlement. Likewise, if some facts are indeterminate—uncertain or controversial—the rules will fail to do their moral work if they refer to such facts. In general, however, rules do their moral work by supplanting moral considerations with factual ones.

We then discuss the bluntness of rules, their over- and underinclusiveness. Because moral principles can never be perfectly captured in application by the general categories of facts that rules pick out, general rules that perform their settlement function will always be morally imperfect in application.

In chapter 3, we devote our attention to issues raised in chapter 1 with respect to the simple rule for settling what ought to be done, "Let Lex decide." Given problems of succession, distance in time and space, changes of circumstances, and disagreements about what rules require, the community will eventually end up with rules designating rule-promulgators (legislators) and rules regarding adjudication and interpretation. These rules will be hierarchically superior to rules promulgated by lawmakers and will thus be "constitutional." Of course, these "constitutional" rules may set up hierarchies of lawmakers, such that those who are superior can promulgate rules (a "constitution") that authoritatively settle what rules the inferior lawmakers may promulgate. The key here is to focus on what the settlement function of rules implies for hierarchies of rules and rule-makers, including what it implies for judicial finality. This chapter will also include discussions of "preconstitutional rules," constitutional change, law and efficacy, revolution and occupation, and multiple legal systems within a territory.

Part II—"Acting under Rules"—consists of chapters 4 and 5. In chapter 4, we elaborate and confront the paradox of rules. This is perhaps the most important chapter, for it asks at the deepest level whether and under what conditions the settlement function is possible. Rules are to settle what ought to be done by supplanting moral considerations. When a rule's prescription diverges from background requirements—as it almost certainly will in some cases—it is neither rational nor morally right for rule-subjects to act as the rule requires. Hence the paradox: it is right to issue authoritative rules but sometimes wrong to follow them.

Various strategies for closing this moral "gap" are unavailing. Reasoning in a way that takes account of the value of rules—"rule-sensitive particularism"—will not solve the problem; nor will a strategy of "presumptive positivism," in which rules are given enhanced but not conclusive weight in deciding what to do. Consent or commitment to follow rules will not eliminate the paradox because consenting or committing to do what is morally wrong cannot create a countervailing moral reason for action.

A more promising strategy is to reject the "reflection" or "correspondence" principle, which requires that only wrongdoers or the culpable be punished. Sometimes a person's act is morally correct only if he is punished for it. More frequently, a person's act is nonculpable even if wrong. Rejecting the correspondence principle would alleviate these problems, but it is an unstable strategy for moral and psychological reasons. Just as rule-subjects cannot rightly follow rules in every case, so too judges cannot rightly punish all those who violate rules.

Another problematic strategy to avoid the paradox of rules is to jettison the publicity principle, which tests the moral bona fides of a course of action by whether it can be publicized to all affected without being undermined, in favor of an esoteric morality that condones misrepresenting to others the moral force of justified rules. In effect, rules claim implicitly that following them is morally justified. To the extent that their prescriptions diverge from background moral requirements in particular cases, the rules are making a claim that is not true. This raises a number of difficult questions. Are rules and their promulgators justifiably deceptive? Are we in the situation of Gregory Kavka's would-be toxin drinker, who is promised a million dollars if he intends tonight to drink a vile but harmless drink tomorrow, after he has received the money, or Kavka's nuclear deterrer, who must truly intend to launch nuclear retaliation should his country be attacked? That is to say, is it only by rationally and morally blinding ourselves to the irrationality and immorality of following authoritative rules when they conflict with morality that we can attain their moral benefits?[3]

In the final section of chapter 4, we shall discuss the implications of consequentialism versus deontology for this paradox about rules, both with respect to punishing the justified generally, and with respect to punishing the justified where the rule violated defines the boundary of a domain of deontologically justified rights.

In chapter 5, we take up disputes over interpretation, such as speaker's meaning versus utterance meaning, the Wittgenstein/Kripke puzzle of rule-following,[4] the indeterminacy critique, and so forth. Again, the focus is on the settlement function of rules, and the question will be, what does this function imply regarding these issues of interpretation, and vice versa? Can we know what has been settled, and how? And do the moral concerns that give rise to the need for authoritative rules—coordination, expertise, and efficient decision-making—point in the same or in different directions for purposes of rule interpretation?

Part III—"Issues of Legal Reasoning"—consists of three chapters. In chapter 6, we explain why analogical reasoning would likely have no role in the settlement function. In cases settled by rules, reasoning would be deductive, not analogical. In cases not covered by rules, analogical reasoning would either track moral reasoning or be indeterminate. Most accounts of analogical reasoning therefore either posit nonrational decision-making or else introduce a new norm type, the analogy-warranting rule (shown in chapter 8 to be exemplified by Ronald Dworkin's notion of a "legal principle"). We argue that such a norm, building on past mistaken decisions, will be morally unattractive and indeterminate. We conclude the chapter by offering a tentative and much more limited defense of analogical reasoning in settling controversies.

In chapter 7, we discuss the nature and role of precedent given the settlement function. A system of rules can perform the settlement function without a doctrine of following precedent. But if it has such a doctrine, what must the doctrine look like in terms of the scope of precedential constraint and the strength of precedential constraint? We argue that with respect to the first question, that of scope, precedential constraint must be a function of rules promulgated by the precedent court legislating with respect to future cases. We discuss both the difficulties of such a view and the impossibility of other views of precedential constraint.

With respect to the second question, the strength of precedential constraint, we raise the general issue of whether there can be constraint greater than none but less than absolute, and, if so, how the strength of the constraint could be formulated to settle *that* issue. We also raise the general issue of in what sense rules designed to settle issues must be entrenched against repeal whenever the lawmaker believes the rule can be perfected. At what point does changing the rules become tantamount to ignoring them, and can there be rules (as opposed to moral principles) that can regulate changing the rules?

Chapter 8 deals with reasoning to and from so-called legal principles. We explicate Ronald Dworkin's account of legal principles and show how Dworkin's legal principles undergird analogical reasoning within the result model of precedent. We attempt to demonstrate why Dworkinian legal principles are morally unattractive and neither should nor even can play a role in legal reasoning. Invoking legal principles may be a response to the paradox of rules and an attempt to find a middle way between the demands of posited rules and the background moral principles the rules are meant to implement.[5] This strategy for dealing with the paradox, however, incorrectly assumes that norms other than posited rules and moral principles might serve some useful function.

The final two chapters of the book comprise part IV—"The Settlement Function and Jurisprudential Debates." In chapter 9, we argue that the standard framing of the positivism–natural law debate is inapt. The settlement account shows that what we call the natural law question—What ought to be done?—gives rise to the need for rules and surfaces again when the actor faces such rules. What we call the positivist question—What rules have been posited?—is not the same question, and the answer to it cannot contradict the answer to the natural law question. We point out how this way of looking at natural law versus positivism illuminates the symbiotic relation between them identified by Roger Shiner[6] and exposes the error in Dworkin's critique of Hart.[7]

In chapter 10, we deal with some miscellaneous jurisprudential issues that are prominent in other works but not in ours. For example, we explain why coercion is not a central feature of our account of law, which, though it deals with the settlement of moral issues, and thus with when force can be used, by whom, and how much, does not rely on antisocial motives as central to an account of law. We discuss the points of view displayed by officials, by rule-subjects, and by the people in accepting the rules designating officials. And we discuss (at greater length than in chapter 3) pathological states of legal systems, primarily those where there ceases to be agreement on the rules of settlement but certain rules remain efficacious due to the superior force of those who accept them.

We also explain why the issues of the objectivity and determinacy of law receive no prominence in our account. Objectivity and determinacy cannot be dealt with apart from ontology. In our account, there are two ontological ingredients: moral principles and posited rules. We offer no general account of the ontology of the former, nor do we need to beyond assuming that moral principles can be matters of disagreement and uncertainty. We do have an ontology of rules: they are whatever rule-makers have determined ought to be done.

Their objectivity is dealt with in chapter 5. The objectivity of rules in the sense of their having *a* meaning that is generally accessible—determinate—is obviously a major desideratum given the settlement function. We contrast our account of objectivity with that of Coleman and Leiter.[8]

Finally, we turn to the obligation to obey the law. We argue that the dilemma that rules create that we explored in chapter 4 fully explains why the obligation to obey the law has been so controversial. We have an obligation to do what is right, and law is a means to that end. But law is necessarily imperfect.

In the final analysis, we see the predicament to be the following: Human actors wish to be guided by Reason, so that they achieve the Good and do the Right. Because they are imperfect as reasoners, however, Reason itself dictates that they seek the constraints on reasoning provided by algorithms that they prescribe (Will) for themselves. Nevertheless, no algorithm imposed by Will is capable of capturing precisely what Reason would dictate, both because the world is too complex to be captured by algorithms and because any algorithm will undoubtedly be imperfect as an algorithm.

The result is a practical paradox. Reason requires resort to Will, but Will can never capture Reason. The paradox lies at the heart of law. It surfaces not only in the perennial clash of jurisprudential titans, natural law (Reason) and legal positivism (Will), but also in puzzlings over interpretation, precedent, legal reasoning, and many other jurisprudential matters, as well as in controversies about legal doctrine, which are replete with synchronic and diachronic clashes of Reason and Will.

Human imperfections require the imposition of constraints of Will and also ensure that those constraints will be imperfect by Reason's lights. This is the central problem that we shall explore in what follows. We hope to show that focusing on this problem provides one of the most powerful lenses through which to view and comprehend legal phenomena.

PART ONE The Circumstances of Law

ONE Disagreement, Uncertainty, and Authoritative Settlement

Imagine a small community, larger than a kinship group, but sufficiently small and geographically compact that everyone knows everyone else and must deal from time to time with everyone else. Perhaps imagining a community of several hundred people will get us started.

Imagine also that the members of this community have roughly similar views about their moral rights and obligations. At least, their views are fairly similar if we characterize those views at a high level of generality. Thus, they generally agree that innocent lives should not be taken, that property rights should be respected, that promises should ordinarily be kept, that undue risks to others should be avoided, and that everyone should contribute a fair share to support actions necessary for the common good. In other words, they agree about moral rights and duties at the level of abstraction at which *we* tend to agree with one another.

Finally, we ask you to imagine, not that everyone in this community is a saint, but that everyone will honor his moral obligations *as he sees them* almost all the time. In other words, the members of this community are fairly strongly motivated to act morally toward one another.

Now this community as we have described it so far sounds pretty idyllic, and compared to most communities of which we are aware, other than the tribal or the religious, it is. Nonetheless, as favorably situated as this community is in terms of general moral agreement and good will, it lacks something necessary to prevent ruinous discord. It lacks authoritative rules.

Let us explain. We have said that the members of this community generally agree about the content of their moral rights and duties at a high level of abstraction. Yet as the moral questions become more specific—Does a fetus have a moral right not to be aborted? Should one be liable without regard to fault for causing an accident? Should a contractual obligation be extinguished when the purpose of the contract has been frustrated? Should resources be divided so as to reflect differences in welfare? and so on—they begin to disagree.[1]

Moreover, even when they agree about the formulation of moral rights and duties, they may disagree about the facts that govern when and how those moral rights and duties apply. For example, although they may agree that no one should put dangerous pollutants in the water supply, they may disagree over whether a certain pesticide dangerously pollutes the water supply. Or, if they agree that those in irreversible comas should be regarded as "dead," they may disagree over whether a certain physical condition constitutes an irreversible coma.

Now these disagreements about moral rights and duties can produce considerable strife and turmoil, even among people of good will. Indeed, the road to the nasty, brutish, and short lives of the Hobbesian state of nature does not require people motivated solely by selfishness and predatory opportunism. Moral disagreement over concrete courses of conduct, coupled with the motivation to do the right thing, can lead to the Hobbesian state of affairs as expeditiously as naked self-interest.

What our otherwise rather favorably situated community needs to avert these bleak prospects, and what it lacks in the picture we have thus far presented, is a method for resolving these concrete moral disagreements and uncertainties authoritatively. That is, the community lacks the capability for *authoritative settlement.* Authoritative settlement is something of a redundancy. The function of practical authority—authority about what ought to be done—is precisely to settle the question what ought to be done. And to settle that question requires that the answer given be treated as if it is correct by those for whom the answer is supposed to settle the question. Once the question is settled, those who want to know what to do need not deliberate but need only consult the terms of settlement. They no longer need to debate the reasons behind those terms, reasons about which they disagreed, thus necessitating the settlement. Moreover, not only are they no longer required to consult the reasons behind the settlement in determining how to act, they are also required *not* to heed those reasons if, from their perspective, those reasons conflict with the terms of the settlement. Given that the objective is a settlement, its terms must be authoritative, which means that they must supplant the reasons upon which they are based.[2]

Let us illustrate the previous paragraph with an example. Suppose Paul operates a factory that dumps a certain chemical waste product into the river. Paula is a downstream water user who believes that the chemical is a dangerous pollutant and wants Paul to stop the dumping. Paul agrees that he has a moral obligation to Paula not to dump dangerous chemicals in the river, but he denies that the chemical is dangerous. Suppose now there is an authoritative settlement of the question "Is Paul morally obligated not to dump because the chemical is dangerous?," and the answer it gives is that Paul is obligated not to dump. If Paul must decide whether he may continue dumping, he need only consult the terms of the authoritative settlement, which will tell him that he may not. He may continue to believe that the reasons behind the settlement—the dangerousness of the chemical—point to a different result. If the settlement is truly authoritative, however, he will not believe that he may still act on those reasons. The settlement has supplanted them in his decision-making.

Now that we have explained what an authoritative settlement entails, we can also describe the benefits it can bring to our community. Before authoritative settlements, members disagreed or were uncertain about such matters as how fast they should drive, when they were relieved from their contractual obligations, and how much each should contribute toward the support of the community's poor. Even if they did not disagree about morality at an abstract level, concrete disagreements and uncertainties about the more particular shapes of moral principles and about factual matters resulted in the types of disagreements and uncertainties just described. And those disagreements and uncertainties are potentially quite destructive. If Agnes believes one should drive fifty-five miles per hour, and on the left side of the road, but Ben believes one should drive seventy-five and on the right, serious collisions are likely to result. If Alfred believes that Victor is in an irreversible coma and should be taken off life support, so that the resources can be used to help others, but Bertha believes the opposite, Bertha might feel obligated to use force to prevent Alfred from disconnecting Victor. Finally, if Alex mistakenly believes that mercury is not harmful in the water supply, he might be tempted to dump it there and avoid the costs of alternative means of disposal.

Authoritative settlement solves the problems of *coordination, expertise,* and *efficiency.* Coordination problems are those that stem from the existence of moral disagreement. Agnes's opinion on how to drive and Ben's might be equally sound, and yet if their opinions differ, and if they are free to act as they see fit, disaster will follow.[3] Alfred and Bertha's disagreement over the status of Victor leads to a coordination problem because it may lead them into "moral combat."[4]

As we are using the term, a coordination problem is any cost that results from moral disagreement or from uncertainty about how others will resolve questions about what they are morally permitted, required, or forbidden to do. Moral combat is a coordination problem, as are attempts by agents to undertake mutually incompatible actions. So, too, are all the costs of upset expectations and the costs incurred to avoid the costs of upset expectations. These latter costs are frequently referred to under the headings of reliance and predictability (or the lack thereof). We view them as but one genus of the species coordination problem.

Any authoritative settlement can solve coordination problems. Declaring Victor to be in an irreversible coma solves Alfred and Bertha's coordination problem. So, too, does declaring Victor not to be in an irreversible coma. Likewise, declaring the rules of the road to include a fifty-five-mile-per-hour speed limit and driving on the right solves Agnes and Ben's coordination problem—though perhaps no better than a seventy-five-mile-per-hour speed limit and driving on the left. Sometimes the problem is exclusively one of coordination, and all that is needed to solve it is an authoritative settlement, whatever its terms.[5]

Usually, however, there are better and worse ways of settling matters. There is a fact of the matter about whether Victor is in an irreversible coma. There are costs and benefits associated with the choice of a speed limit. In these circumstances, a good solution calls not only for coordination but also for expertise. And in Alex's case of dumping mercury, there is no coordination problem at all. Rather, the problem is solely a problem of expertise, or Alex's lack thereof.

Thus, the second benefit produced by authoritative settlements is a reduction in individual decision-making error through the authoritative decision-maker's greater moral and factual expertise. If there are persons in the community whose moral and factual expertise is greater than that of others, then having them authoritatively settle disagreements and uncertainties about what ought to be done solves both the coordination and expertise problems.[6]

Finally, a third benefit produced by authoritative settlements is a reduction in decision-making costs. Even if members of the community could, through lengthy deliberations, arrive at coordinated and correct decisions, the moral costs in terms of time and other resources of such deliberations might outweigh the moral gains. For example, suppose "Drive seventy-five on the left" is slightly preferable to "Drive fifty-five on the right." And suppose that if Alfred and Bertha deliberate for a long time and consult enough other people, they will both arrive at the conclusion that they should drive seventy-five on the left. Nevertheless, the net cost of their deliberations may exceed the net gain over the rule "Drive fifty-five on the right." Without the rule as an authoritative settlement of how they ought to drive, they will have to deliberate. And because they do not know in advance where deliberation will lead them and what the stakes are, they will keep on deliberating until they reach a decision, even if the costs of deliberation exceed the gains. Once a deliberative cost is sunk, it provides no reason against continuing to deliberate. Only settlement by some means or another keeps us from potentially squandering all our resources on deliberating about what to do, much in the manner of Buridan's ass. In other words, authoritative settlement is *efficient*.[7]

Achieving Authoritative Settlements: The First Steps

We have shown why our imagined community needs authoritative settlements of moral disagreements. Lack of coordination and expertise threaten deterioration into a Hobbesian nightmare despite the members' general similarity of moral views and their willingness to act on moral reasons.[8] But how does authoritative settlement get started? Necessity on its own will not generate solutions.

The requisite first step is for all the members of the community to agree that they need ways of authoritatively settling their moral controversies. The logical next step is for them to designate someone as the authoritative settlor. Suppose, for example, that they all agree that Lex has proven in the past to possess the reasoning ability and the knowledge to resolve moral controversies well. They might then all accept the following rule: "Let Lex decide (authoritatively settle) our moral controversies." And let us suppose further that Lex begins his work by resolving Agnes and Ben's conflict and issuing the following rule: "The speed limit shall be fifty-five miles per hour."

Notice that at this point in our story, we have two rules. The first rule—"Let Lex decide"—exists because the members of the community agree to its terms. That is, its existence is based on its *acceptance* as normative.[9]

The second rule—"Drive fifty-five"—exists because it has been *posited* by someone with authority to settle moral controversies, Lex. The posited rule has authority to settle moral controversies because its promulgator, Lex, does. And he has authority because the society accepts a rule to that effect.

Before we continue down the path toward a more elaborate set of rules and more complications, we wish to comment on a point that might be nagging some readers: if the members of this community are plagued by a predictable degree of moral disagreement, how could they agree that Lex has greater moral expertise than anyone else? In other words, if, in the realm of moral expertise, "it takes one to know one," will not the community's moral disagreements preclude agreement on the rule "Let Lex decide"?

We think that so long as the basic moral intuitions of the members are not wildly disparate, there is a reasonable likelihood that they will be able to agree on relative moral expertise despite their moral disagreements. In other domains one can identify experts through experience without becoming an expert oneself. For example, most people make errors in reasoning about risks.[10] They can, however, be brought to understand their errors by others. They will rightly regard those who consistently demonstrate their errors to them as experts in reasoning about risks. Yet although these experts can bring others to understand their mistakes, such understanding will not make those who were mistaken into experts themselves. Left to their own devices, they will err again, and they realize that. That is why they can identify those who point out their mistakes as experts and yet not be experts themselves. Defects in moral judgment may be more difficult to demonstrate than defects in risk assessment, yet moral expertise will often be recognizable with hindsight.

Moreover, even if members of our hypothetical community regard themselves as equally expert in moral reasoning, they may agree that when they themselves must decide what to do, they are subject to cognitive biases and errors that do not affect them to nearly the same degree when they are deciding in a more disinterested posture what others ought to do. Thus, they might agree that anyone who is in the role of Lex will be more morally expert than those facing decisions about how they should act, if for no other reason than the authority's greater degree of disinterest. (This point also suggests as a corollary that Lex's decisions might not be deemed authoritative regarding matters on which Lex has a certain type of personal stake.)[11]

Achieving Authoritative Settlements: Some Complications

At this point we have a rule based on acceptance designating Lex as the community's moral authority ("Let Lex decide").[12] And we also have a rule, promulgated (posited) by Lex and deriving its authority from Lex's authority, that resolves a particular moral controversy ("Drive fifty-five").

Let us imagine that Lex is capable of moving from moral dispute to moral dispute to moral query, resolving them as they arise. If so, Lex need not resolve general moral questions; he need only resolve the particular dispute or question before him. Thus, Lex can tell Paul that Paul may or may not dump a particular pollutant in a particular river. Lex need not resolve more general potential controversies because he can resolve those general controversies' and questions' particular manifestations. Of course, to resolve particular controversies, Lex will perforce employ general moral and empirical principles. The point is that he need not resolve *authoritatively* any issue broader than the specific controversy he confronts.

Nor will there be problems in interpreting Lex's resolutions. For if the disputants misunderstand Lex's pronouncement on their dispute, Lex can correct them immediately. Of course, at some level Lex must be able to communicate his resolution to them; he could not function as a practical authority if his resolutions of moral controversies and questions were completely opaque to the rest of the society. If he is always on the scene, however, then the chances of failure of communication are minimized; for Lex can fine-tune his formulations whenever he perceives that they are being misunderstood.

These two points—the specificity of Lex's resolutions and his ability to minimize misunderstandings of them—follow from Lex's being at the scene of each moral controversy or question.

It is easy to see why this method of resolving particular moral disputes and queries will not prove satisfactory once a community becomes sufficiently populous or far-flung. Indeed, even in the community we have described, with a few hundred people living in a relatively small area, Lex's resolving moral issues in this way will run into difficulties. Lex may die or become incapacitated. Or he may be distant from the location where the decision must be made and thus unavailable for consultation within the necessary time frame.

With respect to Lex's possible death or incapacity, the community will perceive that it needs a rule to take account of that contingency (indeed, with regard to death, inevitability). So the community might agree to a broader rule than "Let Lex decide," such as "Let Lex or Lex's designated substitute or successor decide." Alternatively, this broader rule might not be agreed upon by the community but might instead be promulgated by Lex. In the first case, the rule's authority derives from social agreement on *its* terms. In the second case, the rule's authority derives from Lex's authority, which in turn derives from social agreement on "Let Lex decide." In both cases, however, the broader rule authoritatively settles the issue of who, in the absence of Lex, may take over Lex's function and authoritatively settle controversies over what ought morally to be done.

With respect to Lex's inability to be present at the scene of each moral controversy, one solution is the promulgation by Lex of rules that are more general than the controversies and questions already resolved and thus anticipate and resolve controversies and questions that have not yet arisen. Indeed, Lex's resolution of Agnes and Ben's speed limit dispute—"Drive fifty-five"—goes far beyond resolution of the specific controversies between Agnes and Ben.

Of course, when Lex promulgates general rules to govern controversies and questions that have not yet arisen, there is a danger that he will not foresee the range of future circumstances very clearly, and that his rules will for that reason prove inapt. We have said that Lex is perceived by the community to be a moral expert, but that does not mean that he is or is perceived to be omniscient. To be realistic, we must assume fallibility, not so much in Lex's motivation, but much more importantly for our purposes, in his knowledge and foresight. Moreover, even if Lex could somehow foresee every dispute that might arise, he could not draft a rule that correctly resolved them all and was at the same time reasonably accessible to actors.[13]

The problem of general rules that have infelicitous applications is, as you will in due course discover, what we regard to be the primary problem of jurisprudence. That problem, though it will be a specter in the background of most of the discussions throughout this book, will be the central focus of chapter 4, and we shall defer further explicit discussion of it until then.

Of course, many of the controversies Lex must settle will be quite specific. Even if Lex has promulgated the rule "Do not dump mercury in the river," Alex may disagree with Sue, who lives downstream, about whether a particular substance he plans to dump *is* mercury. Clarifying the general moral principle that enjoins creating excessive risks by means of rules such as "Do not dump mercury in the river" will go some distance toward resolving moral controversy, but it will not eliminate it if there is controversy over the facts to which such rules apply. So Lex will have to decide factual disputes as well as promulgate general rules. Further, because he cannot be present at the scene of every dispute, he must promulgate general rules for how factual disputes are to be resolved and, in the event these "adjudicatory rules" cannot be applied without conflict, designate other persons as having the authority to resolve factual disputes.

We can see now that despite the extreme simplicity of this hypothetical social situation, the set of authoritative rules required for coordination, expertise, and efficiency will have a certain degree of complexity. Beyond the rule establishing Lex as the authority—a rule based on its social acceptance—there will be rules promulgated by Lex that (1) will range from the general ("Do not dump pollutants") to the more specific ("Do not dump mercury") to the very specific ("Do not dump *this* substance *here now*"), and (2) that will designate other persons as authorities for certain questions (adjudications), or authorities under certain conditions (Lex's unavailability).[14]

Finally, Lex's inability to be present at the scene of every dispute or query about what ought to be done means that Lex will not be able instantaneously to correct misunderstandings of the rules he has promulgated to settle the matters authoritatively. Suppose Agnes or Ben is unclear whether "Drive fifty-five" applies in rainy weather, or refers to kilometers rather than miles, or to aircraft as well as cars. So long as Lex is on the scene, he can clarify these matters. If he is not on the scene, however, then it might be useful to have available some rules for how to interpret Lex's rules.

Of course, there is an obvious problem with rules about interpreting an authority's rules. The former themselves must be interpreted; and if they, too, are promulgated by the authority, a vicious regress looms. A rule promulgated by Lex prescribing how to interpret rules promulgated by Lex cannot be self-interpreting. If *it,* too, requires a rule of interpretation, then Lex's rules will be interpreted by reference to Lex's rules, which will in turn be interpreted by reference to Lex's rules, and so on. Rules for interpreting an authority's rules cannot themselves be promulgated by the authority if they are to be the sole bases for interpretation of the authority's rules, including themselves. In other words, they cannot be both exclusive and self-referential.

An example may be helpful. Suppose one problem in interpreting Lex's rules is the problem of determining the language in which they are expressed. That is, suppose that in our small community, people sometimes speak in English and sometimes speak in Shmenglish, a close but distinct language, and that many sounds and marks are meaningful in both languages but mean different things. If Lex decides to clarify his rules by promulgating as a rule for interpreting them—"Interpret my rules to be in English"—then if *this* rule means different things in English and Shmenglish, we cannot know what language to use in interpreting based solely on Lex's rule for interpreting. For example, if the word "English" often means "Shmenglish" in Shmenglish, the rule is unclear about what language to look to until we know what language *it* is employing. If the rule in Shmenglish means something quite irrelevant to interpretation or to any other matter of social affairs, or if the rule is unintelligible in Shmenglish, that is good circumstantial evidence that the rule is employing English, in which case we now know how to interpret other rules. Notice, however, that it is the rule *plus* the circumstantial evidence regarding Lex's language choice, and not the rule by itself, that guides interpretation. And the same point holds even if Lex's rule for interpretation means exactly the same thing in English and Shmenglish. For only circumstantial evidence can tell us whether Lex was using either of those languages or was instead using his own invented dialect, say, Lenglish, in which case his rule could mean something entirely different from what it would mean in English or Shmenglish.

We shall take up the issue of interpretation of authorities' rules in chapter 5. We raise it now only because it may have occurred to you that the meaning of Lex's rules might not be transparent to everyone, and that it would be useful to know how to clarify his rules in his absence, given that he cannot always be present to correct misunderstandings as they arise.

Authoritative Settlement and the Circumstances of Law

You may have noticed that although the first part of this book is titled "The Circumstances of Law," we have not used the word "law" even once to this point. We have spoken of rules, moral authorities, coordination, expertise, and efficiency, but we have not said a word about law, at least not explicitly.

We have not said a word about law because our primary interest is in rules of the kind necessary for authoritative settlement. That interest is, to be sure, spurred by our interest in jurisprudential debates over the nature of law; but, as we said in the introduction, our purpose in writing this book is to throw light on those jurisprudential debates by refracting them through the prism of rules and rule-following. We believe that by looking at authoritative rules—what they are, why they are necessary, and the problems they create—one can gain a better understanding of such jurisprudential topics as the legal positivism–natural law debate, the role of legal principles, reasoning by analogy in law, legal interpretation, the nature of precedent, the determinacy and objectivity of law, constitutionalism, and revolution. Indeed, the chapter titles reveal that we shall be spending most of this book discussing these standard jurisprudential topics. Nonetheless, we do not want to beg any questions about what "law" is and how it relates to authoritative rules, and so we have avoided calling Lex's rules "laws." In the end, we find the focus on rules to be sufficiently rich and suggestive jurisprudentially that we do not need to offer it as a concept of law, much less as *the* concept.

Why then have we titled this part "The Circumstances of Law" rather than, say, "The Circumstances of Authoritative Rules"? Our only reason for doing so is the strong parallel between what we are doing here and what H. L. A. Hart does in chapter 5 of *The Concept of Law*.[15]

In that chapter, Hart imagines a community very much like the one we are imagining, "without a legislature, courts or officials of any kind."[16] And he says that "only a small community closely knit by ties of kinship, common sentiment, and belief, and placed in a stable environment, could live successfully by such a regime of unofficial rules."[17] Hart gives three reasons for this conclusion. His first reason is the reason we have given in this chapter:

> If doubts arise as to what the rules are or as to the precise scope of some given rule, there will be no procedure for settling this doubt, either by reference to an authoritative text or to an official whose declarations on this point are authoritative. For, plainly, such a procedure and the acknowledgement of either authoritative text or persons involve the existence of rules of a type different from the rules of obligation or duty which *ex hypothesi* are all that the group has. This defect in the simple social structure of primary rules we may call its *uncertainty*.[18]

Hart's other two reasons for concluding that the imagined community is defective are the static character of its rules—there are no procedures for changing the rules—and the inefficiency of the diffuse social pressure that is the mechanism for enforcing the rules.[19] We believe, however, that these latter two "defects" are but instances of the first.

With respect to change, there are two types of change that Hart regards as desirable. First, he finds it problematic that an accepted norm that might have been useful at one point in time has now, due to social or technological changes, become anachronistic. At some time prior to Lex, for example, our community might have translated the general moral norm against killing as protecting anyone whose heart and lungs were functioning. When instruments capable of detecting cessation of brain activity became available, so that brain death could be distinguished from heart and lung cessation, most might have favored replacing the old injunction against killing anyone whose heart and lungs were functioning with a new one deeming the brain dead "dead." Yet there was no expeditious mechanism for getting the new injunction established over dissent.

Thus, one desirable feature of the rule establishing Lex as the community's moral authority is that it provides a mechanism for changing anachronistic or otherwise undesirable social norms. It should be clear, however, that this desirable feature is really no different from the first desirable feature, namely, the rule's ability to resolve uncertainty over what ought to be done.

The second type of change that Hart is concerned with is what is often called "private ordering." Andrew may own a piece of property, Blackacre, and he may wish to transfer it to Carole, either in exchange for money or other goods, or as a gift or bequest. If he does so, rights and obligations with respect to Blackacre will change and will become rights of and obligations owed to Carole, not Andrew.

In the primitive community as Hart imagines it, there are no rules prescribing how to transfer property, make contracts, or otherwise change specific persons' rights and duties. Hart believes, therefore, that to cure this defect, as well as the one discussed above (anachronistic norms), there have to be *rules of change* in addition to a *rule of recognition* establishing Lex as the authority about what ought to be done.

As with anachronistic rules, however, the defect Hart regards as requiring a separate kind of rule we regard as solved by establishing Lex as the authority. In the first place, in our hypothetical community, there may well be general views about contracting and other forms of transferring rights and obligations. No formal institutions are required for such norms to arise and be generally or universally accepted. The problem with such informal norms is the same problem that besets the other informal norms: disagreements or questions about their meaning or applications cannot be authoritatively settled. And the same rule that is required for settling questions about what ought to be done and updating such rules—"Let Lex decide"—is sufficient for settling questions about how to alter rights and duties by transfer or waiver.

The third defect Hart identifies in his primitive community—inefficiency in enforcement—is again one that we believe should be thought of as merely a component of uncertainty. General moral principles that establish primary moral rights and duties are also the source of the moral rights and duties regarding both proof and punishment.[20] The questions that Hart points to that he says the primitive community cannot resolve—questions regarding who has violated the norms, who is to punish wrongdoers, and how much are they to be punished—are all indicative of uncertainty over these moral norms' meanings and applications. There is no difference in kind between such questions as, on the one hand, "How great a risk may be imposed on others?," "May mercury be dumped in the river?," and "Is this substance mercury?," and, on the other hand, "How much should a polluter be fined?," "To whom should the fine be paid?," and "Is Alex a polluter?" Agreeing that Lex is the authority about what ought to be done starts the community down the road toward solving the second set of questions just as much as it does so with regard to the first set of questions.

Hart believes that primitive communities need three types of rules—rules of recognition, rules of change, and rules of adjudication—in order to remedy the three defects of uncertainty, unchangeability, and inefficiency.[21] Our simple single rule—Let Lex decide—is, however, adequate to handle all three of these problems, so long as Lex's rules are clear and broad enough to settle what ought to be done, including what ought to be done in light of promises, gifts, and so forth; so long as Lex keeps the rules from becoming anachronistic; and so long as Lex promulgates rules to deal with adjudications that he cannot personally conduct.

In other words, we believe that although Hart does identify problems that would plague his imagined primitive community, these problems are all aspects of a single problem, namely, the absence of authoritative settlement by means of rules. Hart's focus is on the need for what he calls secondary rules, which he then divides into rules of recognition, change, and adjudication—and once a community has such secondary rules, the combination of those rules with "primary" rules of obligation would warrant the claim that the community has a legal system.[22]

Our interest is, like Hart's, in what the primitive community lacks. But what it lacks, in our view, are authoritative rules simpliciter, not particular types of authoritative rules. Moreover, our primary interest, unlike Hart's, is what the rules must be like to settle moral disputes, both in terms of the features they must display and in terms of the attitudes that they must command toward themselves. And it is to the required features of authoritative rules that we turn in the next two chapters, leaving the crucial issue of the attitudes toward them for part 2.

TWO Settlement Requisites and the Nature of Authoritative Rules

In chapter 1 we argued that a community must have a mechanism for authoritatively settling disagreements and uncertainties over what is to be done or else pay a high moral price in terms of lack of coordination, relative lack of expertise, and inefficient deliberation. The mechanism we identified for authoritative settlement was a set of rules: first, a rule designating Lex as the one to resolve moral disagreements and uncertainties, which rule exists because it is accepted by the community; and second, rules promulgated by Lex from time to time to resolve both specific and general disagreements and uncertainties and to handle such problems as Lex's death, disability, or absence from the scene of a controversy.

What this chapter takes up are the characteristics these rules must have if they are to settle issues in a way that secure the moral benefits—benefits of coordination, expertise, and efficiency—that authoritative settlement is meant to secure. In other words, if the rule establishing Lex as the authority and the rules Lex promulgates are to facilitate coordination, prevent error, and obviate the necessity of cost-ineffective deliberation, what features must they possess?

Norm Types: Posited Rules versus Moral Principles

The term "rule" has many meanings in ordinary usage. It should be relatively clear that as we are using the term, most of those meanings are inapplicable. We are, for example, referring to norms that guide conduct. Thus, empirical generalizations, such as "As a rule, most tigers are yellow" or "As a rule, the male bird will fly away before the female bird," although surely rules of a sort, are not the kinds of rules with which we are concerned.[1] Our interest is in normative rules, not descriptive or predictive rules.

Nor are we concerned with what some have called "rules of thumb" or "summary rules."[2] Such "rules" offer practical advice, but they are not practical norms. Examples of such soft, advisory rules are "As a rule, you should drive slowly rather than drive fast" and "As a rule, you should engage in organic farming." Because these "rules" are not practical norms but are only advisory, they can be heeded or ignored but never "obeyed" or "violated."

Our focus is on rules that are practical (prescriptive) norms and thus can be obeyed or violated, what we call "serious rules." Serious rules contain a factual predicate or hypothesis and a prescription.[3] For example, the rule "Do not dump pollutants in the river" can be roughly recast as "If you are considering dumping pollutants in the river (hypothesis), don't do it (prescription)." The most important characteristic of a serious rule, as we use the term, is that it purports to state a prescription applicable to every case that falls within the rule's factual predicate or hypothesis.

Now there are all sorts of practical norms. One major division is between, on the one hand, those norms that are posited by human beings and thus come into existence at particular times and places, and, on the other hand, those norms that are not so posited. The latter, nonposited, norms we shall refer to throughout as "moral principles." We use the term "principles" rather than "rules" to avoid confusion. Whenever we refer to a "rule," we will be referring to a posited rule, not a moral one.

By contrasting posited rules with moral principles, we are not taking any particular position on the metaphysics of morality—the reality to which moral propositions refer—nor on the content of morality. Whatever we think morality is—whether it is a realm of moral fact in the external world, a projection of sentiments onto the external world, or purely emotional responses to the world—and whatever we think its content is—a single principle demanding that we maximize goodness, Rawls's two principles of justice,[4] Nozick's principles of justice in acquisition, transfer, and rectification,[5] Gert's ten moral "rules,"[6] or something else—all we need to assume is that moral principles do not exist by virtue of being posited by particular persons at particular times and places.

Norm Types: Characteristics of Serious Rules

The rules that we are interested in are norms that are posited by human beings, not nonposited moral principles. Posited norms, however, are not all alike in terms of their capacity to settle questions of what ought to be done. If Lex is to perform his function as a practical authority, his norms must be general, determinate, and efficient.

The need for general norms results from Lex's limited capacity for resolving uncertainties as they arise. In the absence of general norms, decision-making must be *particularistic*.[7] Particularistic decision-making means reasoning directly from moral principles to particular decisions—such as how fast Agnes should drive *now,* or whether Paul ought to dump *this* substance in *this* river *now.* Particularistic decision-making is the decision-making that members of our hypothetical community engaged in before they adopted the rule "Let Lex decide"; and the costs of particularistic decision-making in terms of coordination, expertise, and efficiency are precisely what led them to adopt that rule.

Now, so long as Lex can decide each particular question and controversy as it arises—that is, so long as Lex can, by engaging in particularistic decision-making, bring about coordinated, efficient, and morally proper decisions by the rest of the community—the need for decision-making under rules does not arise. Or rather, to be precise, the members of the community need only follow one rule—"Let Lex decide"—each application of which is guided very particularistically by Lex himself.

But, as we said, Lex will be unable to be present at each moment when a decision in light of moral principles must be taken and when the application of those principles is controverted or misunderstood. Lex will therefore have to anticipate such decisions and settle in advance what should be done in those cases through promulgation of general norms—norms applicable to a range of cases that share common features.

Generality is a matter of degree, of course. Rules can range from the most particular ("Drive *this* speed *now*") to the more general

("Drive fifty-five so long as the weather is dry, the road has a shoulder, it is after sunup and before sundown, etc.") to the quite general ("Drive fifty-five").[8] Yet to serve Lex's purposes, the norms he promulgates must be general enough to take the place of Lex himself.

Lex's norms must also be "rules," in the sense of posited general norms that settle determinately the questions and controversies that arise in the application of moral principles. Suppose, for example, that Agnes and Ben are trying to decide how fast they should drive, and they take their concern to Lex. They will not be satisfied if Lex promulgates any of the following "rules" in response: "Drive at a reasonable speed," "Drive safely," "Drive so as to maximize total social utility," or "Drive consistently with maximum equal liberty for all." They will say to Lex, "If we knew what was safe, or reasonable, or utility-maximimizing, and so forth, we would not need to have you settle how fast we should drive; we could decide for ourselves and achieve coordination, expertise, and efficiency." In other words, these posited norms do not settle for Agnes and Ben the particular question they need to have settled in order to coordinate desirably and efficiently.

Typically, norms like "Drive reasonably" and the others hypothesized above are called *standards*.[9] Standards are posited norms that contain vague or controversial moral or evaluative terms in their formulations. Persons attempting to conform to standards must be able to resolve for themselves the application of these vague or controversial moral and evaluative terms.

If Agnes and Ben require an authority such as Lex because they cannot resolve for themselves efficiently, expertly, and consistently the applications of the moral principles that they both subscribe to at a more abstract level, then they will not be helped by Lex's promulgating standards. For the standards do not improve their ability to determine what they need to determine.

Nor will standards be any more helpful if they point to determinate factual matters, but only as "considerations" or "factors." For example, Lex might promulgate the norm "Drive reasonably, taking into account the weather, visibility, traffic, and condition of the road." The difficulty is that in order to decide what is reasonable in light of these factors, Agnes and Ben will most likely still need to resolve how to apply abstract moral principles in concrete situations—

the problem that led them to seek Lex's determination in the first place.

Things are somewhat improved for Agnes and Ben if Lex promulgates a slightly different norm, "Drive reasonably, considering *only* the weather, visibility, traffic, and condition of the road." This norm, unlike the previous one, moves some distance from being a pure standard and toward being a "rule" as we are going to be using the term. For now Lex has told Agnes and Ben more than they already knew. He has told them to ignore all factors that they might think bear on reasonable behavior other than the four mentioned. The part of the norm that can be translated as "Do not consider anything other than weather . . ." is a rule-like norm coupled with a standard ("Drive reasonably").

The quality that identifies a rule and distinguishes it from a standard is the quality of determinateness. A norm becomes a rule when most people understand it in a similar way. When this is so, the rules will give the same answer to unsettled moral questions to every affected individual and so bring about coordination. Although a standard is transparent to background moral principles and requires particularistic decision-making, rules can be applied without regard to questions of background morality. They are opaque to the moral principles they are supposed to effectuate. Thus, a rule is a posited norm that fulfills the function of posited norms, that is, that settles questions of what ought to be done.

A pure rule is a posited norm that settles all questions about what ought to be done that fall within its scope. For example, the posited norm "Drive fifty-five" is a pure rule if it settles for each driver in our community the otherwise unsettled question of how fast he or she should drive. A posited norm that settles some but not all unsettled questions that fall within its scope we shall call an impure rule ("Drive fifty-five unless it is raining, in which case drive reasonably").

The determinateness requirement refers to the moral functions that the rules are meant to serve: coordination, expertise, and efficiency. The indeterminateness of the moral principles regarding how they apply to particular cases is what produces the controversy and uncertainty that results in lack of coordination, costly deliberation, and mistaken (inexpert) conclusions. The purpose of having Lex promulgate rules to settle questions about how moral principles apply in concrete situations is to eliminate the controversy and uncertainty and their associated moral costs. Lex's rules can perform this function only if they are relatively determinate for those who must follow them.[10] In other words, it must be easier for the members of the community to ascertain correctly what Lex's rules require in concrete situations than it is for them to ascertain what their moral principles require. Otherwise, the rules will have failed to fulfill their moral function. And ideally, the rules should be fully determinate: everyone in the community will agree about what the rules require in every case.

We have spoken so far of generality and determinateness. These are separate considerations: a quite specific rule can be either determinate ("Drive fifty-five on Wednesdays between two and five") or indeterminate ("Do not dump unsafe materials in the Grand River this Monday"). Likewise, a very general rule can be either determinate ("Drive fifty-five") or indeterminate ("Drive safely").

Nonetheless, there is a tendency for generality and determinateness to go together. That is so because if Lex posits specific rules, then although they may be determinate, they will have to be quite numerous to cover all the controversial or uncertain cases that will likely arise. And the presence of a lot of specific rules will create indeterminacy about what ought to be done even if the individual rules are quite specific.

The instructions for filing the tax return of a business are a good example. Although the rules governing taxation might individually be quite determinate, there are so many of them that ordinary taxpayers have difficulty figuring out what the rules in the aggregate require. A prolix code of very specific rules can be so difficult to apply that it produces the lack of coordination and inefficient decision-making that determinate rules are supposed to remedy.

So the desire for determinateness will tend to push Lex in the direction of generality. So, too, will another consideration, namely, Lex's inability to foresee all possible concrete applications of moral principles.[11] Lex will only be able to anticipate concrete cases in terms of broader, more general, categories of cases. Thus, his rules will handle cases in terms of the more general categories that he can foresee.

Generality and determinateness enable rules to settle moral questions and controversies. Of course, to fulfill their moral function, rules must not only settle these moral questions, but also settle them efficiently enough that the moral gains of coordination are not exceeded by increased decision-making costs. A rule that produces coordination, where lack of coordination has modest moral costs, but that requires each person to make a thousand time-consuming and hence costly calculations, would be an undesirable rule, despite its ability to settle unsettled moral questions ("Drive fifty-five when the temperature is over 33 degrees Fahrenheit, and skies are sunny to partly cloudy, and it has not rained for twenty-four hours; otherwise drive forty-five").

A final desideratum of authoritative settlement is expertise. That is, we expect a practical authority not only to settle unsettled moral questions, but to settle them well. Obviously, a rule can bring about coordination and efficient decision-making and yet be morally obtuse or perverse. Such a rule, if sufficiently morally undesirable, negates the moral gains of increased coordination and efficient decision-making.

Nonetheless, expertise, unlike the capacity to affect coordination and efficient decision-making, is not a function of a norm's being a rule. That is, expertise is not a matter of whether the posited norm can settle unsettled moral questions but is rather a function of the wisdom of the authority who posits the norm. What is important for a norm's being a rule is its ability to settle unsettled moral questions in a coordinated and efficient way within the community to which the norm applies, not its ability to settle those questions well.

The Determinacy of Rules and the Question of Moral Content

We have said that if Lex's rules are to serve their moral functions and foster coordinated, morally more expert, and more efficient decision-making, then their meaning—what they direct members of the community to do in particular cases—must be determinate. That is, members of the community who disagree about the results of particularistic inquiries—how fast one ought to drive under certain conditions, how much risk to health and the environment one ought to run in dumping materials into the river, and whether one may unplug a person whose brain activity has irrevocably ceased but whose heart and lungs continue to function—must agree about what course of conduct Lex's rules require or permit. Put differently, if uncertainty and disagreement about how moral principles apply in concrete situations are what give rise to the need for Lex and Lex's rules, Lex's rules are responsive to this need only if they themselves do not engender uncertainty and disagreement about their concrete applications.

Some might believe that this determinacy requirement means that Lex's rules cannot themselves refer to moral or evaluative considerations but must refer solely to factual matter. We think, however, that this position, although it is correct in one sense, is incorrect in another and potentially quite misleading.

The position is surely correct in this sense: the application of rules must not require members of the community to resolve the very moral controversies and uncertainties that give rise to the need for rules in the first place. If the rules did this—if, in other words, the rules were really standards—then they could not settle the very questions they were meant to settle. Rather, to apply the rules, members would have to settle the moral questions themselves, which by hypothesis they are unable to do. Lex's rules—that is, Lex's standards—would leave everything as it was.

On the other hand, suppose there are moral or evaluative terms that all members of the community apply the same way across a broad range of circumstances. Suppose, for example, that Lex fashions a rule to deal with the effects on neighboring farms of a farmer's methods of irrigation, plowing, crop rotation, and spraying. And suppose that Lex's rule employs the phrase "the reasonable farmer." Finally, suppose that in our hypothetical community, everyone agrees about how "the reasonable farmer" irrigates, plows, and so forth in almost every conceivable situation. In such a case, Lex's rule—which we may assume is meant to settle some other moral controversy, such as whether reasonable farmers should nonetheless be liable for damages they cause adjoining farms[12]—will be determinate and capable of performing its moral function despite its use of an evaluative term.

Of course, what makes such moral and evaluative terms determinate and thus employable in rules is the social fact of agreement on their concrete applications. One might say that whatever their true referents, it is their conventional meanings—social facts—that the rules are employing. Members of the community do not need to be correct about the meaning of "reasonable farmer." They need only be consistent with one another.

All this is true, but at the same time we think it much less misleading to claim that rules must be determinate within the community rather than to claim that their predicates must be factual.[13] Placing the emphasis on determinateness also has the virtue of remaining neutral on the question whether certain moral terms have referents beyond conventions.

At the same time, emphasis on rules' being determinate can be misleading. Sometimes a somewhat vague prescriptive norm is preferable to a fully determinate rule because the subject of the norm can clarify the vague term at the point of application better than the authority at the time of promulgation. Thus, the somewhat vague rule on a medicine bottle "Take as needed for pain" does convey information to the user and is likely to be applied by him with superior results to those that would occur were the rule promulgator to attempt to clarify the rule further. The subject of the rule has better information about when to take the medicine than the rule promulgator once he knows that he is to take the medicine "as needed for pain." The important point is that a rule should not be vague on the matters that are uncertain and controversial and require authoritative settlement.

Finally, it should be apparent that many factual predicates will cause rules to fail to perform their moral function because those factual predicates are as or more indeterminate than the application of moral principles at issue.[14] Factual predicates may be vague ("*Bald* men must wear hats"), controversial ("No one may destroy the natural habitat of any *species* of animal *threatened with extinction*"), or require so many calculations that mistakes will be very frequent ("One must deduct the income, minus the basis, but prorated by . . . ."). The desiderata of authoritative rules—their moral raisons d'etre—are their abilities to coordinate, to foster efficient practical decision-making, and to improve the substance of practical decision-making. Those desiderata come from determinacy of the rules' prescriptions,[15] not from the rules' exclusive reference to factual matters. The latter is related to determinacy only contingently.

The Built-In Imperfection of Rules

To the extent that Lex's rules are general and determinate, they will not always correspond to the results of ideal particularistic moral reasoning. That is, a particularistic decision-maker will come to conclusions about what moral principles demand in concrete cases that will differ from what general rules require or permit in some of those cases. A particularistic moral reasoner might conclude correctly that he should not exceed fifty miles per hour on one stretch of road but that he should drive sixty on another. The general rule "Drive fifty-five" will permit him to exceed the morally optimal speed in some instances and require him to drive more slowly than the morally optimal speed in others.

This feature of general rules—this bluntness, and the resulting over- and underinclusiveness relative to background moral principles—stems from rules' being what Fred Schauer calls "entrenched generalizations."[16] The fifty-five-mile-per-hour speed limit generalizes over an indefinite number of particular occasions for driving and functions as if one should infer that fifty-five is the optimal speed on every occasion. And that generalization about optimal speed is "entrenched" because "Drive fifty-five" is an authoritative rule—it is meant to supplant the controversial background moral principles for members of the community in deciding how fast to drive. Only if it does so—only if the members consult the rule and ignore the background moral principles in deciding what to do, even if those principles appear to conflict with the rule in the case at hand—can the rule deliver the coordination, expertise, and efficiency it is there to provide.

This bluntness of general rules is therefore both morally desirable and morally problematic. Once Lex is forced by his limitations to promulgate general rules rather than on-the-spot commands, his rules will be blunt norms in the way described because only then can they solve the problems of particularistic moral decision-making—lack of coordination, mistakes, and inefficient decision-making. But the very bluntness that enables them to solve these problems of particularism will also mean that the results they dictate will diverge from those that particularism, applied correctly, would dictate. In other words, blunt rules will be morally flawed even when they are morally desirable.

It is important not to be misled into thinking that rules' moral flaws can be eliminated by having a better set of rules in terms of content. So long as the members of our community are finite in their knowledge and reasoning capacities—so long as they are human beings—the best posited norms for them will be blunt rules. Put differently, for a community with the normal epistemic limitations, a good set of blunt rules will be preferable to particularism and its attendant controversies and uncertainties. But even the best set of blunt rules will produce outcomes at odds with correct particularistic reasoning. (Indeed, even if Lex were able to decide each particular controversy as it arose, and did not therefore need to promulgate any rules, he would occasionally make errors. In those cases, the one general rule in the community—"Let Lex decide"—would entrench a generalization that produced results in the cases of Lex's errors at odds with the background moral principles, which is not to say that "Let Lex decide" would not be the best rule available, nor is it to say that the rule would be inferior to pure particularism.)

This paradoxical aspect of authoritative rules—the fact that such rules are simultaneously morally optimal and morally sub-optimal—and the decision-making conundrums it engenders, will be taken up extensively in chapter 4. Our purpose here is merely to show how that paradoxical nature is a function of rules' entrenching and generalizing nature.

| | | | |

Lex's rules, as well as the rule "Let Lex decide," have as their moral function solving the problems caused by controversy and uncertainty over the application of moral principles. They can fulfill their function only if they are determinate rules, not indeterminate standards. And given Lex's human limitations, the rules can fulfill their function only if they are general and relatively blunt, which means that they will diverge in application from the moral principles they aim to serve.

THREE Hierarchies of Rules

Complicating the Picture

Thus far, the picture we have painted of our imagined community has been a quite uncluttered one. The community possesses a master rule for settling what ought to be done, namely, "Let Lex decide." That master rule exists because the members of the community agree to its terms and accept it as normative. And we have assumed that Lex, in addition to deciding particular controversies over what ought to be done, has promulgated some general rules prescribing what ought to be done in certain categories of cases. Finally, we have assumed that Lex has promulgated rules designating who can authoritatively resolve disputes in Lex's absence.

This simple system of rules will more than likely prove to be inadequate, even for our small, relatively morally like-minded community. For example, in chapter 1 we noted that the community would be well advised, not merely to "let Lex decide," but to anticipate Lex's death or disability. It might ask Lex to promulgate rules for these contingencies. Or, if it can reach agreement on terms, it might incorporate its own views into its master rule, so that the master rule becomes "Let Lex or Lex's duly authorized successor decide," with additional provisions that spell out how duly authorized successors are identified ("Lex's successor shall be a person so designated by Lex, who is at least thirty years old, and whose selection is concurred in by the oldest members of the Smith and Jones families, unless Lex fails to name such a successor before Lex's death or disability, in which case . . . .").

Moreover, it is possible that the community already agrees about what ought to be done in a number of important categories of cases. If so, then in addition to establishing Lex and Lex's successors in its master rule, the community may also set forth its agreed resolution of those cases in the master rule. The master rule—really, the master set of rules—may thus contain procedural rules designating certain authorities other than Lex and Lex's successors—for example, judges and administrators—and also substantive rules resolving important matters, such as questions of liberty ("Lex may not forbid public criticism of his rules"), equality ("Lex may not display favoritism between those descended from Jones and those descended from Smith"), and the like.

Finally, the community would be well advised to provide, if it can agree, or to have Lex provide if it cannot, for mechanisms for changing its basic rules. Although it may agree on the terms of these rules now, it can anticipate changing its mind in the future, but not unanimously. Thus, it may agree that the terms of the agreement may be modified by agreement among some (large) percentage of the community.

Let us take stock. In the simplest scenario, our community has one master rule that it agrees to, "Let Lex decide." All of its other rules settling what ought to be done both procedurally and substantively are rules promulgated by Lex, who presumably also has the authority to amend or repeal the rules he promulgates. In the more complex scenario, the master rule settles by agreement additional questions of what ought to be done, perhaps including questions of succession, administration, rights, and amendment of the master rule itself. In the most complex scenario we shall imagine, the community amends some portion of its master rule through the amendment process described in the master rule.

In the latter scenario, then, we have rules with three kinds of provenance: (1) those rules contained in the master rule that are the products of agreement to (or acceptance of)[1] their terms by the entire community; (2) those rules contained in the master rule that are the products of the amendment process described in the master rule; and (3) all the rules promulgated by Lex (or Lex's duly authorized delegates or successors). Let us call rules of type 1—the products of agreement to their terms—"preconstitutional rules." Let us call rules of type 2 — the products of the amendment rule — "constitutional rules." All other rules we shall call "ordinary rules."

Why do we call rules of type 1 "preconstitutional" and rules of type 2 "constitutional"? We do so because we doubt that any constitution of any important legal system has ever been adopted by unanimous agreement on its terms, nor is any such constitution deemed authoritative only for those alive at its founding and thus capable of expressing such agreement. A community may agree — indeed, unanimously agree — on a mechanism by which a constitution can be established, even though the mechanism itself does not require unanimous agreement on the constitution's terms. Therefore, although the terminology is not crucial, we wish to use the terms "preconstitutional" and "constitutional" to mark the distinction between those foundational rules that are based on community-wide agreement on their terms and those that are not. The latter, however, are "constitutional" and not "ordinary" because they cannot be changed by Lex, the community's ordinary rule-promulgating, rule-repealing, and rule-amending institution. For ease of reference, we shall call the institutional mechanism for promulgating, repealing, and amending "constitutional" rules "Super Lex."[2]

We should also say that none of these rules, preconstitutional, constitutional, or ordinary, need be written. Of course, there are plenty of practical reasons why they should be written, particularly as they become more numerous and complex. What *is* important is that they be understandable by those to whom they are directed. Otherwise, they would fail to perform their moral function of settling what ought to be done. Their being written, however, is not essential to their existence.

Additionally, either the community, in its preconstitutional rules, or Super Lex, in its constitutional rules, would be well advised to provide for an institution to interpret — and to settle disagreements about the interpretation of — the constitutional rules. Disagreements about the preconstitutional rules are in some sense impossible since preconstitutional rules only exist to the extent that they are agreed upon. (We shall elaborate this point and its implications below.) Disagreements over the interpretation of ordinary rules can be resolved by Lex or by Lex's surrogate adjudicators; and if Lex believes the latter have misinterpreted those rules, Lex can clear up the matter.

Disagreements over constitutional rules, however, cannot be resolved by Lex, who is subordinate to Super Lex. And Super Lex may be even more difficult to call to the scene of disagreement than Lex. Therefore, just as either Lex in the ordinary rules or the community in its preconstitutional rules would be well advised to set up institutions to interpret ordinary rules in cases where Lex is unavailable, so too should either the community or Super Lex promulgate rules regarding how and by whom Super Lex's constitutional rules should be interpreted.

Finally, the community's preconstitutional, constitutional, and ordinary rules are all intended to settle controversies over the application of moral principles. It should go without saying that they will fail to perform their moral function if they incorporate the very moral principles whose applications they are meant to settle. At no level—preconstitutional, constitutional, or ordinary—will it suffice to have a "rule" that merely refers to moral principles whose concrete meanings are uncertain and in dispute.[3]

The Motivation for Agreement

In chapter 1 we presented a seemingly unproblematic explanation for why members of our hypothetical community, who disagree about what their moral principles require concretely even if not abstractly, might nevertheless agree on the rule "Let Lex decide." We said that the members might well conclude that the moral gains from authoritatively settling their moral controversies, gains that are cashed out in terms of cooperation, expertise, and efficiency, will outweigh the moral losses from those instances where Lex's decisions are (from their perspective) morally incorrect.

In chapter 4 we shall raise deep difficulties with this picture. Even if all agree that it is morally better to have Lex authoritatively settle moral controversies than to leave those controversies unsettled, what motivation will they have for adhering to Lex's rules and decisions when those rules and decisions require them to act morally suboptimally (from their perspective)? And if they cannot have adequate motivation to adhere, how is it possible for them to agree to adhere?

We defer these and related questions to chapter 4.[4] Here, however, we shall assume that adherence to Lex's rules and decisions is unproblematic in terms of motivation and thus that agreement to adhere is unproblematic on that ground. The issue we wish to explore here is how the members of the community can come to agree on rules that are suboptimal from everyone's standpoint. That issue is important for understanding some of the ways constitutional and preconstitutional rules can change, how revolutions can be domesticated, how separate systems of authoritative rules can exist side by side in the same community (and why this happens less frequently than might be expected), and other mysteries of authoritative systems of rules.

Let us begin with the simplest version of the story. Members of the community disagree about or are uncertain about how their common moral principles are to be applied concretely. They perceive the moral need for authoritative settlement of those disagreements and uncertainties. Jane prefers the rule "Let Jane decide." John prefers the rule "Let John decide." And so on for each member of the community.

Jane's second best rule is "Let Sarah decide." But although it is also Sarah's preferred rule, it must compete with John's second best rule, "Let Jim decide," which is, of course, supported by Jim and John.

Now let us suppose that everyone's third-, second-, or first-choice rule is "Let Lex decide." If everyone understands that other first- and second-choice rules will not command agreement—and if everyone believes that "Let Lex decide" is morally superior to the alternative of no authoritative decision-maker—then everyone has a strategic reason for accepting "Let Lex decide" as the foundational authoritative rule. We say "strategic" to emphasize that perhaps everyone (other than Lex) will view the rule, not as the best rule for settling moral controversies, but as the best rule that they can get others to accept.[5] (In an important sense, of course, because the purpose of authoritative rules is to settle moral controversies, by being the best rule everyone can accept and the only rule that will actually perform the settlement function, this suboptimal rule becomes, for everyone, the optimal rule.)

Now as we complicate the story and move from the one basic rule, "Let Lex decide," to a complex set of preconstitutional rules regarding rights, procedures, and institutions, including the institution of Super Lex with the power to promulgate, repeal, and amend those rules, it becomes more and more likely that the resulting set of preconstitutional rules that must be agreed upon is far from anyone's ideal set of such rules. Some of the rules may be some members' first or second choices, but others will be further down on their list, and some may even be morally repugnant. Still, all have good reason to agree to the entire set, including the rules that they find morally repugnant, if that is the best set of rules to which they can get the others to agree, and if that set of rules is morally preferable to the absence of authoritative settlement. And again, because authoritative settlement requires agreement on authoritative rules, the morally best rules on which agreement can be obtained are in some sense the morally best rules. Rules that cannot command agreement cannot perform their moral function and are thus undesirable, no matter how good those rules would be if they did command agreement.

We thus end up with the following picture. Our mythical community has reached agreement about certain foundational rules, rules that set up Lex as the basic rule promulgator and decision-maker, that prescribe certain rights and procedures and set up certain institutions, and that set up Super Lex as the institution for expanding or changing these basic rules. The members agree to this complex package of rules, but not necessarily because it is anyone's ideal, and not necessarily because there are no rules in the package that anyone finds morally repugnant as opposed to suboptimal. Rather, they agree to the package because it is from everyone's point of view both morally superior to the absence of authoritative settlement and also the morally best such package to which they can get others to agree.[6] And because it meets those conditions, the package is in an important sense everyone's morally ideal package of rules.

Pathologies: Misinterpretation, Revolution, and Fragmentation

STAGE SETTING

Let us assume that Lex has appointed Judge to adjudicate cases arising under Lex's rules. Such adjudications will require Judge both to decide what the facts are and to interpret Lex's rules.

Let us also assume that either the community, in its preconstitutional rules, or Super Lex, in its constitutional rules, has established the institution of a supreme court to decide controversies arising under the constitutional rules, which will include its interpreting those rules.

In chapter 5 we shall take up the topic of how rules should be interpreted. Here we wish to focus on the implications of misinterpretation of the rules, leaving until chapter 5 how misinterpretation is identified.

MISINTERPRETATIONS OF ORDINARY RULES

Suppose Lex posits the rule "Do not dump pollutants in the river," and a case arises involving whether the substance Alex has dumped is a pollutant within the meaning of Lex's rule. Suppose that Judge misinterprets Lex's rule and decides that the substance is (or is not) a pollutant. What are the implications of Judge's misinterpretation of Lex's rule?

Ignoring Judge. The community in its preconstitutional rules, Super Lex in its constitutional rules, or Lex in his ordinary rules may have posited a rule to the effect that misinterpretations of Lex's rules are not authoritative for what ought to be done and may be ignored by everyone. Such a rule, however, although possible, would be quite undesirable, for it would leave an anarchical lacuna, a dispute over what ought to be done that would be temporarily without an authoritative resolution. Judge believes, albeit incorrectly, that Alex is in violation of Lex's rules. Alex may believe the contrary. Lex is at least temporarily absent from the scene of the dispute. Should Alex pay a fine to Judge? Should he resist? Should Judge attempt to throw Alex in jail if Alex resists? Should Alex resist such an attempt? Should third parties intervene, and on whose side? If Alex believes Judge has misunderstood Lex's rule regarding pollutants, and there is another rule that says misinterpretations may be ignored, then Alex and Judge—and interested bystanders—are likely to end up in combat or flight.

Giving Judge's Misinterpretation (Some) Authoritative Status. At a minimum, Lex, Super Lex, or the community should invest Judge's misinterpretations of Lex's rules with authority over the parties to the immediate dispute. That would mean that Alex would have to act as if Judge's misinterpretation were actually a correct interpretation, and he (Alex) were actually guilty of violating Lex's rule, even though he is not. In other cases, however, Judge would be free to reconsider her interpretation of the rule.

A stronger grant of authority to Judge would require Judge in future cases to abide by her interpretation of the rule in Alex's case, even if Judge now acknowledges that her interpretation was incorrect. In other words, Judge would have to treat her misinterpretation of Lex's rule regarding pollutants as a binding precedent. (We take up the practice of following precedent in chapter 7.) Such a grant of authority to Judge would be advantageous for the following reason: Lex's rule was supposed to settle what ought to be done (in a class of cases); the rule was not completely successful because it failed to settle determinately, at least in some cases, the meaning of "pollutants"; Judge's misinterpretation, though at odds with Lex's true views, *does* settle the meaning of "pollutants" within the disputed class of cases and thus settles what ought to be done. So long as Judge is sincerely attempting to interpret Lex's rule properly, and so long as Judge is reasonably able, Judge's settling the meaning of Lex's rule incorrectly may be morally superior to leaving the meaning unsettled for other parties. After all, when Lex is apprised of Judge's misinterpretation, Lex can always clarify the meaning of his rule and correct Judge (or, if he now prefers Judge's interpretation to his original meaning, allow Judge's interpretation to stand).

MISINTERPRETATIONS OF CONSTITUTIONAL RULES

In certain cases, controversies will arise over the meaning of Super Lex's constitutional rules. Suppose, for example, Super Lex has posited a rule requiring Lex to respect "freedom of religion" in the community. A controversy arises over what Super Lex means by "religion." For example, is transcendental meditation a "religion" within the meaning of Super Lex's rule? And suppose the supreme court misinterprets Super Lex's constitutional rule. The proper method of interpretation of Super Lex's rules might itself be prescribed constitutionally by Super Lex; more likely, to avoid the potential regress, it is a matter of preconstitutional understanding or agreement. What are the implications of such a misinterpretation?

Ignoring the Supreme Court. Again, one possibility is that constitutional misinterpretations have no authority whatsoever. Until Super Lex steps in to clarify its meaning, the disputants over the constitutional rule's meaning are free to ignore the supreme court and follow their own interpretations of the constitutional rule. For the same reason we gave with regard to misinterpretations of ordinary rules, however, this result is undesirable. Super Lex's constitutional rule was supposed to settle what ought to be done, but it did not succeed for these parties. The supreme court's decision, although a misinterpretation of the constitutional rule, can settle what ought to be done. Unless the supreme court's misinterpretations are not just incorrect as interpretations, but transgress preconstitutional rules placing limits on officials, giving the supreme court authority over the disputants regarding Super Lex's rules will be morally preferable to not doing so.

Giving the Supreme Court's Misinterpretation (Some) Authoritative Status. Just as with Judge's misinterpretations of Lex's rules, it will be morally desirable for the community or Super Lex to invest the supreme court with authority to bind the disputants before it to its interpretations of Super Lex's rules, even when its interpretations are incorrect. We shall not repeat the argument for such a result.

More interesting is whether those misinterpretations should bind others or bind the supreme court itself in future cases.[7] Many who accept that Judge's misinterpretations of Lex's ordinary rules should bind other actors and even Judge deny that the supreme court's misinterpretations of constitutional rules should be binding beyond the parties to the dispute giving rise to the misinterpretation. Their argument goes something like this: unlike a misinterpretation of an ordinary rule, which Lex can easily correct, a misinterpretation of a constitutional rule may not be so easily corrected. Presumably getting Super Lex to act is much more difficult than getting Lex to act. For example, Super Lex may require a supermajority vote to enact or repeal rules. If Super Lex cannot correct the supreme court's misinterpretations of its rules, and those misinterpretations are deemed to bind all actors, then in effect the supreme court has been given the authority to change the constitutional rules through misinterpretation. Changing those rules is, however, the prerogative of Super Lex, not the supreme court. Therefore, the latter should not be capable of binding anyone other than the disputants before it to its misinterpretations of the constitutional rules.

Notice, however, that the same reason—settlement—that supports making the supreme court's misinterpretation bind the disputants in the case before it also supports making the supreme court's misinterpretations more broadly binding. Even though only Super Lex can change constitutional rules, in cases of disputes over the rules' interpretation, Super Lex has failed to settle the issues that the constitutional rule in question is meant to resolve. That is, the fact that the supreme court could misinterpret the rule demonstrates that the settlement function was not satisfactorily fulfilled. If the supreme court's misinterpretation is less subject to misinterpretation itself than the constitutional rule it misinterprets, then the supreme court has settled the constitutional issue more satisfactorily, at least in terms of settlement, than did Super Lex.[8]

Moreover, the stakes over whether to treat the supreme court's interpretations as authoritative for all actors, even if the actors disagree with those interpretations, are much lower than the stakes involved when Super Lex promulgates the rule. In the latter instance, Super Lex is attempting to settle what ought to be done. In the former, what is at stake is not, at least directly, what ought to be done; rather, what is at stake is what Super Lex has determined ought to be done. Because Super Lex's determinations of what ought to be done may be morally erroneous and yet still bind the community, it is of much less moment to posit a rule to the effect that the supreme court's interpretations of Super Lex's determinations should bind the community. After all, in any given case, the supreme court's misinterpretations might be morally superior to Super Lex's actual determinations, even if, over the great range of cases, the community prefers Super Lex to the supreme court as a promulgator of constitutional rules.[9]

MISINTERPRETATIONS OF AND ACTIONS CONTRARY TO PRECONSTITUTIONAL RULES

Perhaps the theoretically most interesting cases are those in which officials act in ways that contravene the community's foundational agreement on preconstitutional rules. Super Lex may act beyond the authority granted or the restrictions imposed by the preconstitutional rules. The supreme court may contravene those rules directly, or may contravene Super Lex's constitutional rules without any additional authority provided by the preconstitutional rules.[10] (This might occur if the supreme court's misinterpretations of the constitutional rules were not deemed authoritative for anyone either by other constitutional rules or by preconstitutional rules.) Even Lex or Judge might ignore the rules and decisions of Super Lex and the supreme court, who in turn acquiesce in the disobedience, but not through the amendment procedures specified constitutionally or preconstitutionally.

Now the preconstitutional agreement can anticipate, internalize, and domesticate to some extent misinterpretations of and departures from its terms. Just as a constitution can contain a rule giving authority to judicial decisions that misinterpret it, a preconstitutional agreement can include an agreement to abide by certain decisions that contravene the agreement itself.

Nevertheless, a basic community agreement on preconstitutional rules cannot be self-effacing. After all, what is the point of the community's agreeing on preconstitutional rules if the rules can be so easily undermined? We should assume, then, that in most cases, if officials depart from the terms of the preconstitutional rules, they will be acting in complete opposition to what the community has agreed ought to be done. And this is true even if the officials' departures are based on good-faith misinterpretations of the preconstitutional agreement rather than defiance of it.

In such cases the community has in effect two sets of rules regarding what ought to be done: the set of rules whose provenance is the community's preconstitutional agreement, and the set of rules whose provenance is rules or decisions based on some officials' misinterpretations or defiance of the community's preconstitutional agreement.

The community, of course, no longer agrees on the content of its preconstitutional rules, even if it once did. At a minimum, the renegade officials no longer accept the preconstitutional rules that the rest of the community accepts. And when preconstitutional rules are no longer accepted by someone, they cease to be authoritative for that person, even if she accepted them in the past. Preconstitutional rules are thus *pre* in a logical sense, not a chronological sense. They are logically, not temporally, foundational. And if at any moment they are rejected, even by one who previously accepted them, at that moment they—and the rules derived from them—cease being authoritative for that person.[11] The authority of the foundational preconstitutional rules—and thus of all the constitutional and ordinary rules pedigreed by the preconstitutional rules—rests on the continuing acceptance of those rules as authoritative.[12] If those who cease accepting the preconstitutional rules accept the variations of them posited by mistaken or defiant officials, or accept an entirely separate set of preconstitutional rules such as might be established by a conquering army, two or more systems of rules will be competing for authority over the same community. Though each system will settle what ought to be done for those who accept its preconstitutional foundations, none will settle what ought to be done for those who accept another system.[13]

THE RESILIENCY OF THE FOUNDATIONAL AGREEMENT & THE LIKELIHOOD OF NON-RULE-GOVERNED AMENDMENT

It may appear as though authoritative systems of rules, resting as they do on ongoing agreement on preconstitutional rules, are extremely fragile and perhaps impossible to achieve outside a very small community, and even there impossible to sustain for very long. If everyone has to agree to the same preconstitutional rules, not only once, but continuously, then the prospects for an authoritative system of rules that is both durable and capable of governing large populations appear quite dim.

We believe, however, that our earlier discussion of the motivation for agreement on preconstitutional rules shows that systems of authoritative rules are, to the contrary, likely to be quite durable. For if some officials cease accepting the preconstitutional rules, the rest of the community and those officials are each now left with rules that they prefer but that are no longer authoritative settlements of what ought to be done for the entire community. Everyone may prefer a set of preconstitutional rules accepted by everyone to a set that is better from their perspective but that is not accepted by others. Everyone will then have a strong reason to seek agreement between the community and the officials.[14] If the officials are prestigious, and if the officials' departures from the preconstitutional rules are inadvertent, or the preconstitutional rules they accept appear to many to be superior to the original rules, the rest of the community will have strong reasons to acquiesce in the officials' departures and to accept the officials' preconstitutional rules.[15] If those conditions are absent, the officials' revolution is likely to be short-lived, and the original preconstitutional rules will regain universal acceptance.[16]

In either case, there will always be strong pressure toward establishing foundational rules that are accepted as authoritative by the entire community. And this point explains how rules can be amended other than through formal, rule-governed, amendment processes. If the terms of the preconstitutional agreement change because some of those terms are no longer accepted as authoritative by the community and new terms are, then the constitutional and ordinary rules that are derived from the preconstitutional rules will also change. If, for example, the original preconstitutional understanding was that the supreme court would interpret Super Lex's constitutional rules by reference to Super Lex's intentions, and the supreme court now interprets those rules by reference to modern understandings, those constitutional rules can be deemed amended by a method other than the method formally prescribed—action by Super Lex—if the supreme court's interpretive methodology is now accepted by the community as proper.[17]

| | | | |

We have complexified the picture of our hypothetical community, not only to make the picture more realistic but also to introduce some worries about the very possibility of a rule-governed community and some issues that we shall revisit in later chapters. The worries are these: What reason will members of the community have for accepting—as opposed to perhaps appearing to accept—rules that are less than ideal from their perspective? And can any set of rules that rests on continuous acceptance by an entire community be sufficiently durable to serve rules' settlement function?[18] We believe the second question is but an aspect of the first. If there is reason to accept a nonideal set of rules, then all will have reason to accept the set that others will accept, and rules accepted in the past have special salience in this regard. Rules once accepted will thus tend to be durable, at least until there is an obvious refusal by some to accept them, or until they prove too anachronistic or unjust to serve their moral functions. We take up the basic question of how we can have reason to accept and act on nonideal sets of rules in chapter 4.

Other issues we have introduced include revolutionary changes of systems of rules, coexistence of separate systems of rules in a simple community, and impositions of systems of rules by conquest. We take these issues up more fully in chapter 10.

PART TWO

Acting under Rules

FOUR The Problem of Rules

In the preceding chapters, we explained why a community might name an authority, Lex, to settle doubts and controversies. Settlement is necessary although the members of the community agree on general moral principles and recognize the importance of interests other than their own. Even in these ideal circumstances, there will be disagreement and uncertainty about what should be done in response to particular problems of social life, and this in turn will impose considerable costs on the community as a whole.

The means for settlement is a set of authoritative rules. Through rules, Lex can solve coordination problems, prevent mistakes that result from lack of information or expertise, and provide individual reasoners some relief from the task of assessing all possible reasons for or against different courses of action. Some of his rules will serve directly as guides to conduct; others will authorize further settlement by private parties or official decision-makers. The authority for all Lex's rules stems from general acceptance within the community of a basic settlement rule, "Let Lex decide."

To perform their functions effectively, Lex's rules must be determinate enough to avoid moral controversy in the process of their application and general enough to settle questions that Lex cannot attend to as they arise. They must also be "serious" rules—prescriptions to be followed in all cases that fall within their terms, without further consideration of the reasons that led Lex to issue them.

The problem with settlement by means of serious rules is that no matter how wise Lex is and how well he crafts his rules, a general, determinate rule can never achieve the perfection of accurate case-by-case decision-making. The rule's function is to translate moral principles into a set of directions that can be understood by people who previously disagreed or were uncertain about the meaning of the those principles. It follows that the rule must be different from and simpler than the actual moral reasons that support it.[1] Further, the rule cannot provide a correct translation for every case. Lacking omniscience, Lex cannot anticipate all future problems that will meet the concrete conditions stated in the rule; and if he could do this, the rule would be far too complex for practical application. Lex's rules, therefore, will sometimes dictate the wrong result.

The purpose of this chapter is to spell out in detail the paradox generated by imperfect rules and the consequences that follow for the process of authoritative settlement. In summary form the problem is this: it is rational and morally desirable for Lex to issue a rule whenever it appears that the rule will prevent more errors than it will cause. It is also rational and morally correct for individual members of the community to endorse Lex's decision to issue such a rule. Yet the rule inevitably will dictate erroneous results in some of the cases it covers, and it is neither rational nor morally correct for individuals to follow the rule when they believe that its prescription is wrong for the circumstances in which they find themselves.[2] At the same time, these individuals will sometimes err in their calculations and disobey the rule when in fact its prescription is correct. And as long as the sum of these errors is likely to exceed the sum of errors of universal compliance, it continues to be rational and morally desirable for Lex to issue the rule and to demand that it be followed in every case.[3] In other words, a "gap" lies between what Lex has reason to prescribe (and his subjects have reason to want him to prescribe) and what his subjects have reason to do, all things considered.

It is our position that this gap between the morality of issuing rules and the morality of following rules cannot be closed. As we shall show in the following pages, various attempts to eliminate it or explain it away are unpersuasive. Nor is it possible to strike a compromise between serious rules and mere advisory rules or rules or thumb. Rules cannot usefully be given a presumptive value or "weight."

We begin by looking more closely at the different versions of the gap that accompany different functions that rules perform. Next, we review various strategies that have been proposed as ways to close or narrow the gap. Initially, our discussion is confined to the two-way relationship between the rule-making authority, Lex, and the individual actors to whom the rules apply. Later, when we take up sanctions as a strategy to close the gap, we shall complicate the problem by introducing a third party, the judge who applies rules in adjudicating disputes.

A Closer Look at the Gap

Lex issues rules because he anticipates that his subjects will err in various ways in deciding what to do. It is not necessary that they be self-interested or otherwise inclined to act for improper reasons. In fact, if the only problem were improper motivation—if Lex's subjects were immoral but capable of perfect reasoning—a credible promise to punish moral wrongdoers would be enough to elicit ideal conduct. The problem that leads Lex to issue rules is not wrongdoing, but error.[4]

Lex's rules respond to a variety of reasoning errors. Perhaps the simplest type of error results from the actor's lack of information or expertise. In this case, the function of a rule is to require uniform conduct when this is the best course of action for most of those who are subject to the rule. If, among the sum of actions governed by the rule, more harm would result from mistaken judgment than from compliance with the rule, the rule is justified.

For example, suppose Lex knows that frequent strong tides make swimming dangerous at a certain site. In a world of perfect reasoners, no rule would be necessary because all people would correctly judge whether and when they should swim.[5] In fact, most people lack the information necessary for accurate judgment: some may understand the tides well enough to know when it is safe to swim, and others may be strong enough to resist the tides; but too many will err and swim when they should not. As a result, considerable public and private resources will be devoted to rescuing hapless swimmers. As long as Lex's information is superior to that of most of his subjects, and as long as it is not practical to identify the experts among them, the best course for Lex is to enact a serious rule, "No swimming."[6]

This rule, however, is not correct in all its applications. For those who understand the tides or swim powerfully, and who have a reason to swim, compliance may not be the right thing to do. At the same time, a qualified rule, "No swimming unless you know it is safe for you to swim," will not serve Lex's purposes because some people will believe they understand the tides or swim powerfully when in fact they do not. Thus, in a community of imperfect reasoners, we have a gap between what Lex ought to demand and what some of his subjects (the genuine experts) ought to do.

A second type of error is often discussed under the heading of "coordination."[7] To explore the gap thoroughly, it is useful to make some distinctions within this category. One form of coordination error is what we shall call "equivocation." Equivocation occurs when individual actors can proceed in several incompatible ways and there is no reason to prefer one course of action over the other. Each actor will then choose at random, and the resulting actions will conflict. Choices about language, currency, and the flow of traffic are examples of equivocation.

Here, the function of a rule is to avoid conflict by designating one of the alternatives: "Drive on the right." The rule is easily justified because people will surely do better if they act in harmony, and they will lose nothing by conforming to the rule. The interesting feature of this rule is that unlike most rules, it is correct in *all* of its applications. If there truly is nothing to recommend one course of action over another, compliance is always the right thing to do. The rule should be as determinate as possible, so that all will understand what it requires. But it need not be a serious rule because true equivocations do not produce a gap: what Lex demands is exactly what his subjects should do.

A second type of coordination error is a failure of internal coordination. This happens when short-term reasons for action conflict with long-term reasons of greater importance, and yet the short-term reasons prevail because the harm to long-term reasons is incremental. In other words, the long-term reasons are disregarded because the actor cannot assign them a precise position in time and compare them with short-term reasons for action. Procrastination is an example:[8] Brian knows there is a chance that over the course of the summer, his house will suddenly be invaded by ants, and he will need to call an exterminator. This is something Brian would very much like to avoid, and he can prevent it from happening by spraying ant poison outside the house at the beginning of summer. The difficulty is that on any given day, he has better things to do than kill ants; and one day's delay is unlikely to make the critical difference. As a result, he never sprays, and sooner or later the ants arrive inside his house.

Assume that Brian can persuade Lex to provide him with a personal rule: "Spray for ants on the first day of May." The rule solves the internal coordination problem by designating (arbitrarily) a point in time at which Brian must act to protect his long-term interest. A perfect reasoner with perfect information would not need such a rule. He would know precisely when ants were due to arrive, would anticipate his opportunity costs at all points during the intervening period, would be free from any bias, and would spray at the optimal time. An ordinary reasoner lacks information both about when the threat will mature and what opportunities will arise in the interim, and may unduly prefer present satisfaction over future satisfaction.

Thus, if Brian possesses only ordinary powers of reason, and if his long-term interest in avoiding extermination is greater than the interests it preempts on May 1, he will be better off complying with Lex's rule. Yet the rule is not perfect; there may be a better time to spray, when opportunity costs are not as high. If, on May 1, Brian believes the time is not ideal, there is a gap between what Brian thought best when he asked for a rule and what he thinks best when the time comes to follow it.

Most of the coordination problems with which law is concerned require coordination between two or more people. One well-known form of multiparty coordination problem is a prisoner's dilemma. Two parties can gain from cooperation, but each will suffer if one "cooperates" and the other does not. As a result, neither dares to cooperate, and both forgo the potential gain. This problem is intractable even among perfect reasoners, because even if everyone assumes that everyone else will infallibly do what is best, neither action (cooperation or noncooperation) is independently the best thing to do. Either option may be best, depending on what the other party chooses. Further, even if perfect reasoners could overcome the problem, imperfect reasoners cannot. As long as it is possible that one party will fail to understand the potential for cooperative benefit, or believe the other will fail to understand, or be tempted to cheat, or think that the other might cheat, the incentive not to cooperate remains in place.

A rule appears to solve the prisoner's dilemma by requiring both parties to cooperate. Yet the rule "Cooperate" does not in itself close the gap between what it requires and what reason dictates. Whether the actor's reasoning is self-interested, as in the classic form of prisoner's dilemma, or altruistic, as in an altruist's dilemma, the actor has reason to defect from the cooperative behavior required by the rule: if others are complying, the actor will produce a gain by defecting. And if others are not complying, the actor will avert a loss. Either way, reason dictates defection, and a gap remains between what Lex has reason to require and what his subjects have reason to do.[9]

In a more typical form of social coordination problem, reasons for action vary according to the actions of others but are not exclusively or symmetrically dependent on them. In these situations, the function of a rule is to secure the benefits of cooperation by requiring classes of actors to conduct themselves in a designated way. Among well-motivated perfect reasoners with perfect information, a rule would be unnecessary, because everyone's circumstances would be understood by all simultaneously and the best combination of acts would ensue. In fact, actors cannot reasonably calculate the reasons for action that may apply to others whose actions affect them, and they certainly cannot calculate all the errors those others will make in deciding what to do. As a result, cooperative gains will be lost even among well-motivated actors because the actors do not know how to cooperate.

The variety of circumstances in which rule-subjects find themselves means that a coordination rule requiring uniform conduct will not be perfect. Some people will have reasons to disobey the rule that outweigh whatever cooperative benefit their compliance would bring. If these people could neatly identify themselves, Lex would prefer to exclude them. But for the same reasons that lead Lex to issue a rule, calculating the effect of one's action on potential cooperative gains is an extremely difficult task. Because subjects will err in making this calculation, Lex cannot make an exception for those who believe they have sufficient reason to disregard the rule without giving up the benefit of the rule. As long as more would be lost through a general failure of cooperation than through the overinclusiveness of the rule, a serious rule is justified. Yet because some people will in fact have sufficient reason to disobey, there is a gap between what Lex has reason to demand and what those actors have reason to do.

Suppose, for example, that a library has a hundred regular patrons. Most of them find it useful to mark in books as they read. At the same time, most prefer to read unmarked books, and most of these would prefer to forgo marking in exchange for assurance that no one else would mark in books. Further, some of the patrons strongly dislike reading marked books and have taken to checking out new books as they arrive and hoarding them for periods of time. The marking and hoarding of books produces acrimony among the patrons.

If all library patrons were perfect moral reasoners with perfect information, this situation would not arise. No one would mark in books unless his reason for doing so were strong enough to justify all resulting harm to others, and no one would hoard books because all would know that others marked only when justified. There would be no cause for discord. But these are obviously impossible conditions. Stephen, contemplating marking in a book, cannot accurately assess the harm it will cause without knowing how many others will read the book, what their preferences will be regarding marks, and whether any other readers will have reason to mark in the same book. And if Stephen is likely to err in his calculation, Fred, who is thinking of hoarding a book, cannot assume that others will mark only when justified. And Donald, who would like to mark in a book, cannot predict the harm his own marks will cause without assessing the possibility that Stephen or others like him will, rightly or wrongly, mark in the book. Thus, cooperation is not possible, even if all parties are willing.

Lex might now intervene with a rule, "No marking in library books." Assuming general compliance, this rule will prevent unjustified harm and eliminate the incentive for hoarding. Accordingly, it is likely to be well received by all patrons: those who prefer unmarked books will be better off, and even those who do not care about marks in books will have better access to books (no hoarding) and better relations with fellow patrons.

Nevertheless, the results of the rule are not ideal. Stephen may in fact have good reason to mark in a book (time is short, the book is obscure, and he is working on something of great social and political import). Yet if Lex qualifies the rule—"No marking in library books unless your reasons for doing so outweigh any harm the mark will cause"—the same errors will occur and the rule will fail to have the desired effect. Thus, there is a gap between what Lex has reason to demand of Stephen and what Stephen has reason to do.

In each of the situations we have described, individual actors may endorse Lex's rule, believing that it does more good than harm. Yet, with the exception of a true equivocation, actors faced with particular problems may also conclude that the rule's prescription is not the best answer to the question what to do. If so, it is not rational, and arguably not morally acceptable, for them to follow the rule. Yet if people are imperfect in their calculations, either factually or morally, and consequently err more often than not in deciding whether to comply, Lex will prefer that they comply in every case, and his preference will be both rational and morally correct.[10]

It is interesting to note that a gap also exists at the level of the master settlement rule, "Let Lex decide." For example, suppose that everyone agrees that sex should be consensual, yet there is disagreement about what counts, or ought to count, as an expression of consent. Some think that if a woman says no, she does not consent; others think it is fair to assume consent unless she says no three times in a shrill voice; still others think that if the circumstances are inauspicious, even "yes" is not enough to show genuine consent.[11] This situation presents a coordination problem: as long as people diverge in their understanding of what suffices to express consent, there will be instances of sex without subjective consent, instances of lost opportunity, endless debate, and a great deal of rancor.

Suppose also that Lex responds with a rule, "'No' means no." Some of Lex's subjects may endorse the settlement rule, "Let Lex decide" and yet oppose this particular rule. They may believe that his choice of rule is radically wrong, so wrong as to outweigh the potential benefits of coordination. Or they may believe that the benefits of coordination will never exceed the aggregate amount of individual discontent engendered by a rule governing consent to sex. In other words, they may believe that this particular settlement by Lex is not justified by the underlying purposes of the rule "Let Lex decide."

The result is a coordination problem at a higher level of generality. It is also a particularly intractable problem because Lex does not stand behind the rule "Let Lex decide." The source of authority for this rule is the subjects' own acceptance of it. In their general endorsement of the master settlement rule, they surely intend it to be a serious rule, not just a piece of advice to be followed insofar as one agrees with Lex's rules. An advisory rule would not achieve settlement. Yet if rule-subjects believe that a particular rule is not justified by the reasons that support the master rule, they cannot rationally conclude that they ought to let Lex decide.

First Strategy: Rule-Sensitive Particularism

Once a rule is issued, rational and morally motivated actors deciding whether to do as it requires will include among their reasons for action the value of having a rule and the harm their failure to comply might cause to the value of the rule. Borrowing from Fred Schauer, we shall refer to a process of reasoning that takes account of the value of rules as "rule-sensitive particularism."[12] It is sometimes suggested that rule-sensitive particularism can narrow the gap, or even better, that it can lead actors to follow rules precisely, but only when they should.

We believe, however, that the force of rule-generated reasons for action is limited. Moreover, in the case of coordination rules, it is nonexistent unless there is a general practice of nonparticularistic rule-following in effect. We shall discuss the various functions of rules in turn.

When a rule is based solely on superior information or expertise possessed by Lex, the value of the rule is the epistemic value of Lex's judgment about what the rule-subject ought to do. The rule provides actors with a reason to believe that they should do what it requires, but only to the extent that they believe Lex is a reliable source of information and advice. Suppose, for example, that Leo is thinking of going for a swim. He believes he is strong enough to overcome the tides, but he also knows that he might be mistaken. To a rule-sensitive particularist, Lex's rule "No swimming" represents Lex's opinion that it is probably a mistake to think one can safely swim. If Lex is credible on this point, his rule gives Leo some reason, though by no means a conclusive reason, to believe that he is in fact mistaken. Thus, while issuance of a rule does not narrow the objective gap between what Lex has reason to demand and what his subjects have reason to do, it may bring their judgments closer together.

At the same time, it is easy to overstate the epistemic effect of the rule. If Leo is a rule-sensitive particularist, he knows that the rule "No swimming" is only a rule. It is a general prescription that Lex has issued in the expectation that errors of unconstrained judgment would exceed the rule's errors of overinclusion. Thus, the direct effect of the rule is not to create a reason to believe that what it requires is right, but only to create a reason to believe that this is a subject on which people often err. Even if Leo regards Lex as a credible source of advice about swimming, the rule does not express Lex's opinion that he, Leo, ought not swim; it expresses Lex's opinion that most people will overestimate their ability to swim. If Leo firmly believes that he is not like most people, the effect of the rule will be negligible. If he is unsure, he has reason to revise upward the probability that he will err, based on Lex's opinion that the general propensity for error is high. At best, then, the rule provides Leo with an indirect and inconclusive reason not to swim.

Thus, with respect to rules that are based on Lex's superior information or expertise, the most that rule-sensitive particularism can do is to narrow the distance between Lex's judgment and that of his subjects. To the extent of Lex's perceived epistemic competence, the rule creates a reason to believe that the actor's own contrary judgment may be wrong. But this reason is only an indirect reason to act as the rule requires, because the rule is simply evidence of a probability of error. Further, because the effect of the rule is only epistemic, it does not close or even narrow the actual gap between Lex's reasons for issuing rules and his subjects' reasons for action.[13] From the actor's standpoint, rule-sensitive particularism transmutes serious rules into advisory rules of thumb.

When rules solve coordination problems, the value of the rule and its effect on reasons for action take a different form. The easy case for a rule-sensitive particularist is a rule that solves a problem of equivocation. The existence of an equivocation rule generates not only a reason, but a decisive reason, for complying with the rule. A rule that prescribes one of several equally attractive courses of action gives salience to the alternative it selects, and salience provides a reason to believe that others will do as the rule directs. Belief that others will comply with the rule in turn provides several reasons for the actor to comply: like action will avoid confusion and conflict and contrary action will undermine others' confidence in the rule. Further, as a convention develops around the rule, the behavior of others and others' expectations about one's own behavior provide increasingly strong reasons to comply.

As others have noted, the rule itself ("Drive on the right") is not a reason for the actor to drive on the right. The rule merely provides the actor with a reason to believe (salience) that conditions exist (others driving on the right) that generate a direct reason for action (accidents are more likely if one drives on the left).[14] Further, the causal link between the rule's quality of salience and the conditions that create a reason for action depends on the assumption that almost everyone involved will, simultaneously, make the same assumption and perceive the same reason for action.[15] Yet neither of these observations presents a serious difficulty for a rule-sensitive particularist. The mutual assumption of compliance is perfectly fair, even if circular, and the result is a new reason for action, one brought about by the rule.

Coordination problems that involve conflicting interests and beliefs are not so easily resolved. Consider first the case of internal coordination. A rule "Spray for ants on the first of May," gives salience to a particular day, May 1, and it offers the benefits of coordination. Brian knows that if he complies with the rule, he will avoid the need for an exterminator. Yet neither the salience of May 1 nor the promise of benefits can change the fact that when May 1 comes, Brian may have special plans that exclude ant spray and outweigh the incremental danger of waiting until the next day to spray. The same is true of the next day, and every other day; therefore, the coordination problem remains unsolved.[16]

A rule-sensitive particularist might respond that if Brian is careful, he will understand this, and will understand that if he postpones at all he will lose the benefit of the rule. Therefore, he will follow the rule unless the value of doing other things on May 1 exceeds the cumulative value of the rule—that is, the full expected cost and inconvenience of exterminating ants. If in fact the value of doing other things on May 1 exceeds the cost of extermination, then disregarding the rule is the right thing to do. Thus, rule-sensitive particularism will lead Brian to follow the rule exactly when he should.[17]

It is not so clear, however, that good particularistic reasoning would lead Brian to this conclusion. The fact that the rule designates May 1 as the day to spray is not a reason to believe that May 1 is the optimal date. If, on May 1, Brian believes that his plans for May 2, or for any subsequent day, will be less important than his plans for May 1, surely the best thing to do is to put off compliance until that later day. Thus, even if Brian keeps in mind the cumulative value of the rule, "Spray on the first of May," he has reason to revise the rule to reflect what now seems a wiser strategy: "Spray on May 1, or on any day between May 1 and the arrival of ants when your opportunity costs are less than your opportunity costs on May 1."

At this point, however, the potential for error is enormous. Brian may guess incorrectly when ants will arrive (if he could predict this accurately, he would not have a coordination problem). He also may believe that his interest in doing other things is greater than the cumulative coordinating value of the rule, or greater than the opportunity cost of spraying on a future day, when it is not. Errors of this kind are particularly likely because today's interests tend to be more conspicuous in the reasoners' mind than future interests or risks of future loss. And as long as the likely cost of error exceeds the opportunities lost by spraying on May 1, Brian is better off simply following the rule. Nevertheless, it remains true that May 1 may not be the right date. Therefore, taking full account of the value of the rule, there is still a gap between the rule Brian ought to adopt and the action he ought to take.[18]

Descriptively, we do have some success, though nowhere near complete success, in following self-imposed rules. Some of this success may be attributable to a rational estimate of the costs of deliberation. We may set our alarm clocks at a regular time on most days without much thought about the possible alternatives because it is easy to do this, and because experience tells us that further thought is unlikely to be fruitful.[19] Another possibility is that some of our success with self-imposed rules is due to less rational influences, such as guilt, fear of divine retribution, or a test of personal resolve. In any event, understanding the benefits of a coordinating rule is not enough in itself to bring about an ideal level of compliance.[20]

The next type of coordination problem is the prisoner's (or altruist's) dilemma. In a true prisoner's dilemma, involving perfectly symmetrical interdependent interests, the parties will always be better off if all follow a rule that requires them to cooperate than if all defect. Yet unlike a rule designed to overcome equivocation, a rule that solves a prisoner's dilemma does not provide individual actors with reason to believe that it is best for them to conform to the rule. Whether or not others are complying, each actor continues to have reason to defect. Their reasons for action are not affected by the introduction of a rule.

When we come to the typical legal problem of multiparty coordination, in which different actors' reasons for action are related but not perfectly interdependent, the effect of a rule on reasoning becomes more complex. A preliminary point is that if we assume that everyone is a rule-sensitive particularist, there is no reason to believe that others will act as the rule prescribes. Consider the problem of library books. Lex has issued a rule, "No marking in books." The benefits of this rule, if generally followed, include less harm to those who dislike reading marked books, an end to hoarding, and an end to discord (at least if all endorse the rule). Yet for particularists (including rule-sensitive particularists), the possibility remains that some readers, at some times, will have—or will believe they have—reasons to mark in books that outweigh any harm their marks will cause (including, for rule-sensitive particularists, any harm they will cause to general confidence in the rule). Given the complexity of this calculation, a sensible rule-sensitive particularist will also anticipate that, in a community of rule-sensitive particularists, many will err and think they are justified in marking in books when they are not; and he must anticipate that everyone else will anticipate this as well. This puts the rule-sensitive particularist back where he started. He has no reason to assume that others will follow the rule, and therefore no reason to think that his own conduct will undermine a set of benefits that the rule, if generally followed, might produce. Another way to put this is that if everyone is and is known to be a rule-sensitive particularist, there is nothing left of serious rules about which particularists can be rule-sensitive. In a world of particularists, serious rules would be nothing more than rules of thumb.

Things change if many of the population accept the rule as a serious rule and follow it without engaging in a particularistic assessment of reasons for action. At this point, our rule-sensitive particularist must consider the effect that his own failure to comply may have on the potential benefits of the rule. Suppose again that Stephen is contemplating marking in a library book. Lex has enacted the rule "No marking in books," and most of the patrons of the library follow it unquestioningly. The first consideration for Stephen is the direct harm his mark may cause, given a general practice of not marking in books. This calculation differs from the calculation of harm prior to the rule, because Stephen will now be marking in a book that probably would not otherwise have been defaced. His mark also may trigger a hoarding response that otherwise was unlikely to occur, and may cause acrimony that would not otherwise arise.

In themselves, these effects are relatively minor—after all, we are talking about one person marking in a single book. If Stephen is up to something very important, and the mark will prevent his losing a critical thought, he may be justified in marking the book. Yet as a rule-sensitive particularist, Stephen must also consider any indirect influence his action will have on the actions of others. Stephen's marks should have no effect on the conduct of an inveterate rule-follower, because, by definition, this rule-follower does not engage in particularistic consideration of reasons for and against marking in books. Yet to the extent that rule-following depends on a general sense of the usefulness of the rule, Stephen's marks, if noticed by rule-followers, might push them toward the tipping point at which they will cease following the rule.[21] The effect on general compliance is incremental, but it is something for Stephen to consider in deciding what to do.

Perhaps more important is the effect of the act on other rule-sensitive particularists. No rule-sensitive particularist can count on the prospect that other rule-sensitive particularists will comply, or comply optimally, with the rule—they will balance reasons for action and will frequently err in doing so. Yet rule-sensitive particularists will tend to comply more often when they believe the community includes a large proportion of rule-followers. They will do so because their own violation now causes harm that might not otherwise occur, and because they understand that their action could jar some rule-followers out of the habit of following the rule. If these rule-sensitive particularists notice that someone has violated the rule, they will decrease their estimate of the number of rule-followers in the community, and they will worry less about the effect of their own violation on the general practice of rule-following. If Michael, a rule-sensitive particularist, sees that Stephen has marked in a book, he will know that there are at least some other rule-sensitive particularists out there, and this will lead him to discount the harmful impact of his own violation of the rule. In this way, the potential effect of Stephen's act on Michael becomes another reason for Stephen not to violate the rule.

Thus, rule-sensitive particularism regarding a coordination rule can narrow the gap and bring the particularist closer to an ideal level of compliance with the rule. At the same time, it will never close the gap because the opportunities for error in rule-sensitive calculations are too great. As long as the errors of noncompliance are likely to exceed the errors of compliance, Lex has reason to issue a serious rule.

Further—and this is a point we want to emphasize—rule-sensitive particularism in regard to coordination rules narrows the gap only when most people avoid particularism and treat legal rules as serious rules. Another way to put this is that rule-sensitive particularism cannot be publicized as the correct approach to rules. It can only be effective when rules are presented, and generally accepted, as serious rules. In a community comprised entirely of rule-sensitive particularists, it has no advantage at all. In such a community there can be no serious rules, only rules of thumb.

There is a further benefit associated with rules that cuts across the categories we have identified—the time and energy a rule-follower saves by avoiding deliberation about what to do. Yet this is a difficult benefit to translate into rule-sensitive particularism. Full-scale rule-sensitive particularism, comparing saved costs of deliberation with the probability of error if one follows the rule, means there will be no saving in deliberative costs. One must know what the outcome of deliberation would be to make the necessary comparison. Of course, a quick determination that the costs of deliberation are likely to be high and can be avoided by following a rule yields a reason to follow the rule that would not exist but for the issuance of the rule. Yet this is a reason to *follow* the rule—that is, not to engage in rule-sensitive particularism. Further, the extent of deliberation required to reach a correct result will vary significantly among actors and contexts. Thus, even if Lex rightly believes that in general, the costs of moral deliberation will exceed the costs of following the rule, this may not always be the case. A gap still exists between the justified demands of the rule-maker and a rule-sensitive particularistic assessment of what individual actors ought to do.

Second Strategy: Presumptive Positivism

Fred Schauer and others have suggested that the best response to rules is neither to follow them unthinkingly nor to engage in a full particularist assessment of reasons for action but to give rules a special presumptive weight in decision-making.[22] Actors should assign Lex's rules a higher value than they, or the reasons behind them, normally would have in the actor's balance of reasons for action. This approach, its proponents suggest, will bring the conduct of rule-subjects closer to the moral ideal than either blind obedience or rule-sensitive particularism.

We believe that while presumptive or weighted rule-following is a useful idea, it does not solve the problem of rules. Depending on the form the presumption takes and the decision-making context, it will sometimes collapse into rule-sensitive particularism, and even when it does not, its superiority over blind rule-following is contingent at best. Further, presumptive rule-following, because it is a modified form of rule-following, will never completely close the gap.

An initial question about presumptive rule-following is precisely what it entails. Explaining what he calls "presumptive positivism," Schauer states at one point that an actor should disobey a rule "when, and only when, the reasons for overriding [it] are perceived by the decision-maker to be particularly strong."[23] At another point, he says that an actor should disobey a rule "when the result it indicates is egregiously at odds with the result that is indicated by [a] larger and more morally acceptable set of values."[24] Donald Regan suggests that, while rules should not be treated as transparent (such that the subject engages in a full analysis of the reasons behind them), an actor should disobey "if [the actor] just happens to be able to see clearly that *in that case* it leads to a wrong result, or that the normal justification for it does not obtain."[25] In the context of legal precedents, Stephen Perry argues that a decision-maker should disobey a (precedent) rule only when the reasons for doing so "exceed a threshold of strength which [is] higher to some specified degree than what she would ordinarily look upon as sufficient to tip the balance of reasons."[26] As a phenomenological description of presumptive positivism, Schauer proposes "a casual look, a glimpse, a peek, a preliminary check, pursuant to which a decision-maker follows the recognized rule unless some other factor overtly intrudes on her decision-making process."[27] In Regan's terms, "The fact may simply force itself upon [the actor's] consciousness that the rule should be ignored in some particular case."[28]

These descriptions and comments suggest several possiblities. First, the mechanism for presumptive rule-following might be a simple threshold, referring only to the strength of the reasons to disobey. We might say, for example, that actors should follow rules unless the reasons for violating them have a strength of at least 10.[29] Leo should break the rule and swim in order to rescue a child (110), but he should not break the rule because he is hot (2). Stephen should mark in the book he is reading if his project is enormously important and time is very short (12).

Alternatively, the mechanism for presumptive rule-following might be a comparative threshold, so that the question is whether the reasons to disobey are much stronger than the reasons to obey. The comparison might be proportional, asking whether reasons to disobey are disproportionate to reasons to obey; or it might involve a fixed margin, asking, for example, whether the reasons to disobey are stronger by 10 than the reasons to obey. Now Leo must compare the importance of rescuing the child with the dangers of attempting to swim, and Stephen must compare the importance of preserving his research with the harm he will cause, including harm to coordination, if he breaks the rule and marks in a book. The critical difference between this and the simple form of presumptive rule-following is that the simple form requires only that the subject assess reasons for *violating* the rule.

Looking first at the simple threshold ("Obey unless reasons to disobey have a strength of 10"), this should in fact avert a large range of errors in reasoning. Specifically, it will prevent all those errors that result because the actor assigns a value higher than the reasons for following the rule, but less than 10, to contrary reasons that actually are less important than the reasons for following the rule. Whatever

Leo may think about the dangers of swimming, he is unlikely to swim simply because he is hot (2). Assuming that the reasons for following the rule are well below the threshold, the effect of the threshold is significant because actors must make large errors before they will disobey the rule when they should not. Leo will not swim unless he has overestimated by a factor of 5 the value of cooling off.

Yet the effects of this simple threshold form of presumptive rule-following are both limited and erratic. There remains a possibility that actors will make large errors and break rules when they should not.[30] Leo might overestimate by a factor of 5. Further, although the reasons for following the rule are not part of the subject's calculation, the possibility for error increases as the strength of these reasons approaches the threshold. If the dangers of swimming are quite high (say, 9), it takes only a small error for Leo to violate the rule when he should not.[31] For example, if the reasons for diving in to save his favorite hat are in fact worth 8, but Leo mistakenly assigns them a value of 10, he will swim when he ought not.

A related point is that, if a simple threshold is what proponents of presumptive rule-following have in mind, it is a very blunt approach to the problem of rules.[32] Rules vary considerably in their importance: there are rules about murder and rules about cleaning up after dogs. For various reasons, not least of which is the difficulty of defining a universal metric for the strength of reasons, it is not practical to specify a violation threshold for every rule. Yet a single threshold for disobedience of all rules is unsatisfactory. Applying such a threshold without regard to the reasons in favor of the rule is phenomenologically implausible, and it could do more harm than good. If actors allow important reasons for breaking rules to override even more important reasons for following the rules, and if the resulting errors exceed the errors of blind (exceptionless) rule-following, Lex would be better off with serious rules.

A comparative form of presumptive rule-following—in which the actor follows the rule unless reasons to disobey are disproportionately stronger than reasons to obey, or stronger to some fixed extent—permits the actor to "peek" at the whole set of applicable reasons for action. This seems more sensible in psychological terms, and it has the virtue of allowing the threshold to vary from rule to rule. Yet a comparative presumption substantially complicates the rule-subject's inquiry. This not only increases deliberation costs, but also provides more room for errors of individual judgment. Of course, the inquiry is supposed to be limited to a "peek," but a peek at reasons both for and against following a rule is simply a sloppy form of particularism.

To see how errors might arise, suppose that the formula for presumptive rule-following holds that actors should follow rules unless the reasons to disobey are twice as strong as the reasons to obey. Consider first how this formula would apply to a rule that is based on Lex's superior information and expertise. If Leo thinks the tides are dangerous, or if he is not sure where he might encounter dangerous tides and considers Lex a good source of information, he will assign a nonnegligible value to the reasons for complying with the rule (danger). Doubling this value may indeed be effective to prevent serious errors. If Leo assesses the dangers of swimming at 9, he may swim to rescue a child (and this may be a mistake), but he will not swim to rescue his hat. If, on the other hand, he believes the rule "No swimming" is an overbroad rule designed to protect weak swimmers, he will assign little or no value either directly to danger or indirectly to the epistemic value of the rule. At most, the rule will appear as a warning that many people err, and even this may not come to mind in a "peek." If the value Leo assigns to reasons for following the rule is close to nothing, doubling that value is unlikely to keep him out of the water. And if Lex believes that many people will reason this way, and most will be mistaken, Lex is still better off with a serious rule.

The possibility for errors of judgment is more striking in the case of a coordination rule. A "peek" may not be enough to reveal coordination benefits at all, and if it is, the presumption ("twice as strong") may prove illusory. Recall that the benefits of coordination provide a reason to follow a rule only if the existence of the rule gives the actor reason to believe that others will follow it. Only then will his own violation cause harm that would not otherwise occur and undermine general faith in the rule.

We have already explained why the existence of a coordination rule does not give a rule-sensitive particularist reason to believe that others will comply if those others are also particularists. The process of calculating the probable distribution of reasons for action throughout a community is too complex to permit anyone to count on the conduct of other particularists. As a result, unless most in the community are rule-followers, there is no reason to comply with the rule. Doubling this changes nothing.

Perhaps if everyone were a presumptive rule-follower, and if this were generally understood, and if the probable distribution of reasons for action were such that very few people would have, or think they have, important reasons to disobey the rule, there would be reason to expect a general practice of rule-following. This in turn would provide some reason to follow the rule (violation would cause harm that would not otherwise occur, including harm to the practice of rule-following), which could be doubled as the presumption requires. Yet this is unreliable. If chances are that a significant number of people will break the rule, rightly or erroneously, the prospect of coordination collapses and the presumption has no effect.[33]

Returning to the library example, if all library patrons are presumptive rule-followers, who mark in books only when they believe the reasons for doing so are twice as strong as the reasons against, Stephen must anticipate that some people will mark in books, and that some of these will have erred in applying the presumption. If he expects that more than a few will break the rule, then he cannot count on general compliance and will believe that his own marks will make little or no difference. Doubling his reasons to comply then means nothing.

The possibility that reasons for compliance will vanish completely under particularistic scrutiny might be avoided if the presumption took the form of a fixed margin between reasons to obey and reasons to disobey, rather than a proportional comparison. For example, the formula for presumptive rule-following might hold that actors should follow rules unless the reasons for breaking them are stronger by 10 than the reasons for obeying them. Assuming (dangerously) that people can make sense of "10," this ensures that the reasons for obeying a rule will never be overridden by reasons perceived to be worth less than 10, and that something more than 10 will be required when the reasons for compliance have some purchase in the mind of the actor. Stephen will not mark in the book unless the importance of this to his project is at least 10; and if Leo rates the danger of swimming at 4, he will not dive for his hat unless he thinks the hat is worth 14. A range of errors is thereby avoided (those in which Stephen assigns a value of 1 to 9 to reasons that are less important than following the rule, and those in which Leo assigns a value of 5 to 13 to the rescue of his hat when in fact the hat is worth less than the costs of diving).

Yet there is still room for error, particularly when reasons for compliance depend on successful coordination. The margin (10) may not be enough to prevent a mistaken comparison of reasons for and against compliance, and if this happens often enough, Lex would be better off with a serious rule. A fixed margin also suffers from problems of bluntness that are nearly as serious as those of a simple threshhold presumption. If Leo estimates that reasons to obey have a value of 100 (serious danger) while reasons to disobey have a value of 110 (rescuing a child), the margin for error is rather narrow. If he estimates that reasons to obey have value of 4 (moderate danger) and reasons not to obey have a value of 14 (saving his hat), the margin is proportionally much greater and the likelihood of error is less. The odd result is that the less is at stake, the better the presumption works.

We have explored at some length the potential weaknesses of different versions of presumptive rule-following, insofar as these are viewed as ways to bring conduct closer to the moral ideal. In each case, it remains possible that Lex's subjects will conform less well to applicable reasons for action than they would if they followed rules blindly. If so, Lex has reason to insist on obedience to serious rules.

A more fundamental problem is that presumptive rule-following, even when it is superior to blind rule-following, does not eliminate the gap. From the point of view of rule-subjects, a presumption that limits inquiry into the justification for the rule, or artificially inflates the reasons to obey, will sometimes produce outcomes at odds with their best judgment, all things considered. When this is the case, following the rule will not appear to them to be the right thing to do. In other words, a presumption in favor of rule-following is in fact an additional rule, which subjects may have reason to disobey. Thus, even if we assume that presumptive rule-following is the best choice from Lex's point of view, what Lex has reason to demand will diverge from what his subjects have reason to do.

Third Strategy: Exclusionary Reasons

Joseph Raz has argued that legal rules can be understood as "exclusionary" reasons for action.[34] In his view, legal rules function as "second-order" reasons that exclude a set of "first-order" reasons from the process of moral deliberation. A rule of this kind is derived from the same first-order reasons that normally would govern its subjects' decisions, but because subjects are likely to err, it preempts these first-order reasons and replaces them with the prescription of the rule.[35]

Suppose, for example, that Lex enacts a rule, "No swimming," because he believes most people will misjudge their abilities to swim. If this rule creates an exclusionary reason for action, it will prevent Leo from considering how well he can swim and how much he values his sinking hat. It also—argues Raz—provides Leo with a new first-order reason not to swim: Lex said so. Rule-sensitive particularism does not enter into the analysis. The rule functions not only as a reason to forgo swimming, but as a reason that supplants all the reasons for or against swimming that Lex might have considered in issuing the rule. The exclusionary effect of the rule may not be absolute—it may not, for example, exclude emergencies such as a drowning child. But whatever reasons fall within its scope are removed from consideration.

The idea of exclusionary reasons captures very nicely what Lex would like to accomplish through rules—if rules did operate this way, there would be no gap and no obstacle to obtaining the benefits of rules. In our view, however, there is no magic in the issuance of rules that can bring about this kind of exclusion. The premise of the exclusionary theory seems to be that it is rational, at the time of action, to view the reasons that support Lex's rules—the likelihood of error and the epistemic superiority or coordinating abilities of Lex—not just as reasons that affect beliefs about reasons for action, but as reasons not to act on the balance of reasons.[36] Yet it is not clear by what mechanism epistemic superiority, which is a reason that affects beliefs about reasons for action, or the need for coordination, which is a first-order reason for action, can also exclude the normal array of first-order reasons to act and require the actor to follow the rules.[37] And if there is no such mechanism, the problem of rules remains: although Lex has good reason to issue serious (or exclusionary) rules, his subjects, after taking into account the reasons for having a rule, may conclude—based on the very moral reasons the rules purport to exclude—that they ought not obey.

It might be argued that rules can acquire serious or exclusionary effect if rule-subjects consent to be governed by the rules or commit themselves to treat the rules as serious rules.[38] On this view, consent or commitment prior to action operates as a constraint on later action. The rule-subject is now morally obligated to obey and therefore precluded from acting on reasons to disobey.[39]

We can pass over any questions about the motivation to consent. We have assumed that Lex's subjects are anxious to conform to moral principles and understand that, in the long run, the best way for them to do this is to follow Lex's rules. Therefore, they are willing to consent to Lex's authority and commit themselves to obey.

For our purposes, the more critical difficulty is that consent or commitment to follow rules simply does not create a moral obligation to follow rules in particular cases. Consent and commitment are species of promises. If a promised act falls within the zone of morally permissible conduct—conduct that is neither morally prohibited nor morally required—then a prior promise may create a weighty reason for action. It has this effect because the ability to create new moral rights and duties in voluntary transactions with others is an important source of liberty and autonomy. The intrinsic value of the practice of promising becomes a reason to perform the promise. Yet this reasoning cannot apply when the promised act is not a matter of moral indifference but a moral wrong. If Jules promises to kill George—or consents to do so, or commits himself to do so—this cannot possibly generate a reason to perform the act. In these circumstances, the practice of promising—or consenting or committing—has no moral value and adds nothing to the quality of the act. So, too, if it would otherwise be wrong to follow a rule in particular circumstances, prior consent or commitment does not change this conclusion.

It is true that consent or commitment to rules has potentially good consequences, if only it could be made binding. Yet the potential benefits of consent or commitment to follow a rule are no more or less than the potential benefits of the rule itself. They add nothing to rule-sensitive particularism. In Donald Regan's words, "It simply does not follow from 'It would be a good thing if *X*' that '*X*.'"[40]

Assume for example that Lex has issued a rule for Brian, "Spray for ants on May 1." Brian may understand that following this rule will save him from a predicament he badly wants to avoid. Therefore, he may be willing on April 30 to commit himself to follow the rule. But this commitment does not change the fact that he may have better things to do on May 1 and believe that his opportunity costs will be lower on some later day. Nor does prior commitment screen these facts from his view. Similarly, Stephen and other library patrons may agree that everyone will be better off if all follow the rule "No marking in library books." Therefore, they may undertake to follow it. But when a good reason arises to mark in a book, Stephen has no reason to honor his commitment unless he believes that all things considered, the reasons for marking are outweighed by the reasons against. The commitment itself—even if universal—is not a reason at all, much less a determinative one, to act against the balance of moral reasons.

Of course, people do commit to projects and relationships, and with some success. Perhaps, as Regan suggests, the reason for this success is that we invest in the projects we commit to, which in turn reinforces our interest in continuing them.[41] Or perhaps we follow up on commitments because honoring them gives us an important sense of self-control. In both these ways, a commitment might generate reasons to honor it later. But in the case of Lex's rules, it seems unlikely that rule-subjects will be moved either by a developing interest in obedience or by the need to exercise their will to honor a previous commitment to obey. And in any event, reasons of this kind, even when applicable, are not conclusive or exclusionary. At best, they are reasons in favor of honoring the commitment, to be compared with reasons to the contrary.[42]

A commitment to obey legal rules may also serve as an expression of respect for and identification with a community, particularly when that community is defined in part by its laws. The desire to maintain this expression of respect might in turn provide a reason to honor the commitment later when one would otherwise be inclined to disobey.[43] Stephen may feel that compliance with the rule against marking in books is intrinsically good because it confirms his continuing loyalty to Lex and the community of library patrons who endorse Lex's rule. But there is a problem in this reasoning: if the act of rule-following is morally wrong, it is not clear how it can have moral value as an expression of allegience to the community. In any event, even if Stephen's attitude is plausible, it creates at most an ordinary reason, and not an exclusionary reason, to follow the rule. And as long as the reasons generated by a commitment to obey rules can be overridden by other, stronger reasons to disobey, there is still a gap between what Lex should demand and what his subjects should do.

Fourth Strategy: Sanctions

Assuming we cannot close the gap by defining rationality in a way that encompasses rule-following or by introducing the notion of consent, we are left with the fact that it is sometimes rational and morally appropriate for Lex to demand action that differs from what it is rational and morally appropriate for his subjects to do. If Lex expects that many will err in their particularistic judgments of what to do, and believes they will do better overall if they follow his rules, his best course is to issue serious rules. If Lex's subjects also understand that they will often err, and believe they will do better overall by following Lex's rules, they will endorse the issuance of rules and approve of the practice of following them blindly. Yet if any particular actor believes that the balance of reasons favors not following a rule in the circumstances at hand, he is not rational if he follows the rule. And if he is correct in his belief, it is not right for him to follow the rule.

Another possible way to narrow the gap is to impose sanctions on those who violate rules and thereby alter subjects' reasons for action. A threat of punishment can have this effect if the punishment is sufficiently onerous to enter into the subjects' moral calculus. It is possible that concerns about harm to oneself should count only as prudential, rather than moral, reasons for action, and if so they will have no effect on Lex's subjects, who seek to do what is morally right. But if we assume that at some point, a threat of punishment assumes moral significance, either because punishment will cause grave harm to the actor or because it will cause indirect harm to others, then sanctions can tip the balance of reasons in favor of compliance with rules.

An initial problem with sanctions as a strategy for closing the gap is the practical impossibility of perfect sanctions. Not all rule-breakers will be caught, and the penalties imposed on them will be no more than rough estimates of what is necessary to tip their balance of reasons.[44] Yet even if we assume that Lex could perfectly calibrate sanctions for violations of rules, there are serious rational and moral obstacles to enforcement of sanctions, which prevent them from eliminating the gap.

The fundamental difficulty is that sanctions are not self-executing. Lex must rely on judges to impose sanctions after the fact in response to particular events or disputes.[45] Because these judges act retrospectively, their view of any case will differ from Lex's view. Unlike Lex, they know just what acts have occurred and what immediate consequences those acts brought about. If we assume that Lex's judges, like his subjects, are disposed to do what is morally right, it will be difficult for them to punish actors who appear from the judges' perspective to have acted correctly.[46] This in turn means that as long as rule-subjects expect judges to do what is morally right, they will not expect universal enforcement of rules because universal enforcement inevitably entails moral error. Subjects who believe they have acted correctly, and believe judges will act correctly in administering sanctions, will not expect to be punished for breaking the rules. Therefore, unless Lex's subjects predict moral error by judges, the threat of sanctions will not close the gap.

The difficulty that judges face in enforcing rules has nothing to do with the identity of judges. Instead, it results from the different point in time at which they judge moral questions. If Lex himself were presiding over individual cases, he would have the same difficulties that judges have in imposing sanctions, and if rule-subjects expect him to act morally, they would not expect full enforcement of rules.

Suppose a judge, Heidi, is presiding over the case of Leo, who has been rescued from dangerous waters at considerable public expense. Leo is charged with swimming in a prohibited place, in violation of Lex's rule. One way for Heidi to approach this case is to punish Leo if she finds that he broke the rule. If she chooses this approach, we shall call her a rule-bound judge.

A second possibility for Heidi is to punish Leo if, but only if, she finds that his act, viewed objectively, violated applicable moral standards. If Leo broke the rule, but was right to do so, then Heidi will be lenient and decline to impose sanctions. By this standard, however, Leo's act is right (justified) only if he has correctly identified one of the instances in which the rule's prescription is wrong. If Heidi follows this course, we shall call her a strict moral judge.

The third choice is to punish Leo only if he acted culpably and therefore deserves punishment. Heidi will be lenient to Leo if she finds that, at the time he acted, he reasonably believed that his action was morally correct.[47] If Heidi proceeds in this way, we shall call her a compassionate moral judge.

Because of the gap, Lex's preference is for rule-bound judges. If Lex has drafted his rules well, his subjects will do better overall if they expect to be punished for every violation of a rule. The prospect of leniency for morally correct violations, or for nonculpable violations, reintroduces the possibility of well-motivated but mistaken violations of rules.

At the same time, it will not always be rational or morally correct for Lex's judges to punish those who have broken the rules. If Heidi takes the compassionate moral approach to imposing sanctions, the disparity between Lex's position and Heidi's turns out to be quite stark. We have assumed throughout that Lex's subjects are motivated to comply with moral standards, although they sometimes err in applying those standards. In these circumstances, a compassionate judge could never punish an actor for violation of a legal rule. By hypothesis, the actor's only moral failure is a failure of information or calculation. Leo may have believed a child was drowning when the object in the water was really a hat. More mundanely, he may have believed, on sound evidence, that he was strong enough to resist the tides.[48] Either way, it is hard to say that punishment is morally deserved.

Thus, on the compassionate moral view, punishment for violation of rules is justified only when the actor deliberately flouts not only the rule but also the moral principles that stand behind it. As a result, a system of sanctions administered on this basis will do nothing to narrow the rational and moral gap between Lex and his subjects. Unless Lex can induce rule-following in some other way, rules will be effective only against those who intend to do wrong. Needless to say, this state of affairs is not satisfactory from Lex's point of view if he expects that many of his subjects will make well-intentioned mistakes. It is particularly unsatisfactory in coordination cases, in which the value of the rule depends on a general practice of blind obedience to rules.

Suppose instead that our judge, Heidi, takes the strict moral position, imposing sanctions against rule-breakers when their actions, viewed objectively, are morally wrong. Under this approach, Heidi is sometimes lenient, but only if she concludes the actor has done the right thing. She will not ordinarily punish Leo for swimming in a restricted area if he has succeeded in saving a child.

Our first observation about this approach to sanctions is that it raises the awkward possibility of punishment for wrongful obedience to legal rules. If the standard governing sanctions is strictly one of justification—objective conformity to moral requirements—it would seem to follow not only that judges would decline to punish those who act correctly in violation of rules but also that they *would* punish those who obey rules when they ought not. Of course, this is a harsh result for those who have relied on duly enacted legal rules. But reliance is relevant only to culpability, and culpability is of no concern to a strict moral judge.[49] Therefore, if judges are fastidious in applying a strict moral standard of decision, they could inject a peculiar anomaly into the system of rules—the prospect of sanctions for those who always comply.[50]

Moreover, although strict moral decision-making may have a greater effect on subjects' reasons for action than compassionate decision-making, it will not eliminate the gap. For Lex, the purpose of sanctions is to create a new reason for compliance with rules that will tip the balance in favor of following rules. But if judges impose sanctions based on the moral quality of individual action, subjects who believe they have good reasons to violate rules will not anticipate punishment unless they also anticipate either that their actions will be misassessed by the judges or that their actions constitute moral error. Under a strict moral standard, subjects will expect to be punished if their own judgment is incorrect, but this will at most affect those who are unsure of their conclusions. If we also take into account the logical corollary of strict moral adjudication—the possibility of sanctions for mistaken compliance—even those who are unsure of themselves have reason to follow their best judgment regarding what to do.

At this point, a proponent of strict moral adjudication might say that we have missed an important aspect of proper moral evaluation of a violation of rules. Accurate moral adjudication must be rule-sensitive. That is, it must take into account not only the immediate effects of individual actions but also the existence of rules and of judges authorized to impose sanctions. If strict moral judges are rule-sensitive in this way, it might be thought that actors will expect more frequent enforcement of rules and have more reason to conform to their terms. In this way, sanctions imposed on a strict moral basis would be effective in narrowing the gap.[51]

An initial point about rule-sensitive adjudication is that judges will seldom be influenced by the epistemic value of rules. For example, the value of the rule "No swimming" lies in Lex's superior information about dangerous tides. Heidi is presiding over the case of Leo, who broke this rule. If Heidi is both a strict moral judge and a rule-sensitive particularist, she will take into account the likelihood of her own error and the epistemic reliability of Lex. Yet she knows, as Leo knew, that the rule is simply a rule: it is designed to secure greater moral accuracy from the majority of its subjects, at the cost of moral inaccuracy in some of its applications. Moreover, she knows, as neither Leo nor Lex could know in advance, what actually happened after Leo dived in. Therefore, if Heidi thinks Leo was right, she will attribute little if any epistemic value to the rule in this case. And if Leo knows Heidi will proceed in this way, he has no reason to act in any way except the way he believes to be right.

Yet this is not the end of the matter because Heidi must also consider the impact of her decision on the overall effectiveness of the rule. The process of reasoning this entails is somewhat complex. First, Heidi must identify the potential value of the rule, if it is consistently obeyed. The value of the rule "No swimming" lies in its capacity to prevent errors in the run of cases. Leo may have been right to break the rule, but most who break it will be wrong. The value of a rule such as "No marking in library books" lies in its capacity to prevent harm through coordination. If no one marks in books, readers will be happier and strategic or acrimonious responses can be avoided.

The next question for Heidi is what effect her leniency might have on future actors. Assuming that Heidi's decisions are open to the public, her decision to withhold sanctions against an actor who was justified in breaking a rule may encourage disobedience by others who believe they are justified but who are not justified in fact. This in turn may lead Heidi to revise her conclusions about the act she is evaluating. If Leo's act, when left unpunished by Heidi in a decision accessible to others, will cause others to break the rule when they ought not, and if the ensuing harm to others outweighs the reasons that appear to justify Leo's act, then Heidi may reason that Leo's act is not justified after all. Finally, if Leo anticipates that Heidi will reason in this way, he must also anticipate that he will be punished. In this way, the threat of sanctions imposed on strict moral grounds does indeed create new reasons to obey rules. Or so the argument might go.

There are several weaknesses in this line of reasoning. The first is that it may be undermined by errors at various levels of decision-making. Judges may err in calculating the effects of their decisions on the value of rules. In fact, errors of this sort are particularly likely because, for a judge deciding a single case, the impact of the decision on the parties immediately involved will be more salient and "available" than remote effects on future actors.[52] If errors of judgment exceed the errors that would result from strict adherence to the rule, moral adjudication may produce morally inferior decisions. And if judges systematically undervalue the negative effects of their decisions and err in favor of leniency, actors such as Leo cannot anticipate rigorous enforcement and have less reason to follow the rule. Finally, even if judges are very reliable in assessing the effects of lenient decisions, individual actors may err in predicting what judges are likely to do. For all these reasons, a significant gap may remain in place.

An even more important difficulty in narrowing the gap through sanctions is that the effect of one judge's leniency on the value of a rule depends on the practice of other judges. In other words, whether the rule itself is justified on the basis of epistemic superiority or coordination, enforcement raises a problem of coordination among judges. Just as one person's marking in a library book causes little harm if others are likely to mark in the book, so Heidi's leniency in one case will have little effect on future actors if other judges are likely to be lenient as well. Neither the existence of the rule nor the existence of judges with power to impose sanctions changes this conclusion. If all judges are moral judges, and not all judges are perfect reasoners, Heidi has no reason to believe that others will consistently enforce the rule, no reason to believe that her own leniency will cause harm, and therefore no reason to revise her assessment that Leo's act was justified. Accordingly, Leo has no reason to expect punishment for an act that, but for the effect of judicial leniency on future actors, would be morally correct.

This conclusion might change if most judges were not moral judges but rule-bound judges. In these circumstances, Heidi's leniency might have several negative effects on the value of rules. If noticed by rule-bound judges, it might lead them to question their own practice of enforcement. If noticed by other rule-sensitive moral judges, it might lead them to lower their estimates of the number of rule-bound judges and therefore to lower their estimates of the harm their own leniency would cause to a practice of rule-following. Finally, the more leniency is discernible by rule-subjects such as Leo, the less reason they will have to expect punishment if they break rules and the less reason they will have to comply. Each of these effects is a reason why Heidi, as a rule-sensitive moral judge, should expect her own leniency to Leo to impair the value of the rule "No swimming," and therefore a reason for her to conclude that Leo's act was not justified. Yet each depends on her initial observation that most judges enforce rules according to their terms, without regard to possible justifications for breaking rules.

In a certain range of cases, rule-sensitive moral adjudication also suffers from an internal paradox. The reason for this is that punishment can have a corrective function with respect to moral costs that follow from the example of an unpunished violation of rules: punishment can make morally right a violation that otherwise would be wrong because it would undermine the value of the rule. For example, suppose Heidi is presiding over the case of Stephen, who was apprehended marking in a library book. She reaches an initial conclusion that Stephen's act was justified: despite a rule, "No marking in books," and a general practice of compliance with the rule, his reasons for marking outweigh the harm to future readers—though not by much. Then Heidi recalculates, taking into account the effect that Stephen's example and her own decision not to punish Stephen may have on others, including both rule-subjects and other judges. This tips the scales, so that Stephen's act now appears to have been unjustified. Heidi is now inclined to punish. But if she imposes sanctions on Stephen in a public decision, these sanctions will eliminate the exemplary effects of both his act and her own leniency. The act is once again a justified act.[53]

This creates several problems for judges. The possibility that acts may be justified when punished poses an additional moral difficulty for Heidi, who, as a moral judge, is opposed to punishing justified acts. It also complicates the process of calculating the effects of judicial decisions. A public judicial decision to punish Stephen may deter similar rule violations by others—that is, violations that are justified if punished but unjustified if not. Heidi must anticipate how other judges would respond to these potential acts before she can determine her own best response.[54] Finally, the logic of strict moral adjudication raises the possibility that, if punishment of Stephen leads others to obey rules when a violation would be justified if punished, these others should be punished for wrongful compliance.

Viewed from the perspective of actors, the existence of acts that are justified when punished presents yet another difficulty in closing the gap through sanctions. A morally motivated actor will prefer to violate the rule and be punished, if the combination of violation and punishment will produce the best moral outcome overall. If Stephen believes that marking in a book would be the right thing to do, but for the negative effect of Stephen's example and Heidi's leniency on other rule-subjects, and if punishment negates the effects of the example, Stephen's best moral choice is to violate the rule. In such a case, sanctions encourage rather than discourage Stephen's disobedience. If we add to this the point made earlier, that morally motivated actors will not be influenced by the prospect of sanctions unless the sanctions are severe enough to create moral rather than prudential reasons to obey the rule, we reach the following result: sanctions will deter only if the expected moral cost of punishment (the harm punishment inflicts on the actor and indirectly on others) is greater than the moral benefit of violating the rule if the actor is punished (the benefit of the act, without regard to any exemplary effects, which will be canceled by punishment).

For the various reasons we have described, sanctions imposed on moral grounds will not close the gap between what Lex has reason to demand through rules and what his subjects have reason to do. Compassionate judges will not impose sanctions against rule-breakers who intended to do what was morally right; therefore, their decisions will have no effect on the gap. Strict moral judges will impose sanctions more often than compassionate judges because their leniency is limited to cases in which they believe the rule prescribed the wrong result. But their own errors and the errors of actors in guessing what they will do will keep the gap in place. Moreover, strict moral decisions will not even narrow the gap unless the practice of rule-bound adjudication is widespread enough to give moral judges reason to enforce rules against actors whose acts would be justified but for the effects of a lenient decision. This means that if Lex hopes to narrow the gap by means of sanctions, he must insist that all judges enforce rules in all cases. In short, he needs to impose a rule on judges, "Always enforce the rules."

Yet this rule suffers from the problems of all rules. It is imperfect in that it will sometimes be wrong for judges to punish rule-violators, either because they are not culpable, or because their acts were justified, taking into account the residual effects of their own acts and of judicial decisions not to impose sanctions on them. When this is the case, rational, well-motivated judges have reason to be lenient. At the same time, Lex's position remains constant. As long as judges err in their moral judgments, and rule-subjects err in their predictions of what judges will do, and these errors exceed the errors that would follow from universal enforcement of rules, Lex has reason to insist on enforcement.

In other words, there is a gap between what Lex has reason to demand of judges and what judges have reason to do. This gap cannot be closed by imposing sanctions on judges: sanctions imply that someone must judge the judges, and this brings all the same difficulties into play. And as long as there is a gap between Lex and his judges, sanctions will never close the gap between Lex and his subjects.

One possible way to avoid the judges' moral objection to imposing sanctions on those who are morally justified or who are not culpable is to return to the notion of consent. Lex's subjects want to conform as closely as possible to moral requirements and understand that the best way to do this is to follow Lex's rules; accordingly, they may consent to be governed by the rules. As we explained earlier, prior consent to rules does not make it right for the rule-subject to follow a rule when the result it dictates is wrong. Nevertheless, if rule-subjects also consent in advance to being punished for disobeying rules, this may change the moral position of judges. If potential defendants have waived their claims to retributive justice, it may no longer be wrong for judges to enforce the rules in every case.

We are reluctant, however, to assume that Lex's subjects would consent to punishment for any and all violations of legal rules or that if they would consent, that this would eliminate the moral difficulties of full enforcement. Consenting to full enforcement of rules means consenting to be punished, not only for one's own moral lapses, but also whenever a consistent practice of punishing rule-violators will prevent moral lapses by others. Unless the morality Lex's subjects embrace is strictly utilitarian, however, they may not be willing to go this far.[55] They may understand that others will do better if their own violations are punished, and even that they themselves will do better in the long run if rules are universally enforced; but it does not follow that they are willing to suffer punishment when they are right and the rule is wrong. Therefore, we cannot infer even hypothetical consent, much less actual consent, to punishment of justified or nonculpable violators merely because punishment might produce net moral gains.

There is a more fundamental reason why we cannot posit such consent. In consenting to sanctions, rule-subjects are counting on sanctions to cause themselves and others to relinquish their best moral judgment on a wide range of subjects. To the extent that sanctions succeed in improving behavior, they do so by tampering with the actor's judgment. Those who act under a threat of sanctions do so not from the conviction that what they are doing is right, but in response to an artificial, prudential reason for action introduced by Lex.[56] And it is dangerous to assume that individuals would consent to give up moral autonomy in order to improve their actions.[57]

Fifth Strategy: Deception

So far, we have explained the nature of the gap between what Lex has reason to demand through rules and what his subjects have reason to do, and we have suggested that various strategies for diminishing this gap are unreliable. Rule-sensitive particularism leaves open the possibility that it may be wrong to follow the rule, and it has no impact at all unless the actor believes Lex's expertise is superior to his own or understands that most others follow rules blindly. Presumptive rule-following also leaves open the possiblity of justified violations and may collapse into rule-sensitive particularism. Sanctions are undermined by the moral and psychological difficulty of punishing those who are justified, and if they are not universally enforced, they will fail to close the gap.

To the extent that these strategies fail, the only way to maintain a system of rules is by one or more forms of deception. The primary form of deception in which Lex might engage is deception of rule-subjects about the nature of rules and the relationship of rules to correct moral conduct. One implication of the gap we have described is that authoritative settlement by means of rules cannot withstand the test of publicity. The function of rules is to translate moral principles whose meaning is contested into directions that will be understood by all in roughly the same way. But if this is generally known, the rules will fail in their purpose.

For example, Lex might issue the following statement: "Based on our knowledge of dangerous tides and of the average person's ability to swim, we advise that if you are a typical swimmer, if today is a typical day, and if there is no emergency at hand, you ought not swim." This statement is morally correct, but it is also an invitation to rule-sensitive particularism. As we have explained, rule-sensitive particularism will not contain errors in the way Lex intends.

If, instead, Lex issues a serious rule, "No swimming," he is not being fully candid about what his subjects ought to do. The implication is that in every case covered by the rule, the correct choice is not to swim. And of course this is false: Lex knows that his rule is not a statement of what action is always right but a statement of what action will be best if taken in all cases.

We do not mean to suggest that authorities commonly engage in active subterfuge. Rule-makers may cast rules in serious form ("Do X") without further explanation. They may back up their rules with a threat of sanctions, which in common understanding suggests that the rule's prescription corresponds to what one ought to do. Officials may even make efforts to teach or persuade rule-subjects to follow rules without further moral consideration. But for the most part, the deception on which serious rules depend will not be deliberate misrepresentation by officials, but a sort of collective self-deception. Rather than a Lex who clearly perceives the nature of rules, there may simply be officials who are accustomed to think of rules promulgated by authorities as serious rules, and rule-subjects who have a generally good opinion of the rules and prefer to avoid difficult moral inquiries. In other words, people may simply obey without reflection unless shocked by unusual facts into full moral deliberation.

A second form of deception occurs at the level of adjudication. If Lex wants to narrow the gap by means of sanctions, he must represent to rule-subjects that punishment will correspond precisely to the terms of his rules. Only this will push rule-subjects in the direction of compliance. Yet as we have explained, judges have moral reason not to punish all rule-breakers.

One way for Lex to respond is to encourage habits of blind enforcement among judges (or do nothing to dislodge these habits when they arise spontaneously). But this will not always work, and when it does not, the alternative is to allow judges to reach decisions that are not consistent with the announced rules of conduct. Lex may issue a rule, "No swimming," but permit judges to withhold sanctions when swimmers are justified or when they are not culpable. Of course, if the more lenient decision rule is known to the public, sanctions will fail to narrow the gap.

Yet if the serious rule of conduct is widely publicized, while the lenient decision rule is kept from public view, Lex may be able to achieve the results he wants without requiring judges to impose unjust sanctions.[58] In other words, if rule-subjects are deceived about the relation between rules and sanctions, Lex can avoid both error and injustice. Again, this need not be a conscious exercise in deception by Lex or his judges: judges may simply apply lenient decision rules without realizing that there are inconsistencies between these rules and the rules of conduct as generally understood. And if the operative decision rules are sufficiently obscure or complex, actors may not come to expect leniency. Borrowing Meir Dan-Cohen's term, strict conduct rules and lenient decision rules can coexist in a condition of "acoustic separation."[59]

It is not difficult to identify areas of acoustic separation in legal doctrine. Crimes may be defined in clear and simple terms, while excuses are comparatively murky and complex and therefore unlikely to be widely understood.[60] On the civil side of law, a parallel can be found in the historical distinction between "law" and "equity," which still has some influence today.[61] Few laymen (and not all lawyers) understood the tricky subject of "equitable" defenses. The result was a set of relatively firm conduct rules backed by a firm threat of sanctions, coupled with little-known decision rules that allowed judges to engage in quiet leniency.

Deception, then, holds some promise as a way to narrow the gap. Lex can fool his subjects, or allow them to fool themselves, into treating rules as exclusionary or conclusive reasons for action. At the level of adjudication, Lex and his judges can take advantage of acoustic separation to combine effective conduct rules with just sanctions.

At the same time, there are serious practical, political, and moral objections to a strategy of deception. On the practical side, deliberate deception raises questions about who should have access to the truth and how these insiders can be controlled.[62] Self-deception, on the other hand, is mysterious. How do people initially come to relinquish moral reason? And once they do, how are morally desirable rules devised, and how are the moral principles themselves sustained over time?[63]

Deception about the relation of conduct rules to sanctions combines the problems just mentioned with a significant risk of discovery. Because judicial decisions can never be hidden entirely from the public, acoustic separation will never be complete. If enough people come to understand that judicial decisions do not correspond to conduct rules, not only will the strategy fail, but there is likely to be a general loss of faith in authoritative rules.

Another reason to be concerned about deception in regard to rules is that it may affect the quality of public debate on questions of law and morality. Suppose that Lex enacts a rule, "No marking in library books." Although there may in fact be instances in which marking in a book is the right thing to do, Lex presents this as a serious rule because the potential for error would otherwise undermine the coordinating effects of the rule. If Lex's subjects obey the rule without further thought, either because they are misled by the serious form of the rule or because it is their habit to obey, there will be less discussion of precisely when one is justified in marking in a book. Acoustic separation has the same effect. If excuses and "equitable" defenses are obscured from public view, there will be less debate about when one should engage in a prohibited act or breach a contract.

Thus, successful deception puts an end to discussion of the moral questions that lie behind the rules. For Lex, this can mean the loss of important resources. If Lex relies on public debate for information about the success of his rules and ideas about how they could be improved, less debate means less feedback. Loss of this information becomes a cost of authoritative settlement.

Aside from its practical consequences, deception—whether it takes the form of official dissembling or collective self-deception—is morally disquieting. Deception of any kind is often condemned as destructive of autonomy. It interferes with the reasoning process, and therefore the moral judgment, of the person deceived.[64]

Of course, it is notoriously difficult to say what ethical obligations the ideal of autonomy imposes among people or between a government and its subjects. Deceit, danger, and necessity are all forces that endanger autonomy, but they are also among the many circumstances of life that that engage autonomy and give it value. Thus, it is not sensible to insist that autonomy is a state or condition that must be kept inviolate.

Further, common practice suggests that not all forms of deception are morally unacceptable. Most would agree that it is right to lie when lying will prevent a more serious wrong ("No, there is no gun in the drawer"). Many think it is acceptable to lie in small ways that avoid inflicting pain ("Yes, your haircut looks fine"). Some, at least, think it is fair to lie for sex ("Yes, I will love you forever"). Closer to the problem of rules, we often simplify when giving moral instructions to children or explaining something to a person who we doubt will understand everything we might have to say on the subject. Yet in doing so, we are deceiving others about their reasons for action, in much the same way that rules may deceive rule-subjects.[65]

Nevertheless, there is reason to be concerned about a practice that depends either on a deliberate attempt by authorities to displace autonomous moral judgment or on the disposition of individuals to relinquish their own autonomy. One possible way out is to insist that violation of authoritative rules is contrary to moral duty. Therefore, the judgment Lex seeks to displace—judgment about whether to follow his rules—cannot be a valuable exercise of autonomy.[66] Yet everything we have said about the gap demonstrates that rules designed to enforce moral principles as effectively as possible will not be perfectly in accord with moral duty. If we are right in our view of authoritive rules, then moral duty may sometimes require a violation of the rules.

Another possible answer to moral doubts about the deception associated with legal rules is that the object of these rules is to improve moral performance and to increase the prospects for autonomous life. A rule, "Do not lie," may be more effective in protecting autonomy than a more candid statement—"Do not lie when lying would unduly interfere with another's autonomy"—if people are likely to err about the demands of autonomy. Therefore, some interference with autonomy is justified in the interest of moral principles that include autonomy itself. Another way to put this is that if the question were put before them, Lex's subjects would understand that official deception ultimately yields morally desirable results and a social environment favorable to autonomy; therefore, they would consent to be deceived.

In this context, of course, "consent" must be hypothetical. If rule-subjects understood what they were consenting to, they would not be deceived. And in order to recognize the moral force of hypothetical consent to a strategy of deception, one must assume that people would or should relinquish their moral judgment because this would serve the greater good.

The question of consent comes down to this: Imagine you are offered a drug that would put an end to your powers of moral reason and simultaneously improve your moral behavior.[67] Would you take this drug, or does it represent a form of death? If the answer is that you would not take the drug, then deceptive rules and deceptive remedial practices are morally unsatisfactory.

At the same time, deception appears to be necessary if rules are to settle moral controversy and prevent moral error. Rule-sensitive particularism will not serve the purpose unless general compliance with rules has already reached a critical level for some other reason. Sanctions will not serve the purpose as long as judges engage in moral reasoning. It follows that either deception or delusion is an inevitable feature of successful rules.

Rules and Deontological Rights

We have already identified several of the moral difficulties associated with the gap. The basic problem is that rules sometimes require action that is wrong. The two strategies most likely to narrow the gap—

sanctions and deception—not only promote the moral errors of rules but generate independent moral problems of their own. Sanctions involve judges in punishing those who are not culpable and sometimes also those who are justified. Deception is an offense to the autonomy of rule-subjects.

These moral difficulties are especially acute if one takes a deontological view of morality. The moral justification for rules, and for strategies to put them into effect, is consequentialist in nature. When complied with, rules induce a set of moral errors in order to avoid a greater number of moral errors. And to bring about compliance, those who act rightly in violating the rules, or would be acting rightly but for the exemplary effects of their acts, must be punished or deceived in order to reduce wrongful violations by others.

Further, if the act in question falls within a domain of deontological rights, the effect of rules and of strategies for their enforcement is a utilitarianism of rights. Suppose, for example, that there is a deontological right to commit suicide, and to obtain another's assistance in committing suicide, if one is terminally ill and in serious pain. Others have a corresponding right to assist suicide in these circumstances. There is also a right not to be killed against one's will, and a corresponding duty not to kill.

Assessing this array of rights, Lex concludes—correctly, we shall assume—that in practice, people will err too often about when others are ready to die. Therefore, he enacts a rule, "Never kill or assist in the death of another person." If, by means of sanctions or deception about the moral force of the rule, Lex succeeds in bringing about compliance with this rule, he is trading the rights of some against the rights of others. And this, of course, cannot be consistent with the notion of rights as side constraints.[68]

A Possible Technological Fix? Automatic Retaliation Devices

Suppose it were possible technologically to have a device that perfectly detected all rule violations and automatically imposed draconian punishment on the violators, even when their violations were all-things-considered justified. The certainty of draconian punishment would likely deter all but the most saintly (or perhaps martyr-like) actors, and would deter even saints in all but those extreme cases where the perceived moral benefits of rule violation were very high (such as where the actor believed that rule compliance would produce moral catastrophe).[69]

Such an automatic retaliation device (ARD) would close the gap better than ordinary sanctions because it would bypass the moral reasoning of human judges. Unlike Heidi, who might not punish the justified violators or even the nonculpable ones, and who might even punish rule-followers in some cases, the ARD would impose its draconian punishment on all and only rule-violators.[70]

One problem with the ARD, which it shares with all sanctions, is that it operates on the actor's fear of punishment, not his assessment of the moral reasons at stake. That is, as Gerald Postema puts it, it operates by corruption of the decision-making process.[71] This problem could be remedied by making the sanctions so draconian that it would be *immoral* for the actor to trigger them no matter how great the moral loss to be averted by rule violation. Because conceivably a rule violation might save many lives, or avoid excruciating pain or terror for many persons—only the size of the community and the limits of the human capacity to suffer set a cap on the potential benefits of rule violation—the punishment imposed by the ARD would have to be unimaginably horrible to operate other than by overriding moral reasons with prudential ones. And because the worst an ARD could dish out could still be exceeded by the effects of rule compliance, the ARD could not guarantee that it would deter all rule-violators.

Perhaps, however, we can get around the worries about corruption and martyrs if we program the ARD, not to impose draconian punishment on the rule-violator, but to impose draconian harm on innocent persons whenever a rule is violated for moral reasons. Thus, if Stephen believes the balance of moral reasons tips in favor of violating the rule against marking on books and proceeds to mark, then even if he is correct in his assessment *as far as it goes,* the ARD would inflict horrible torture and death on Sue and Howard. Because Stephen would ex ante perceive that this would occur, and that it would outweigh any moral benefits from marking, he would conclude that the balance of moral reasons actually favored rule compliance, not rule violation.

We could further imagine that everyone in our community, cognizant of the benefits of the universal rule compliance that it would bring about, would consent to being an innocent ARD hostage. That is, they would consent to being put at risk in the way that the ARD puts innocent people at risk.[72] We leave it to the reader to decide whether such consent is plausible and whether it obviates any moral objections to the ARD.

Conclusion

We can sum up what we have said in this way: It is morally desirable for Lex to impose serious rules on his subjects. But because it is not always morally appropriate for his subjects to follow the rules, Lex can do what is morally desirable only if he is willing to do what is morally wrong. To act in the best interest of his subjects, he must punish them for justified acts, deceive them, corrupt their moral judgment, and violate the rights of some in order to minimize rights violations overall. This is the problem of authoritative rules, right up to and including the rule "Let Lex decide."

Serious rules offer the prospect of moral gains. The more complex and diverse the society, the greater the moral gains serious rules can achieve. The question is whether in light of the gap—and its associated practical and moral problems—serious rules are a possibility for us, at least so long as we can see clearly what the gap entails.

It is not our position that every serious rule generates a gap between the rule-making authority and its subjects. We have already identified one category of rules—coordination rules of the equivocation type—in which there is no gap because there are no significant reasons why anyone would disobey the rule. One course of action is as good as another. There may not, however, be many rules of this kind.[73]

Another type of rule that does not generate a gap is a rule that simply restates a categorical moral imperative. The rule "Do not commit rape" might be an example. Among Lex's morally motivated subjects, no one would violate this rule because a violation would always be morally wrong. However, legal or conventional rules ordinarily must be more determinate than the moral imperatives on which they are based. Again, therefore, we doubt that there are many rules in this category.

In addition to these small groups of gap-resistant rules, there are instances—probably many of them—in which Lex may prefer not to issue a serious rule. If Lex lacks sufficient information to determine whether a rule will prevent more error than it causes, or if the benefits of coordination are small in comparison with the costs of bluntness and uniformity, a serious rule may not be justified.[74] In such cases, Lex may prefer to enact an indeterminate standard, or an advisory rule, or no rule at all, and so allow individuals or judges to rely on their own judgment and expertise.

Yet there remains a wide range of cases in which determinate, serious rules can produce substantial moral benefits, and in which the gap we have identified presents a serious problem. All cases in which the need for settlement is greater than the error that will follow from adherence to rules fall within this range.

The point we have tried to make is that the mere fact that serious rules will produce moral gains, and that it is therefore rational for us to want serious rules, does not mean that it is rational for us to have them. Rationality may preclude our having serious rules. In this way, serious rules may be like "the intention to drink the vile potion tomorrow" in Gregory Kavka's "toxin puzzle."[75] Although it would be rational to want to intend tonight to drink the potion tomorrow—because, in Kavka's story, an intention tonight guarantees a lot of money tonight—we may be unable so long as we are rational actually to form the intention to drink the potion, given that we know it will be irrational for us to drink it tomorrow. Serious rules may be analogous in this sense: we cannot really intend to follow them when we know that in some of the future cases that fall within their terms, it will be irrational to do as they require. Just as with promising and its benefits in a society comprised entirely of utilitarian maximizers, so long as we see the true nature of serious rules—and thus the gap that undermines their normativity—we may be unable to establish them, no matter how much we lose morally without them.

FIVE Interpretation of Rules

In order to settle controversies over the meaning and application of moral principles, the members of our imaginary community have adopted the basic rule "Let Lex decide." Lex carries out the task of settlement by means of authoritative rules, which translate moral principles into comparatively determinate instructions for action. Lex's rules provide coordination and expertise and simplify decision-making. Through this combination of benefits, they reduce the sum of moral errors: if the rules are well-designed, Lex's subjects will perform better according to applicable moral standards if they follow the rules in every case than if they judge for themselves what to do.

As we demonstrated in chapter 4, however, if Lex's rules are to succeed in settling controversies, his subjects must accept them as serious rules. That is, Lex's subjects must follow Lex's rules without examining how well the rules serve their moral ends in each particular case that arises. If all or most subjects act as "rule-sensitive particularists," the benefit of Lex's expertise will be at least partly lost, the coordination effect of the rules will be seriously impaired, and decision-making will not be simplified.

Because Lex cannot be present at the site of every controversy, he issues rules prospectively and in general terms. As a result, when the time comes to apply the rules to particular cases, there may be disagreement about what the rules require. By hypothesis, Lex is unavailable to solve the problem himself.[1] Thus, to settle disagreements about the meaning of rules, and to complete the settlement of controversies over what to do, Lex must designate interpreters with authority to determine how Lex's rules apply. As we shall explain, not everything interpreters do is properly called interpretation; but for now we can give them the title of interpreters. The settlement function, which we take to be the central and perhaps exclusive function of Lex and his rules, has implications for what the job of interpretation entails.[2]

Interpretation and Authoritative Settlement

THE BANAL TRUTH THAT WORDS HAVE MEANING

As an initial point, we reject skepticism about the possibility of communication through language. As we will explain shortly, we do not confine the meaning of rules to the conventional meaning of the words of which they are composed. Nevertheless, settlement requires that controversial moral principles be made more determinate, and Lex accomplishes this through language. Therefore, it is essential that language be capable of carrying determinate meaning.

We do not view this basic requirement as a serious obstacle to settlement or to interpretation of rules. Assume that Lex has issued a rule, "No talking in the library," published the rule in the community's rule book, and designated Michael as the rule's interpreter. Matt, a library patron, leans over to Jacques, another patron, to discuss an important idea in a low voice. Now, it may be that there are no objective facts about the world that correspond to the meaning of the words "No talking in the library."[3] And certainly, Lex's words cannot operate independently of a fairly complex social context: Michael must share with Lex (and with those to whom Michael's interpretation is addressed) the conventions of written language, a body of social experience, and certain assumptions about what Lex is doing when he records a series of words about talking in libraries in the community's rule book. Yet there is little question that in Matt's case, and in most cases that might arise, common understandings about the use of words are such that the words "No talking in the library" can relay from Lex to Michael a sufficient idea of what Lex believes should be done.[4]

If Michael has been named to determine the meaning of Lex's rules, what meaning should he seek out? The meaning of a rule can be equated with the dictionary definitions of the words used, the real nature of the things to which the rule's terms refer,[5] the way in which readers (variously described) would understand the rule, the intentions of the authority that issued the rule,[6] the purposes the rule was designed to serve, the overall moral judgment of whoever is called on to apply the rule,[7] or some combination of these. In our view, however, the objective of authoritative settlement dictates that the only meaning that should count as the meaning of Lex's rules is the meaning Lex intended the rules to have.

To explain our position, we return to the functions of authoritative rules. The justifications for Lex's rules lie in Lex's expertise, the benefits of coordination, and simplification of the process of decision-making. If we were interested only in coordination and efficient decision-making, we might be less concerned with what Lex thinks ought to be done and more concerned with making sure Lex's rules would always be interpreted by everyone in the same way. Thus, for the purposes of coordination and efficiency, an interpretive method that confined the meaning of rules to the dictionary definitions and typical usage of the words Lex used to compose them, in conjunction with the standard rules of grammar and punctuation, would be satisfactory; in fact, it could produce greater determinateness than alternative methods.

Of course, natural languages are full of ambiguities that are resolvable only by reference to authorial intent.[8] Remove the author and coordination and efficient decision-making will suffer. Indeed, if no author and authorial intention are assumed, we cannot identify even the language that the marks or sounds represent.[9] We might try to remedy this ambiguity by agreeing upon an authoritative rule that stipulates the language that Lex should be taken to be employing; but unless we know something about Lex's intentions, even that rule will not resolve the ambiguities in whatever language Lex is deemed to be using.[10]

In any event, we are interested in more than coordination. The controversies Lex addresses can be settled in better or worse ways, and one of the benefits the community seeks from his rules is avoidance of moral error through the application of Lex's superior expertise. Members of the community presumably have selected Lex because they have confidence in his moral expertise. Lex's expertise also is likely to be enhanced by his central position, which provides him with an overview of the consequences of rules, resources with which to gather information, and access to a variety of opinions.

Thus, when Lex enacts the rule "No talking in the library," we want to know what Lex intended in using those words. We are not interested in what the marks "No talking in the library" mean in Swahili, French, or Esperanto—at least if we do not believe Lex was attempting to use those languages.[11] Indeed, we may not even be interested in what the marks mean in standard English if we know that Lex uses nonstandard English, or is prone to malapropisms, or to misspeaking.[12] What we want to know is what Lex meant, or, more precisely, what he intended for us to take his marks to mean.[13]

It may be useful to imagine that Lex is like a famous chef who has written a cookbook. Because we seek to take advantage of the chef's culinary expertise, when we read her recipes we are seeking to discover what she meant by the marks on the pages. If, for example, she mentions "salt" as an ingredient in a recipe, we will want to know whether she meant ordinary salt or kosher salt. If she intended for us to take her to mean ordinary salt, then the fact that the same marks could have been made by a chef who intended for us to use kosher salt is irrelevant to following the recipe correctly. If it is *her* recipe that we want, then we want to know what *she* intended.[14]

Likewise with Lex and his rule "No talking in the library." Lex and his subjects are engaged in an attempt to achieve a common understanding. Lex intends for certain cases to be resolved in a particular way, and he wants to communicate this intention to those whose acts he wishes to prescribe. The latter in turn want to know what Lex intends for them to do. Lex and his subjects will employ semantic conventions and pragmatic conventions to achieve this communicative goal of having the subjects understand what Lex intends for them to understand in his communication of his rule.[15]

Assuming, then, that Lex's expertise is important to successful settlement, the settlement must be what Lex has deliberately chosen it to be.[16] This in turn implies that if Lex settles controversies by means of authoritative rules, the relevant meaning of those rules must be the meaning intended by Lex.

At this point, it may be useful to pose a series of questions about interpretation that will help to clarify our analysis. First, should the meaning of Lex's rule—"No talking in the library"—be treated by the audience (Michael) as what Lex intended by uttering the rule to prescribe for a range of cases, as opposed, for example, to what some other speaker might have meant by the same sounds or marks? We have already given our answer to this question: we are interested in what Lex intended his marks to mean.

Second, is there in fact something Lex intends to prescribe for his subjects in those cases not actually contemplated by Lex when he issues his rule? Put differently, does Lex have an intention regarding what ought to be done in cases not before his mind when he communicates?

Third, is it possible for Lex's subjects to understand Lex's intention sufficiently similarly to make that intention determinate for a range of cases despite the subjects' perhaps differing evaluations of what ought to be done? In other words, even if Michael and others disagree with Lex over what activities in the library's vicinity ought to be forbidden, is it still possible for them to grasp what Lex has intended regarding those activities?

Fourth, assuming that Lex has a determinate intention that the audience can grasp regarding a range of cases, when might Lex's intent be indeterminate, perhaps even for Lex himself? Such cases of indeterminacy must be contrasted with cases in which Lex's intended meaning is determinate, but either over- or underinclusive or mistakenly expressed.

Fifth, does the fact that Lex not only intends through his rule to bring about certain actions or refrainings by his subjects, such as not talking in the library, but also intends that his rule be taken to be a *rule* rather than a standard, help make the rule more determinate for the audience?

And finally, in interpreting Lex's rules, what is the role of rules or norms of interpretation that come, not from Lex, but from the basic agreement constituting Lex as authoritative for what ought to be done?

THE MEANING OF INTENT

One problem with an intent-based approach to rule-meaning is that intent about what should be done can be conceived of in a number of different ways. Minimally, one might say that Lex's intent in enacting a rule refers to conclusions he reached about the situations he was consciously adverting to at the time of the rule's enactment. Suppose, for example, that Lex has issued the rule "No talking in the library" after spending an afternoon in the library's main reading room and noticing that conversations among library users about books they were reading were disrupting the work of others in the room. Accordingly, his intent can be characterized as intent to put a stop to conversations among patrons in the reading room.

It quickly appears, however, that this conception of intent is insufficient. Lex governs by means of prospective general rules because he cannot anticipate or come to the scene of every dispute. Necessarily, therefore, Lex must intend that his rules be applied in situations to which he has not specifically adverted. For example, if two workers fixing a copy machine during business hours begin a conversation about what they had for lunch, it is not difficult to conclude that they are breaking the rule as Lex intended it to operate.

Thus, the intent Michael seeks must, to some extent, include inchoate intent. We prefer the term "inchoate" to the term "hypothetical" because the intent we have in mind is not what Lex would have intended if he had adverted to the problem now at hand, nor what he would intend if he were now present. These are questions that cannot be answered without specifying the counterfactual circumstances more fully, and there are an indefinite number of ways to do so.[17] Rather, Lex's inchoate intent is what he intended, when he enacted the rule, with respect to unadverted-to problems of the kind that have now arisen.

THE EXISTENCE AND DETERMINACY OF LEX'S INTENTIONS

The Existence of Inchoate Intent. Let us now turn to our second question, namely, whether there is in fact something Lex intends to prescribe in cases not actually before his mind when he issues the rule "No talking in the library." Admittedly, it is difficult to conceive of intentions about what should be done in circumstances Lex never contemplated as genuine mental states. Yet the opposite view, that inchoate intent does not exist, is untenable. All intentions are directed at the future, and the future is never fully in view when intentions are formed. Thus, unless our intentions were to some extent inchoate, we could never intend anything. As a result, skepticism about inchoate intent must entail skepticism about the existence of any intentions at all. And if all intentions are ruled to be illusory, human experience and behavior become very difficult to explain.

Moreover, because all intentions involve matters not specifically adverted to by those whose intentions they are, the relation of Lex's subjects to Lex's intentions is really no different from Lex's own relation to his intentions. And just as Lex can say, "I intended my rule to cover case X, even though I was not adverting to case X at the time I promulgated the rule," so likewise can Lex's subjects conclude the same. In fact, language, because of its generality, is well suited to convey intentions that are sufficiently accessible to support a practice of interpretation. If Lex issues a rule "No talking in the library" picturing a conversation among patrons in the reading room, Michael can conclude with some confidence that Lex both intended and expressed his intent that the rule should apply to workers fixing the copy machine.

Our conclusion that the meaning of Lex's rules should be equated with Lex's intent, including his inchoate intent, raises another critical question: at what level of generality should intent be defined for purposes of interpretation? Lex's intent about what should be done can be understood as referring to particular cases, categories of cases, immediate ends, or ultimate ends. Thus, Lex's intent in issuing the rule, "No talking in the library," can be described as intent to prevent an imagined scene of patrons talking in the reading room, intent to regulate talking in the library, intent to reduce noise in the library, intent to promote an atmosphere conducive to study, intent to govern well, or intent to do what is right. Each of these is, in a sense, a true description of what Lex intended. Moreover, they are only some of the points along a continuum of generality, with an infinite number of gradations in between.

We have already concluded that the relevant intent must be something more than intent to govern the particular cases to which Lex adverted. At the other end of the continuum, our account of the functions performed by Lex and his rules places important limits on the extent to which Michael, as interpreter, can refer to the full range of Lex's intentions in issuing a rule. Rules cannot be equated with the ends they serve without losing the benefits of their form.

For this purpose, there is a difference between interpretation of rules and interpretation of vague standards (such as "equal protection" or "due process of law"). In the case of a standard, the role of Lex (or Super Lex) is to identify ends and values to be pursued while saying very little about the means of pursuing them. In other words, the rule-maker is not attempting a complete settlement of controversy. Accordingly, until more determinate rules have been issued to give content to the standards, there is no reason to limit the range of interpretive inquiry into the authority's intent.

Our principal concern in this chapter, however, is with interpretation of determinate rules—rules that are designed to settle disputes and curtail consideration of the best means for promoting certain values or ends. Rules work by restating moral principles in concrete terms, so as to reduce the uncertainty, error, and controversy that result when individuals follow their own unconstrained moral judgment. If the meaning of rules is derived from the moral principles the rules are designed to serve, there are, in effect, no rules and no means for curbing moral error. Another way to put this is that an important part of what Lex intends in issuing a rule is that it be a serious rule and not just an expression or reminder of the principles that motivated him to issue it. Thus, Lex's rules must have, and must be intended to have, a meaning that is independent of Lex's intent at its highest level of generality.

If, for example, Lex has issued a rule, "No talking in the library," in order to promote study, it is not open to Michael to "interpret" the rule to forbid leaf-blowers in the library courtyard, no matter how much they detract from studious activity. Nor can he conclude that a group study session among the only three patrons in the library is permitted because it causes no offense to the purpose that led Lex to issue the rule. These may be instances in which the rule is underinclusive or overinclusive when measured against the underlying moral principles, but underinclusiveness and overinclusiveness do not affect the rule's meaning: they are simply consequences of Lex's deliberate choice to use a rule.

We would be overstating our case, however, if we insisted that

Michael must never refer to the purposes underlying Lex's rules. We have already noted that the basic process by which people grasp the meaning of others' words involves some reference to the speaker's purpose(s) in using the words. At the least, to make sense of a rule, Michael must learn enough about Lex and his purposes to know that Lex intends to communicate, in English, an instruction to be followed by those who are subject to his authority.

We believe it is possible for Michael to advert in a limited way to Lex's purposes, so as to grasp what Lex intended to do by enacting a rule, without equating the purposes of Lex's rules with their meaning. Nevertheless, we shall briefly take up two analyses that raise questions about this distinction and hence about whether intent can serve as the basis of determinate rules.

The Multiplicity of Lex's Intentions. The first of these analyses, which comes from Gregory Bassham, suggests that when Lex issues his rule "No talking in the library," he has not one intention regarding what ought to be done, but several. Moreover, these various intentions can conflict.[18] Bassham distinguishes between, on the one hand, the authority's—Lex's—beliefs about the binding effects of what he has authored and, on the other hand, other changes in the world that Lex expects or hopes will be accomplished by those binding effects.[19] For example, suppose that Lex believes that if the "No talking" rule is enacted and enforced, library use will increase or Lex will be reelected as the authority. Neither of these beliefs, even if mistaken, affects the binding effects of Lex's rule.[20]

Within the former category of Lex's beliefs about the legal effects of his enactment, Bassham distinguishes among (1) scope beliefs, (2) counterfactual scope beliefs, and (3) semantic intentions.[21] Scope beliefs are the actual occurrent beliefs that Lex holds at the time of enactment about the binding effects of that enactment.[22] Put differently, they are Lex's actual beliefs about what changes he has adverted to and determined should be implemented.

Counterfactual scope beliefs are the beliefs about such binding effects that the authorities would have held, had they considered the particular application (of their text) in question.[23] Bassham gives as an example of a counterfactual scope belief the belief the framers of the U.S. Constitution would have held on whether skyjacking is an "infamous" crime within the meaning of the grand jury clause of the Fifth Amendment.[24] Obviously, the framers would not have had actual beliefs about skyjacking in 1791. Nonetheless, Bassham considers it meaningful and sensible to ask what beliefs they would have held on the legal status of skyjacking under the Fifth Amendment, had they considered skyjacking. Strict intentionalists are, for Bassham, all who would interpret legal texts solely according to scope and counterfactual scope beliefs, although the strictest of strict intentionalists look only to scope beliefs.

The authorities' semantic intentions are their intentions regarding the *meaning* of their legal texts.[25] Now this in itself is quite unhelpful because scope beliefs and counterfactual beliefs could be the exclusive determinants of the texts' *meaning,* in which case semantic intentions would merely be intentions to effectuate scope and counterfactual scope beliefs. Bassham points out, however, that a legislature that bans toxic substances may have in mind a particular concept of toxicity, or a particular definition or description of toxicity—semantic intentions—as well as some particular examples of toxic substances that they believed they were banning (scope beliefs).[26] It may turn out that the particular examples of toxic substances may not in fact be toxic according to the contemplated definition of toxicity. Or it may turn out that both the particular examples of toxic substances *and* the contemplated definition of toxicity are inconsistent with the best theory of the nature of toxicity as a concept.

Bassham labels as "moderate intentionalists" those who would follow the authorities' semantic intentions when these conflict with the scope and counterfactual scope intentions.[27] As between "spare," realist semantic intentions (intentions to use terms consistently with the true nature of the terms' referents), and "rich," conventionalist semantic intentions (intentions to use the terms according to the definitions or descriptions the authorities have in mind), Bassham suggests that intentions of the framers of the U.S. Constitution were usually rich, not spare.[28] He concludes that the most defensible form of intentionalism in constitutional interpretation is moderate intentionalism in which the framers' rich semantic intentions trump their scope and counterfactual scope intentions.[29]

Although Bassham would deal with these various types of authorities' intentions—scope, counterfactual scope, and semantic, rich and spare—by choosing which one should be dispositive,[30] we suggest that the question is not one of the interpreter's choice. The question is, what did the authorities intend to communicate that they had determined ought to be done? In our view, that is a datum about the world, not a matter of choice.

Choosing which one of Bassham's categories of intentions should be the basis of interpretation appears artificial for two reasons. First, whenever the various intentions conflict, there is no reason not to ask which intentions the authorities would wish to dominate in such a case. If semantic intentions conflict with scope intentions, there is no reason to choose semantic intentions as what the authorities "intended" if the authorities would have chosen their scope intentions to dominate their semantic ones.

Secondly, we believe that Bassham's distinctions—and other analogous ones—ultimately collapse. Consider, for example, the distinction between sense and reference within semantic intentions. Ultimately, what a term refers to cannot be determined without a definition or description. But definitions and descriptions purport to be *of* something.[31] (We would not know the thing that "death" refers to without some description of it, though likewise we think that death can be misdescribed.) Moreover, the distinction between semantic intentions and more particular scope beliefs and counterfactual scope intentions breaks down. Our definitions and descriptions can be fallible generalizations from particulars, and the particulars can be fallible inferences from generalizations.

In the end, we see no reason why a broad notion of inchoate intentions cannot subsume all of Bassham's categories of authorities' intentions. What we want to know—given some fact situation, the authorities' semantic understandings, the true nature of that to which their terms refer, and so on—is what they determined the binding effect of their action should be. Because the authorities' exemplars may be inconsistent with the definitions of the terms they employ, and the definitions may be inconsistent with the true nature of the terms' referents, the question is, which did they intend to dominate in cases of such inconsistency?[32] In some cases, perhaps, referents will dominate definitions and exemplars.[33] In other cases, definitions or exemplars will dominate.[34]

Our proposal is akin to Bassham's notion of counterfactual scope beliefs and intentions but broader and, as we explained earlier, not strictly "counterfactual." What the authorities mean by an enactment is what they intend its binding effects to be over a range of circumstances, not all of which they have adverted to. If the enactment is a prohibition of some behavior ("No talking"), its meaning is the authorities' intended binding effects—prohibition or no prohibition—in the circumstances in question. If Lex had in mind particular tokens of talking in the library when he enacted his rule, but, if asked whether his rule prohibits other tokens that were not in his mind at the time, would reply that it does, his inchoate intention and thus the meaning of his rule is that those latter tokens of talking in the library are prohibited.

"Translating" Lex's Rules in Light of His Mistakes. We are at this juncture in the argument. The meaning of Lex's rules must comport with Lex's role as a governing authority. That role is to determine what ought to be done, and Lex's determination is what he intends to communicate to citizens and officials through his rules. The meaning of the rules, therefore, just is what Lex wishes to communicate through them. And although various inconsistent beliefs and intentions may be embodied in Lex's rules, when that is the case, the meanings of the rules are still what binding effects Lex would declare the rules to have when confronted with such conflicts and inconsistencies.

Searching for Lex's inchoate intentions—which intentions, we have argued, are the key to interpreting legal texts—leads to the further problem of distinguishing between translations and corrections of Lex's intent. In imagining what Lex would say about the binding effects of his rules, we can envision his conceding that "I meant X but I now see that X was a mistake." In our view, this should not alter the conclusion that the rule means X. But it raises the following issue: is it possible to distinguish between (1) what Lex *did determine* with respect to a factual situation that he was not adverting to at the time he authored his communication about what ought to be done, and (2) what Lex *should have determined* with respect to such a situation? In other words, can we distinguish between inchoate intentions and what appear from the subjects' perspective to be correct beliefs and intentions?

Consider one of the most carefully argued and persuasive attempts to describe proper interpretation in circumstances not envisioned by the authoring authorities. In "Fidelity in Translation," Lawrence

Lessig equates interpretation in such circumstances to translation.[35] Translation, says Lessig, requires two steps.[36] The first step is to read the text for the meaning it carries in its original context—how the authorities envisioned their determination would operate. The second step is to translate that meaning into the current context of application. Interpretation as translation requires that the meaning of a text be preserved as the contexts of application change. So long as the text's meaning in application is preserved through contextual change, the interpreters can be said to be carrying out what the authorities determined and communicated ought to be done rather than to be acting on their (the interpreters') own view of what ought to be done.

Lessig then goes on to describe translation of legal texts—how meaning in application is preserved through contextual changes.[37] The original context from which meaning is derived consists of the presuppositions of the authorities.[38] These, categorized broadly, consist of presuppositions about matters of fact, presuppositions about matters of law, and presuppositions about values. For example, the framers of the Fifth Amendment posited a privilege against self-incrimination in a factual setting in which there were no police forces and police interrogators such as those we find today.[39] Therefore, even if the framers envisioned the clause's application to be restricted to interrogations at or before trial by magistrates or prosecutors, their meaning for the clause is preserved by applying it to the modern context of interrogation, namely, custodial interrogation of the defendant by the police. A difference in factual presuppositions between 1791 and today gets us from the Fifth Amendment to *Miranda v. Arizona*,[40] such that we can say that the *Miranda* decision is what the framers of the Fifth Amendment determined. In Lessig's terms, *Miranda* is a faithful translation of the Fifth Amendment's privilege against self-incrimination.

Lessig gives as an example of a change in legal presuppositions the case where a legal text is implicitly premised on the existence of other legal doctrines, doctrines that in the interim between the promulgation of the texts and the applications in question are judicially overruled or legislatively repealed.[41] As an example of a change in legal presuppositions that arguably requires a change in application, Lessig points to the expansion of federal power under modern judicial interpretations of the commerce clause, a change in legal presuppositions that arguably affects whether the Tenth Amendment, reserving to the states all powers not delegated to the federal government,[42] which might originally have been nothing but a legal truism, now has some affirmative legal bite in order to preserve a meaningful domain of state sovereignty.[43]

The problem with Lessig's approach, as Lessig himself recognizes, is that it threatens to efface the distinction between interpretation—fidelity in translating the authorities' determinations—and emendation, correcting those determinations that are, from the interpreter's point of view, mistakes.[44] In cases of interpretation, the authorities' role to determine what ought to be done is respected. In emendation, that role is usurped by the interpreter, who becomes the ultimate authority.

To see why this is so, imagine any case in which the interpreter has a view on what ought to be done, a view that superficially conflicts with what the authorities have determined. To take one of Lessig's examples,[45] consider that in 1864 Congress wrote a provision into the United States Code limiting the fee to ten dollars that a veteran could pay an attorney for representation in a veterans' benefit suit. In 1864, ten dollars could purchase adequate legal services. Congress's intention was merely to limit what attorneys could charge veterans, not to exclude attorneys from veterans' benefits proceedings altogether. Today, however, because of over a century of inflation, the ten-dollar limitation would operate to exclude legal representation. The question then is, does fidelity in translation require us to read "ten dollars" to mean the cost of the amount of legal services that ten dollars would have bought in 1864?

Lessig is aware of the importance of this question, and he addresses it in the context of setting limits to his model of translation.[46] The important limit for our purposes is what Lessig calls "structural humility."[47] Humility in translation requires that the translator not improve the original text, that is, not correct mistakes that the text contains. The translator's job is to find equivalence in meaning between contexts, not to improve the meaning.

Not all improvements are inappropriate, however, but only improvements that affect the task for which we hold the authors responsible.[48] Thus, it is okay for a translator of poetry to improve the poet's handwriting but not his poetry. We do not judge the poet by her handwriting. On the other hand, it is not okay to improve the handwriting in a child's paper if penmanship is part of the child's work to be evaluated. Lessig summarizes the point: "What humility requires, then, is a claim about the background understanding of what it is the author is being held responsible for. Against this background, humility counsels the translator to stay clear of presuppositions that touch the author's responsibility."[49]

Of what presuppositions of legal authorities must legal interpreters stay clear? Lessig answers that they must stay clear of "political" or value presuppositions but not factual or legal ones.[50] In other words, the interpreter, in faithfully translating a legal text, may correct for factual and legal presuppositions that turn out to be false, but not for value presuppositions with which the interpreter disagrees.

How does Lessig's analysis operate in the context of Congress's ten-dollar cap on attorneys' fees? Remember, the important questions for Lessig are whether there has been change in presuppositions (a change that would have resulted in a different text), and whether the changed presuppositions are factual or evaluative. The presupposition at issue that Lessig attributes to the 1864 Congress—that ten dollars will purchase adequate legal representation—surely appears to be a factual one in Lessig's schema. Therefore, the faithful interpreter, who holds Congress responsible for its value choices but not its factual beliefs, would "interpret" ten dollars to mean whatever dollar amount is now necessary to purchase what ten dollars would have purchased in attorneys' services in 1864. Moreover, one would suppose that similar results might be in order for the constitutional requirement that the president be thirty-five and serve four-year terms, and that senators serve six-year terms, or even that posted speed limits are to be taken literally.

Lessig does not justify his conclusion that we should hold authoring legal authorities responsible for their value presuppositions but not for their factual and legal presuppositions. Lessig realizes that correcting for all now-perceived-as-erroneous presuppositions of the authoring legal authorities in effect makes the interpreters, not the authoring legal authorities, responsible for governance.[51] Thus, he attempts to cabin such corrections by distinguishing between correcting erroneous value beliefs and correcting erroneous factual beliefs. Lessig's distinction, however, is unsatisfactory, both because the relation of fact and value is too messy, and because—as the attorneys' fees example suggests—we wish to make the authorities responsible for factual determinations.

To take the latter point first, many disagreements that interpreters have with the authorities whose laws they must interpret are disagreements about matters of fact. Does the fifty-five-mile-per-hour speed limit save lives? Will congressional term limits increase political accountability? Will ceilings on insurance rates actually work as forecast? And although Lessig's examples of fidelity in translation involve correcting factual and legal presuppositions that were correct when made but became incorrect over (a relatively long) time, there is no reason in principle that we can see why Lessig would not want interpreters to correct factual and legal presuppositions that were erroneous when made. Or, conversely, why should we not hold legal authorities responsible for failing accurately to predict the future and, if at the same time we hold them responsible for failure, accurately to assay the present?

In Lessig's scheme, it turns out to be impossible for the legal authorities to say that the law they enacted was premised on a factual or legal error that should cause it to be repealed. For, faithfully interpreted, the law's factual and legal presuppositions are all corrected; repeals because of factual or legal error are never necessary. Because, however, we believe that such repeals are often necessary, there must be something amiss in Lessig's view of interpretation. Put differently, we think there is frequently a gap between what the authoring authorities *did determine* ought to be done and what, *in light of the facts,* they *should have determined.* Lessig's model of fidelity in translation, however, renders such a gap a conceptual impossibility.[52]

Lessig's distinction between factual and legal presuppositions, which can be corrected by the interpreter, and value presuppositions, which cannot be corrected, is also problematic. It seriously underestimates the number of value disagreements that ultimately can be reduced to disagreements about facts or to mistakes in reasoning. For example, Lessig argues that something has gone amiss if we correct as erroneous the constitutional framers' presupposition that bicameralism is a "better" form of government than unicameralism.[53] That presupposition was a value judgment for which the framers should be deemed responsible. It is hard to imagine, however, how that "value" judgment is anything other than a judgment about facts—that is, about how efficient, liberty-protective, and responsive the two types of government will be. And the value presuppositions behind the preference for the superior form of government in terms of efficiency, liberty-protection, and responsiveness have arguably not changed a bit since the constitutional framing.

Lessig himself admits that the line between value and factual presuppositions will not be a clear or even a stable one.[54] Ultimately, the important question is, for what do we hold the authoring legal authorities responsible? Unfortunately for Lessig's analysis, he makes no case for the presupposition that we should hold authoring legal authorities responsible for their values but not their factual beliefs. Indeed, if the legal authorities' role is to make shared abstract moral notions much more determinate, the role of authorities in determining factual matters is in some sense more important than their role in determining values.

We began this discussion of Lessig by asking whether it is possible to distinguish between what the authorities did determine and what the authorities should have determined with respect to factual situations to which they did not advert. Lessig fails to distinguish these things, namely, when what the authors determined changes with the context of application and when what they determined is shown to be mistaken by the context of application. Lessig's fidelity in translation effaces that distinction with respect to factual distinctions and assumes it with respect to value determinations.

Yet if we are correct about the existence of inchoate intentions, the distinction between actual intentions and correct intentions is possible in principle. The obstacle that remains is whether the inquiry into inchoate intent is sufficiently determinate to support a set of meaningful rules.

The Determinacy of Inchoate Intent: The Kripkenstein Critique. We come now to our third question, whether it is possible for Lex's subjects, despite their disagreements with Lex and among themselves over what ought to be done, to understand Lex's intention in sufficiently similar ways to make Lex's rules relatively determinate. After presenting a preliminary answer, we move to our fourth and fifth questions, when Lex's rules may be indeterminate, and whether the fact that Lex intends a rule (as opposed to a standard) makes the rule more determinate for its audience.

On the question of determinacy, we turn to what is labeled the "Kripkenstein" critique of determinate intentions because it is based on Saul Kripke's interpretation of Wittgenstein.[55] Basically, the Kripkenstein critique stems from recognition that no mental state content, present or past, can *by itself* ever make it true that by uttering certain words, one has intended some future act. For example, when we issue the rule "Add 68 and 57," what makes it the case that by "add" we intend that arithmetic operation that will produce the answer 125? According to the critique, nothing in our past uses of "add" precludes the possibility that we might now mean an arithmetic operation that produces the answer 5. For what we did in the past is, for example, consistent with the result "125 for every day before today, 5 for every day thereafter."[56]

The conclusion to draw from the Kripkenstein critique is not the skeptical one that determinate intentions and rules are an impossibility because there are no mental facts that can anchor determinacy.[57] Rather, the conclusion to draw—and that is almost universally drawn, though by differing routes—is that determinate intentions and rules are matters of *knowing how* rather than *knowing that*.[58] We learn through interaction with others how to follow rules, including those we set for ourselves.[59] When we "interpret" what we have intended with respect to situations to which we have not fully adverted—which situations exist for all intentions—we do not look for mental facts in addition to those we call the intentions; rather, we just grasp, as we have learned to do, the full range of intentions in light of the actual mental state and its context.[60] Assertions about intentions are not like assertions about the speed of light, true or false independently of our social reality. Rather, assertions about intentions and their products, such as rules, are anchored in part in the world beyond social practices (the actual mental states) and in part within the world of social practices. And this is as much true of those whose intentions are in question as it is of those who seek to discover those intentions.

Indeed, the Kripkenstein critique of determinacy is bound to fail because we experience determinacy of intentions and communication daily. We follow rules correctly, be they mathematical or linguistic, and with many rules, we rarely disagree about what they require.[61]

Whether we are Marxists or monarchists, we stop at stop signs, put commas after introductory dependent clauses, and get 125 when we add 67 and 58. Even this chapter is in some sense unnecessary to our project because determinate rules are an everyday fact of life. What the Kripkenstein critique accomplishes is not the undermining of determinacy; rather, at most it forces us to seek the ground of determinacy not in mental states alone, but in mental states coupled with skills learned as part of forms of life.

Infelicities of Rules. That brings us to our fourth problem, which arises when Lex's rules are imperfectly expressed, or accurately expressed but overinclusive and underinclusive, and when they are indeterminate, not only to Michael, but to Lex himself. Our analysis up to this point shows that when Lex decrees "No talking in the library," the rule that he intends can be determinate, even if it diverges from Lex's more general purposes. Those purposes form part of the context in which Lex's rule is understood and thus help determine the rule's meaning; yet, although purpose and meaning are related, they are not the same thing. What Lex *means* by his rule can come apart from his purposes in promulgating it.[62] As we see the situation, there will be instances in which we should read Lex's rule one way rather than another because the reading we reject would make the rule absurd or grossly unfair or self-defeating. There will be other instances in which Lex did mean something that we believe (and even he believes) he should not have meant. Finally, there will be instances in which we—and perhaps even Lex—are not sure what he meant, and no additional evidence can resolve the uncertainty. In the first two instances, Lex's intended meaning is determinate. In the last, it is indeterminate.

Consider Lex's rule "No talking in the library." Suppose Matt sees a fire breaking out in the stacks, one that could quickly imperil the other patrons and the staff. Nonetheless, he refuses to shout "Fire!" When later asked why, he cites the rule.

Here we are inclined to say that Matt has misunderstood the rule. No one could reasonably believe that Lex intended silence in such a circumstance. Although his words do not expressly except situations like Matt's, the context of the rule makes it clear that it is not intended to cover warnings of imminent danger.[63]

Or assume again that Lex has enacted the rule "No talking in the library." Cases arise in which (1) janitors talk while cleaning up after hours; (2) two patrons talk in the bathroom; and (3) a librarian provides a tour to new patrons, pointing out the arrangement of volumes and services. All these cases are covered by the dictionary meaning of Lex's words, yet we believe (with decreasing confidence as we move through the three examples) that Lex did not intend his rule to govern them. At the same time, we do not think Lex made a mistake in drafting the rule; rather, we think he did not intend his words to include these cases. In reaching these conclusions, we inevitably are referring to the purpose of the rule: the reason we believe these cases are excluded is that they are too remote from Lex's aim of promoting study and perhaps too much at odds with an even higher aim, to do what is best.

Consider now a case in which Matt shouts out updates on the progress of the World Series to the other patrons and the staff. When it is pointed out to Matt by some irate patrons that there is a no-talking rule in force, Matt replies that he assumes the rule is intended to promote patron enjoyment. Because Matt believes that the patrons will ultimately be glad that they received information on the World Series, he claims to be adhering to Lex's intent.

Here, even if Matt is correct about the importance of the information, he has surely misread Lex's intent. Lex intends "No talking" in this situation, even if at some level of generality of purpose, he has chosen a rule ill suited to its purpose.[64]

In a closer case, suppose that Matt and Jacques engage in a conversation about material they have been reading, believing (correctly) that no other patrons are present in the library. It may well be that prohibiting this conversation is inconsistent with Lex's general objective of promoting study. Yet Lex's probable inchoate intent is that the rule should apply, even at some expense to its purposes, in order to maintain clarity and guide those who might be mistaken about who else is around.

In the situations we have described so far, the meaning of Lex's rule is sufficiently determinate, although the rule is infelicitous in one way or another. In other cases, however, Lex's intent may be indeterminate. Suppose, for example, that the question is whether Matt can orally inform the patrons and staff of some exciting once-in-a-lifetime event that is occurring outside the library, such as that the president is passing by. An average member of the community may be genuinely uncertain about whether Lex intends his rule to proscribe this. More significantly, Lex himself may be uncertain of his intent. Lex can reliably conclude that the rule he intended does not forbid warnings of fire and does not allow any speech that the patrons might ultimately come to value more than silence; in the third scenario, however, Lex may be uncertain whether the rule he intended forbids the speech. Here, we conclude that Lex's intent, and thus his rule, is indeterminate.[65]

Of course, there is no perfect line between indeterminate rules and those that are determinate but infelicitous. Nevertheless, we are confident that if interpretation is conceived of as a search for authorities' actual but inchoate intent, and not as a process of correction, then, over a substantial range of cases, the basic social and linguistic understandings that allow us to grasp meaning will yield answers to questions about how Lex intended us to understand his rules.

Does the Intent to Promulgate a Determinate Rule Affect Determinacy? This point leads us to our fifth question, namely, does the fact that Lex intends his rule forbidding talking in the library to be a determinate rule render his intentions determinate in situations where they would otherwise be indeterminate? In our last scenario, for example, might this intention regarding determinacy resolve Lex's uncertainty whether he intends to forbid someone's informing the patrons of a once-in-a-lifetime exciting event so that Lex, upon reflection, would conclude that he did indeed intend to forbid this, even if he also believed that an exception for such a case would have been warranted?

We believe that Lex's intention to promulgate a determinate rule can and should affect conclusions about his inchoate intent—that is, what he intended the rule to mean in cases he did not advert to at the time of enactment. The intention to issue a determinate rule, which is part and parcel of Lex's role in producing coordination and eliminating the costs of others' decision-making, forms part of the background against which we infer the intended meaning of Lex's rules. A vital part of Lex's decision-making is the judgment that, for all the reasons explored in chapter 4, a determinate rule will best serve the purpose he has in mind. This does not preclude implied exclusions or indeterminacy, but it explains why when Lex promulgates a particular speed limit—say, sixty-five miles per hour—to achieve the goals of safety and convenience, we do not understand "sixty-five" to mean some other speed, even if we are positive that another speed better serves those goals.[66]

|||||

A useful way to summarize the foregoing is by reviewing the various ways that Lex's rule may be infelicitous. First, the "No talking in the library" rule will, like all rules, be over- and underinclusive with respect to its background moral reasons. This infelicity was the focus of the previous chapter, and it is an uneliminable feature of rules. Even if Lex's rule is ideal as a rule—the best rule that anyone could formulate in advancing its moral goals, including coordination and efficient decision-making—it will diverge in some instances from what it is morally best for Matt to do, all things considered. In this case, Lex's rule is determinate, although it produces a result that diverges from Lex's purpose.

Second, Lex's rule may be infelicitous in a much more prosaic way: there may be a better rule available that Lex has overlooked. Perhaps Congress in the *Church of the Holy Trinity* case[67] really did intend to ban the importation of all laborers, including ministers, but upon realizing this would have viewed doing so as a mistake. Perhaps Congress could have fashioned an equally determinate rule that would have excepted ministers and perhaps other categories of laborers. Even that rule would undoubtedly have had some infelicitous applications, but it could still be a superior determinate rule to the one that Congress enacted. Again, Lex's rule is determinate. The results of the rule may be less than optimal, but there is no further role for interpretation.

Third, Lex's rule may be imperfectly expressed, and yet its meaning is determinate for most or all of Lex's subjects because they can grasp the meaning he must have intended. For example, when the words "All laws are . . . hereby repealed" are attached as boilerplate to a state statute, it is evident that the words should not be taken to repeal all prior laws, including the law against homicide, but instead should be treated as a drafter's slip, inadvertently omitting "that are inconsistent with the provisions herein."[68] Of course, a rule of this kind may be indeterminate for some people, either because they have failed to master how to communicate and to decipher communications, or because they lack access to the interpretive evidence that is available to most. Someone who is uncertain whether Lex's rule permits him to shout a fire warning just does not understand what almost everyone else does. The fact that the rule is inaccessible to some subjects, however, does not generally undermine the enterprise of promulgating determinate rules. Thus, someone who had no knowledge of American history might excusably read the seventeenth amendment—"The Senate of the United States shall be composed of two Senators from each State, elected by the people thereof, for six years"[69]—to have provided for direct election of senators only for a period of six years from the amendment's adoption; those familiar with American history and/or the actual way we elect senators, however, will see the awkward syntax of the amendment as just that—a mistake, a slip—and read it as if "for six years" followed immediately after "elected."[70] (Of course, one must always avoid conflating using evidence of Lex's mistakes and short-sightedness to discover what he meant by his rule and using such evidence to justify disobeying Lex's rule. For if these uses are conflated, cases of justified disobedience collapse into cases of obedience.)

Fourth, Lex might infelicitously draft a rule that renders it indeterminate for everyone except him. That is, it may be clear to Lex what he meant, but unclear to others. For example, in *United States v. Locke*,[71] Congress had required the filing of certain claims "before December 31" of the year in which they arose. Although it is certain that requiring claims be filed *before* December 31—as opposed to *on or before* December 31—is bizarre, it is not certain whether Congress intended this bizarre requirement. Congress, on the other hand, might be quite certain either that it did intend it, though it should not have, or that it did not intend it. In such a case, there is no role for interpretation because interpretation is not possible: the rule has no meaning accessible to those outside of Congress.

Finally, Lex himself may be uncertain about what he intended. We have given the example of whether Lex's "No talking in the library" rule applies to informing patrons of an exciting, once-in-a-lifetime event. Lex's intended meaning may be indeterminate in such a case, even for Lex. Again, interpretation is not possible and Lex's rule is, for this purpose, without meaning.

Noninterpretive Assignments of Meaning

The objective of settlement through authoritative rules dictates that interpretation should be understood as a search for Lex's intent in issuing rules. Nevertheless, officials acting as interpreters may perform other, related functions in assigning meaning to rules: they may supply meaning in the absence of discernible intent, and they may sometimes override Lex's intent. When officials supply meaning that is not grounded in intent, or that override intent, they are not acting as interpreters: they are claiming authority to design or amend rules. While it may be necessary for officials to go beyond interpretation in applying rules, their extrainterpretive activities are in tension with the ideal of deliberate settlement by an authority chosen by the community.

Intent-based interpretation is not always possible, even though Lex has issued a rule. In some cases, notably when Lex is not a single-minded authority but a decision-making body with multiple members, intent fails because the intent of individual decision-makers does not coalesce around a particular outcome. Suppose, for example, that a three-member legislature issues a rule, "No talking in the library." There is evidence that one legislator voted for the rule to promote the use of sign language, another voted for the rule to keep the library quiet, and the third voted against the rule. A library tour in which the librarian gives an oral presentation to newcomers might be prohibited by the first legislator but implicitly excluded by the second. Thus, there is no intent, attributable to a majority of those who voted for the rule, about what should be done in this case.[72] Alternatively, intent-based interpretation may fail because there is no reliable evidence from which Michael can determine Lex's intent, or because Lex's intent is genuinely indeterminate.

When intent-based interpretation is impossible for these reasons, one response is to say that the rule has no effect: it is void, at least as applied to the case in question. This is not an ideal outcome, however, because it raises the possibility of ghost rules that appear to have been issued in proper form and appear to govern the dispute at hand, but in fact have either no applicable meaning or no meaning at all. The result is uncertainty about the status of rules and a failure of settlement.

Assuming the rule is still in force, the alternative is to say that Michael, the interpreter, should select a meaning within the range of meanings the words of the rule will bear. It is important to understand, however, that if Lex's intent fails, and Michael nevertheless proceeds to give meaning and effect to Lex's rule, conceived of as the sounds or marks Lex promulgated, Michael's decision is not based on what Lex determined ought to be done. Instead, Michael is exercising independent authority, which, if it exists at all, must be derived from an external source. That source might be a rule issued by Lex, or a constitutional or preconstitutional rule approved by the community.[73]

Although a delegation of rule-making authority to Michael may be the best solution when the alternative is to leave a dispute ungoverned, it has several flaws. Most obviously, it shifts decision-making power from the preferred authority, Lex, to an authority who has at best been designated to decide in case of default. Another difficulty is that the resulting rule reflects neither Lex's nor Michael's original determination of what should be done. The rule actually issued by Lex ("No talking in the library") has no content and thus imposes no direct, authoritative constraint on Michael's determination of what should be done. At the same time, Michael's moral calculation must take into account the effects of the words Lex chose. He cannot start fresh, because rule-subjects may have been affected by the issuance of what appears to be a rule. The result is a hybrid product of Lex's words and Michael's moral judgment.[74]

Another possible role for Michael, one that exceeds what can properly be called interpretation of Lex's rules, is to apply rules or norms that override Lex's intent in issuing rules. We are not referring here to constitutional rules or norms, which are issued by a Super Lex and operate in much the same manner as Lex's rules.[75] What we have in mind are preconstitutional norms that limit the exercise of authority by any official in whom it is vested (including Lex). These preconstitutional norms arise by agreement among members of the community and operate at the same level as the basic rule, "Let Lex decide."

Assuming such preconstitutional norms exist, the most plausible candidates are rules of form that enforce fundamental rule-of-law values—values requiring that rules be accessible to their subjects and predictable in their effect.[76] For example, the community might adopt a preconstitutional rule holding that the standard English meaning of Lex's words should prevail over wildly idiosyncratic usages that capture Lex's actual intent. The result is a loss of Lex's expertise, but the ends of settlement may be better served by a rule selected arbitrarily than by a rule that fails to meet the basic requirement of accessibility. As in the case of failed intent, when Michael applies such a norm and gives the words of Lex's rule their dictionary meaning, he is not interpreting Lex's rule, but imposing a new rule.[77] In this case, however, the authority Michael exercises is not authority to make rules in Lex's place, but authority to interpret and apply the preconstitutional norms that constrain Lex.[78]

Another possible preconstitutional norm or set of norms would limit the evidence of Lex's intent that Michael may consult. For example, courts might exclude certain items of legislative history from use in interpreting acts of Congress. Because all communication is understood in context, such norms cannot be so strong as to strip Lex's rules completely of the context that gives them meaning. Rather, such norms can operate only at the margin, say, by requiring Michael to ignore evidence of Lex's intent that will not be generally available to or accessible by most persons subject to Lex's rules,[79] or that poses certain dangers of manipulation and hence distortion of Lex's intent.

It is possible that a community would also adopt preconstitutional norms holding that Lex's rules should be "interpreted" to avoid results that are seriously unjust or absurd. For a community interested in settlement of moral controversy, however, norms of this kind seem inadvisable. If Michael measures each application of Lex's rules against a standard of justice (which presumably is the ultimate end of the body of rules) or absurdity (meaning moral absurdity), the rules are no longer capable of settling moral controversy. Instead, the controversy is reopened in the process of assigning meaning to the rules. The principal difference is that settlement authority shifts from Lex to Michael, who was not the community's first choice to serve as moral decision-maker. It seems preferable, therefore, that moral absurdity and injustice should not supplant, but should serve only as evidence bearing on, Lex's intended meaning.[80]

In short, as a supplement to interpretation, our community will need rules permitting noninterpretive assignment of meaning to

Lex's rules in some circumstances. It must have rules that vest rule-making authority in Michael when Lex's intent is missing or indecipherable, and it probably should have rules of form, such as a rule that prefers the dictionary meaning of Lex's rules to intentions that are markedly in conflict with the ordinary understanding of the words Lex has used. Yet decisions made in pursuance of rules of this kind should not be confused with interpretation of Lex's rules: they represent an independent exercise of authority, either directly by Michael, or by the community through its preconstitutional rules.[81] Moreover, because such decisions are at odds with the basic rule, "Let Lex decide," and with the objective of deliberate settlement that captures Lex's expertise, authority to assign meaning to Lex's rules should be granted and exercised sparingly.

| | | | |

In one sense, this entire chapter, despite its length, is too short. It is too short in that each of the topics it covers is worthy of book-length treatment. We have only skimmed the surface of how Lex's various intentions can be folded into *an* intended meaning and of what separates determinate from indeterminate intended meanings.

The chapter is also too long in that determinate rules—rules that we all understand in the same way, regardless of our own differing assessments of what should be done—are a reality. Indeed, they are ubiquitous. We commonly understand others' requests and demands, even when we disagree with them, and we understand them the same way. Occasionally, we are puzzled because we suspect but are not sure of a malapropism, a grammatical infelicity, a slip, a material and unforeseen change of circumstances, or a seriously mistaken assumption about the world. Often, further evidence resolves our uncertainty. But sometimes the uncertainty remains, and the request or order is operationally indeterminate, not just for its addressees but sometimes for its author as well.

Lex, therefore, may not always succeed in promulgating a determinate rule. There is nothing in the nature of the enterprise, however, that renders it impossible either some or most of the time.

PART THREE

Issues of Legal Reasoning

SIX Reasoning by Analogy

Lex's function is to settle controversies. He can do this in part by enacting rules, subject to the difficulties outlined in chapter 4. Even if these difficulties could be overcome, however, rules alone cannot settle every controversy. There inevitably will be further controversies about the application of rules to particular cases, some of which cannot be resolved by private agreement. There will be also controversies that do not fall within the terms of any rule, either because Lex has not considered the problem, or because he has determined that there is not sufficient warrant for a rule. Lex may have no informational advantage or may conclude that the costs of a uniform rule outweigh the benefits of coordination.

In all these cases, Lex will need the assistance of judges who preside over particular unresolved disputes and determine their outcomes one by one. Unlike Lex, these judges look backward at events that have already occurred and consider those events in temporary isolation from other circumstances and events. Part of the judges' task is to interpret rules and make the factual determinations necessary to apply them. Another part of their task is to settle, by some other method, controversies that are not controlled by rules.

In theory, Lex might decide that judges should decline to act in the absence of a rule and should instead leave the controversy to be resolved through other methods, including force. More realistically, however, Lex will prefer a peaceful resolution to a continuing quarrel and so will authorize his judges to decide in favor of one party or the other. He may also authorize judges to promulgate rules for future cases, but we will defer that topic to chapter 7.

The purpose of this chapter is to consider what forms of legal reasoning judges engage in when they perform their adjudicative functions. The basic tools available to the judge, as to any reasoner, are deductive reasoning, empirical reasoning, and moral reasoning.[1] By empirical reasoning, we mean the various methods used to establish facts about the world and human behavior, including observation, induction, and construction and testing of hypotheses. By moral reasoning, we mean the method of "reflective equilibrium," in which moral intuition is combined with reflection on and refinement of moral principles that justify one's intuition.[2] A judge seeking reflective equilibrium begins with an intuitive judgment about the morally best outcome of the case and constructs a tentative moral principle to explain that outcome. Next, she tests the moral principle "downward," by reasoning deductively to other outcomes and considering whether those outcomes are intuitively sound, as well as "upward," by constructing and testing justifying moral principles at a higher level of abstraction. The judge then refines both moral principles and moral intuitions until she reaches a coherent view of the case.

Reasoning under Rules

When the case before the judge is controlled by a rule and the meaning of the rule is clear, the only form of reasoning required is deduction. Suppose, for example, that a customer in a shop finds a package of money on the floor of the shop. A dispute arises between the customer and the owner of the shop over who should keep the money. Research uncovers a preexisting rule: "The finder of lost property is entitled to possession against all but the true owner." If all agree that the customer found the money and that the money was lost, simple deduction will yield a decision for the customer.[3]

Of course, the meaning of a rule is never perfectly clear. What does it mean to "find" property? If "finding" money means being the first person in possession after its owner parts with it, then perhaps the shop owner can claim to have "found" the money because it was lost within the confines of his shop.

We have already discussed interpretation of rules in chapter 5. The goals of interpretation are much disputed, but as far as methods of reasoning are concerned, most approaches to interpretation rely at least in part on ordinary empirical reasoning. Conventional usage, for example, is a fact amenable to simple research. Authorial intent is a fact as well: it may not be observable, but one can draw inferences based on what one knows of the circumstances of authorship. Ordinary moral reasoning may also enter into the process of interpretation, either directly or indirectly. For example, if interpretation focuses on author's intent, and it appears that the author intended the rule to produce morally sound results, moral reasoning provides evidence of the meaning intended. If, as some others have argued, moral reasoning plays a direct role in determining the meaning of the rule.[4]

Reasoning in the Absence of Rules: Moral Reasoning

When judges are authorized to resolve disputes that are not controlled by any rule, the most straightforward approach for the judge is to use ordinary moral reasoning, supplemented by ordinary empirical reasoning, to reach the best outcome. For example, in the case of the money on the floor of the shop, the judge might sense intuitively that the customer should win. From this intuition, together with facts about human motivation, she might construct a tentative decisional principle, "Finders of lost property are entitled to keep the property as against all but the true owner." This principle is justifiable at a more abstract level by the proposition "Honesty and enterprise deserve reward." As initially stated, however, the judge's decisional principle produces questionable results in at least one class of hypothetical cases. If any finder acquires a right against all but the true owner, trespassers might profit by searching through others' property, an unsatisfactory outcome if rectitude is important to desert. Accordingly, the judge might amend her decisional principle to "Those who find lost property in a place where they are lawful invitees are entitled to keep the property as against all but the true owner" but confirm the outcome for the honest finder of money in the shop. In other cases—for example, the case of a trespassing finder—the judge might need to revise the outcome she arrived at originally to bring it in line with an acceptable decisional principle.

Reasoning in the Absence of Rules: Analogical Reasoning

It is often said that judges and lawyers do not reach decisions by straightforward moral and empirical reasoning. Instead, they engage in a form of reasoning known as analogical reasoning.[5] Roughly, a judge reasoning by analogy surveys decided cases, locates similarities between those cases and the case before her, develops a principle that captures the similarities, and decides her case accordingly.[6] This analogical method is considered the special art of lawyers, an art that sustains the common law and justifies treating law as an independent discipline, apart from science or moral philosophy.[7] It has also been praised as a way to align decisions with the fair expectations of parties,[8] as a way for law to avoid the rigidity of fixed rules,[9] as a source of "integrity" in law,[10] and as a means for low-level compromise among people who disagree at the level of abstract moral principle.[11]

Nevertheless, it is not always clear what analogical reasoning means. Some suggest that a judge reasoning by analogy relies on an intuitive grasp of similarities and differences among cases, evolved through long experience with legal disputes.[12] But something more substantive must lie behind the intuition: it simply is not possible to reason from one case to another without a tying rule or principle that determines which factual similarities are important and which are not.[13]

The best explanation of how analogical reasoning works and why it might have rational force comes from Scott Brewer. Brewer describes analogical reasoning as a process much like reflective equilibrium, except that prior decisions stand in place of moral intuitions as the source of a tentative decisional principle.[14] According to Brewer, a judge facing a problem case studies other cases that appear, intuitively, to be related. She then draws from these cases an "analogy-warranting rule" that can explain the prior outcomes as well as determine the outcome of the case before her. Next she tests the analogy-warranting rule upward against more abstract "analogy-warranting rationales" and downward against the outcomes it might dictate in other real or hypothetical cases. If the analogy-warranting rule successfully reconciles the cases, and also survives the process of testing against rationales and further examples, then in Brewer's view, there is reason to believe that the analogy-warranting rule is probably sound and the result it gives for the problem case is probably correct. A conclusion reached in this way is not proven inductively; nor is it proven deductively, because the analogy-warranting rule has never been established as true. Nevertheless, Brewer maintains that the testing process gives the conclusion at least some rational force.[15]

To see how this might work, suppose that a bank depositor finds a packet of money on a chair in the safe deposit vault and reports it to the bank.[16] The bank proceeds to notify customers, but no one claims the money. The depositor and the bank both claim a right to possession of the money. The judge, reasoning by analogy, first searches for prior cases involving lost money. She finds the case of the shop customer who found money on the floor of the shop, in which the customer prevailed over the owner of the shop. She also finds a case in which a barber's customer found money on a table in the barbershop, and the court held in favor of the barber.[17]

After some study, the judge might draw from these cases an analogy-warranting rule to the effect that "mislaid" money—money deliberately set down and then forgotten—should be awarded to the owner of the place where it is found, while "lost" money—money inadvertently dropped—should be awarded to the finder.[18] The judge could then test this rule by searching for analogy-warranting rationales. For example, special treatment of mislaid property might be justified on the ground that if the money was deliberately mislaid, the owner is likely to remember and return to the site. If so, a decision that gives possession to the owner of the site makes it easier for the owner of the money to find and retrieve it. Property rights are more secure, and secure property rights contribute to general prosperity. If the judge is persuaded that these reasons support the "mislaid" analogy and does not foresee examples in which it would produce absurd results, the result is a decision for the bank.

Under Brewer's interpretation, analogical reasoning is not simply a form of deduction from canonical rules.[19] Rather, it combines deduction with "abduction"—the critical step in which the judge draws from prior decisions an analogy-warranting rule that captures their similarities and differences.[20] Abduction itself appears to be an intuitive exercise—Brewer describes identification of an analogy-warranting rule as an "uncodifiable imaginative moment."[21] As the rule is cross-checked against rationales and further examples, however, the process becomes something more than simple intuition.

We shall assume that analogical reasoning is indeed a form of reasoning, and that it works in the manner Brewer describes. As a form of reasoning, however, it has serious flaws. Analogical reasoning is structurally similar to reflective equilibrium, relying on a process of reference back and forth between the abstract and the concrete. It differs from reflective equilibrium, however, in a critical way: the foundation for analogical reasoning is not the reasoner's tentative moral intuition; it is, rather, the prior decisions of other reasoners, which stand as unalterable data from which the present reasoner must work.[22] Because human reasoning is subject to error, those decisions will sometimes be wrong. Yet they remain the starting point for analogy, and the result is to build past error into the process of decision-making.[23]

For example, recall that in the case of money found in a bank vault, our analogical judge began with two previous cases: one in which money found on a shop floor was awarded to the finder and another in which money found on a table in a barbershop was awarded to the barber who owned the site. Given these cases, an analogy-warranting rule that likens the bank case to the barbershop case seems sensible. In each case, the money appears to have been "mislaid" rather than inadvertently lost, and thus it is more likely in these cases that the owner will return. But suppose that the original barbershop case was based on an empirical mistake: owners are in fact less likely to recover their property when possession is awarded to the owner of the site because finders now have an incentive to hide their finds rather than report them at the site. Or perhaps the distinction between "lost" and "mislaid" property is unworkable in most cases. If so, then the bank case may be like the barbershop case, but in both cases the conclusion is wrong.

Our criticism of analogical reasoning, then, is that it corrupts the process of deciding what outcome is best in the absence of a controlling rule because it incorporates the errors of past decisions. Therefore, unless analogical reasoning has some other virtue independent of its rational force in determining what outcome is best, it is inferior to ordinary moral reasoning through the process of reflective equilibrium. In saying this, we do not mean to suggest that past decisions are irrelevant to sound decision-making. Past decisions, especially decisions by judges, have effects on the world. If a past decision has generated reliance, or if we want to encourage people to rely on official decisions, we may need to act as if the decision were correct, even if it was wrong. But at least in principle, the effects of past decisions can be taken into account, for precisely what they are worth, in the course of ordinary moral reasoning. And as long as this is done, there is no need to assume they are in fact correct and to reason (faultily) from there.

Of course, ordinary moral reasoning through the process of reflective equilibrium is also subject to error because the reasoner is always fallible. Yet reflective equilibrium at least permits refinement of the reasoner's initial intuitions if the reasoner comes to perceive that they are flawed. Moreover, it represents the reasoner's best efforts to reach a correct conclusion. The method of analogy, in contrast, deliberately embraces what may be moral error. Rather than asking what the morally correct outcome is, it asks the perhaps incoherent question "What would be the morally correct outcome in a world in which certain morally incorrect outcomes were morally correct?"[24]

It might be objected that rules also build errors into the process of decision-making, and yet we have defended Lex's use of rules. As we explained in chapter 4, however, the justification for rules lies in a favorable balance of error. Lex has reason to issue rules and to demand that actors and judges treat them as serious rules on one condition: the errors the rules avoid by correcting for information deficiencies and providing coordination must exceed the errors they cause through their bluntness. There is nothing in the nature of prior decisions to ensure that analogical reasoning based on those decisions will have advantages of the kind associated with rules. Prior decisions are simply decisions by reasoners no better equipped than the present reasoner to reach a moral conclusion.

A Qualified Defense of Analogical Reasoning

Despite what we have said so far, it may be possible to defend the practice of analogical reasoning in law in a manner that is structurally similar to the defense we have given of rules.[25] Ordinary reasoning, as we have said, is subject to error. Analogical reasoning is rationally inferior to ideal ordinary reasoning because it assimilates past error and lacks rational force. At the same time, if analogical reasoning is accepted by judges and lawyers as the customary method of judicial decision-making, it may have indirect advantages over straightforward moral and empirical reasoning.

One such indirect benefit of analogical reasoning is that it encourages judges to reflect on examples, experiment with justifications, and consider consequences. This is a procedural rather than a substantive virtue. Reflective equilibrium is superior, in principle, to analogical reasoning, but there is no guarantee that judges who view their task as one of ordinary moral reasoning will engage in the full reflective process. Judges work under time constraints and will be tempted to cut corners. If judges do not think of themselves as moral reasoners, but instead assume that they must search for analogies and try to reconcile their decisions with decisions of the past, they will at least assume the posture of reflective equilibrium. In other words, if they accept analogical reasoning as a professional custom, and perhaps as an obligation, they will be more likely to consider the examples provided by past cases and to hypothesize justifications for their decisions that can stand the test of varying facts. The method is flawed, but it may nevertheless produce better results than hasty or intuitive moral decision-making.

A habit of comparison and testing is particularly useful when judges prepare to announce general rules for future cases. Some amount of rule-making by judges is necessary for purposes of coordination, but judges are not as well situated as Lex is to make rules. A judge presiding over a dispute confronts a single set of facts, colored by the personalities and circumstances of particular parties and at the same time simplified by the rules of evidence and procedure. If the judge decides to announce a general rule, she will surely consider its consequences for future situations, but the facts and parties before her are likely to dominate her attention.[26] Her perception may also be affected by hindsight, which distorts determinations of probability by exaggerating the likelihood of the events that actually occurred.[27]

In these circumstances, the process of abducing a rule from past cases and testing it against rationales and further examples can counteract the judge's natural focus on facts before her and illuminate the wider effects of the rule. Of course, a judge is always free to study past cases for assistance in designing rules, without assuming that their outcomes are correct. But under pressure, a custom of analogical reasoning may force the judge to engage in research that she would not otherwise pursue, and therefore cause her to give more thought to the remote consequences of her rule.

Another possible advantage of analogical reasoning is that it ensures a degree of protection for reliance on past decisions that might not otherwise be adequately accounted for in the course of moral reasoning by judges. Reliance creates a reason for the judge to align her decision with decisions reached in the past, both out of respect for the moral claims of those who have relied and because a public expectation of consistency among official decisions is in the best interest of society. In principle, there is nothing to prevent a judge's taking proper account of reliance without resorting to the method of analogy. But the same bias in favor of immediate and salient facts that makes it difficult for judges to craft good rules also makes it likely that judges will undervalue the importance of reliance, particularly reliance by parties not before the court.[28] It is here that analogical reasoning enters in, as a safeguard for reliance. A judge who is accustomed to reason by analogy will naturally make efforts to conform to the pattern of past decisions. In doing so, she may needlessly accept past errors. But she may also, unthinkingly, afford more protection to reliance then she would otherwise have done.

Interestingly, this argument assumes not only that actors have relied on the precise terms of prior decisions, but also that they have extrapolated from those decisions to analogous cases, using much the same method that Brewer and others attribute to judges. This makes the argument somewhat circular: if judges did not reason by analogy, actors would have no incentive to do so; and if actors did not reason by analogy, there would be no reliance-based argument for judges' reasoning by analogy. One response to this is that in the world as we know it, actors (or rather, their lawyers) do make predictions based on reasoning by analogy from prior decisions. Another is that there may be good reason to encourage this type of prediction. A convention of analogical reasoning by lawyers and judges expands the capacity of judicial decisions to provide guidance and coordination. Actors not only can rely on canonical rules, but also can predict with some confidence what direction the law is likely to take.

We have suggested that the practice of analogical reasoning has at least two indirect advantages over ordinary moral reasoning: it encourages judges to test decisional principles against examples, and it compensates for the tendency of judges to undervalue reliance on prior decisions. Whether these indirect benefits justify the built-in errors of analogical reasoning is hard to know. Certainly, the advantages of analogical reasoning are somewhat speculative. With respect to reliance, for example, suppose that prior cases have classified delivery wagons as common carriers and held their owners strictly liable for goods lost or damaged during transit. In these circumstances, it is quite plausible that a common practice of analogical reasoning on the part of judges and lawyers would lead a railroad to anticipate that it will be treated as a common carrier and to plan accordingly. On the other hand, if we consider the position of a bank trying to assess its rights to money found in a safe deposit vault, the analogical method may not be of much help in supporting predictions. Recall that in prior cases, money found on a shop floor was awarded to the finder, and money found on a barbershop table was awarded to the owner of the site. A court presiding over the bank's case may equate the bank with the barber on the ground that the money was "mislaid," but it is a stretch to say the bank's lawyer can predict such a result with confidence.

In any event, the case for analogical reasoning depends on its capacity to avoid or counteract errors indirectly. We have no final answer to the critical question, whether the errors avoided are greater than the errors that analogical reasoning causes by incorporating the mistakes of past decisions.[29] Our point is that if analogical reasoning is justified at all, it is justified on second-best grounds, much like those that support Lex's use of rules.

Before we leave the subject of indirect benefits, we should mention one other advantage sometimes associated with common law methods. This is the epistemic value of a process of elaboration to which many judges contribute over time. Each judge draws on the work of others, and the pattern of past decisions acts as a check on radical experiments that might be misconceived. The resulting body of law represents the joint work and collective wisdom of various reasoners responding to different sets of real facts.[30]

Whether or not such evolutionary decision-making has epistemic value is a controversial question. We shall assume that it does. Nevertheless, we think it is a mistake to link the epistemic value of evolved law too closely to analogical reasoning. Arguments based on collective wisdom are strongest when judges do not simply consult the outcomes of prior cases but also build on the explicit or implicit reasons that motivated prior judges to decide as they did. In some cases a prior judge may have stated a rule or justification that guided the decision; in others, justification may be detectable from judicial allusions to ends or from cross-citations to other cases. If the present judge relies on these rules or justifications to reach her own decision, she is indeed drawing on the insights of past reasoners; and if a number of those reasoners have concurred, their insights may have epistemic weight. But this is not analogical reasoning as we have described it. Rather, it is deduction from explicit or implicit rules. The difference between this deductive method and the analogical method we have been discussing is that the judge is not "abducing" her own analogy-warranting rule from past decisions—that is, imagining a rule that fits the results of those decisions. She is searching empirically for the rules or reasons intended by past judges, then applying them to the case before her. We will return to this point in the next chapter, when we discuss the "rule" and "result" models of precedent.

SEVEN Reasoning in Light of Precedent

Lex needs judges to adjudicate particular disputes both under rules and in the absence of rules. In the last chapter we discussed the methods of reasoning judges might employ in deciding cases, including deduction from rules, ordinary moral and empirical reasoning, and the analogical form of reasoning often associated with adjudication. We are wary of analogical reasoning, although we recognize that as a commonly accepted judicial and lawyerly process, it may have indirect benefits.

Closely related to the problem of judicial reasoning is the problem of precedent: what, if any, authoritative effect should the prior decisions of judges have on judicial decision-making? Having given judges the power to resolve particular disputes, Lex might confine them to that role. Of course, the resolution of any dispute will have an effect on the parties involved, and, to the extent the outcome is visible to the world, it will affect the expectations of other parties as well. These effects may in turn have moral implications for future cases. But the resolution of a single dispute need not have any binding effect on future judges.

Alternatively, Lex might enlarge the settlement function of judges by giving their decisions authoritative effect in future cases. In other words, he might give judicial decisions an effect similar to that of serious rules: future judges must follow them even when they believe the prior decisions are wrong. In this chapter, we shall consider what it might mean for a judge to "follow" prior decisions, and to what extent such a practice is justified.

We organize the various competing approaches to precedent into three models, which are set out below.[1] Before we begin, however, we want to emphasize a simple point about precedent that is sometimes overlooked. A prior decision has no *authoritative* effect as a precedent unless the decision itself, and not just its effects in the world, causes future judges to make decisions they would not otherwise make, all things considered. A judge may study a prior decision, decide it was correct, and apply it to the case before her, but this does not mean she is treating the prior decision as authoritative. The authority of precedents becomes important only when judges think the precedents are wrong.

Three Models of Precedent

THE NATURAL MODEL

Under what we call the natural model of precedent, judges give prior decisions just the force they naturally would have in a full assessment of reasons for decision.[2] The natural model is not a model of authoritative precedent; rather, it is a description of ordinary moral reasoning in the presence of prior decisions. In other words, the natural model describes the reasoning of morally motivated judges who are not constrained to follow decisions with which they disagree.

The natural model does not imply that past decisions have no impact on present decisions. Past decisions, even mistaken ones, can generate reasons for decision that count in the moral balance. The most important of these is that official decisions induce reliance.[3] Reliance-based reasons are of two kinds. First, actors who have acted in reliance on the implication that future cases would be decided consistently with past cases may have individual moral claims that they not suffer the harm of dashed expectations. Second, and relatedly, consistency in official decision-making has social benefits because it enables people to plan and rely. For both reasons, the likelihood of reliance may persuade a judge to follow a precedent she believes to be wrong.[4] But this is not the same thing as following a precedent when the judge believes she will err by doing so.

To give a simple example: Suppose that in case 1, a car owner parked his car in a parking lot and took away the keys, then returned to find that the car had been stolen by an unknown thief. The car owner then brought an action against the owner of the lot, and a judge decided that the lot owner was not legally responsible for the theft.[5] Case 2 now arises involving the theft of a car from a "park and lock" type of lot. At least if we know nothing more about the two cases, the possibility that parking lot owners have relied on the decision in case 1 and the utility of a consistent division of responsibility between car owners and lot owners are reasons for a judge to decide for the lot owner even if she believes that case 1 should have been decided differently because lot owners are in a better position than car owners to watch over cars. But a judge operating under the natural model of precedent is not bound by the prior decisions. If she believes that the benefits of holding the lot owner responsible exceed the harm such a decision will cause by contradicting the expectations of lot owners, the natural model leaves her free to follow her own judgment.

A judge operating under the natural model of precedent does not limit her consideration of reliance to the results of prior cases. In fact, rules announced in prior opinions and explanations judges have given for prior outcomes are more likely to provoke reliance than outcomes alone. Outcomes are fact-dependent; and although they may generate expectations through a process of analogy, their implications are limited by the inevitable factual differences among past and present cases.

In addition to reliance, another reason sometimes given for conforming to precedent is to maintain equality among litigants: like cases should be treated alike.[6] We are not convinced, however, that equality justifies following a prior decision that appears to be wrong.[7] One difficulty is that the meaning of equality among litigants is elusive. No two cases are identical, and the determination whether they are relevantly alike for purposes of equal treatment is a moral question that must be answered by the second judge.[8] Further, the process by which facts are presented and reported in the course of litigation tends to obscure real differences among cases.[9] Situations that appear very similar in appellate records may have differed in morally important ways as they actually unfolded. A park-and-lock arrangement in an enclosed building with security gates may lull car owners into thinking their cars are under guard, but if this fact is never raised by the parties, the case may appear identical to past cases dealing with open lots.[10]

Assuming that there are such things as like cases, however, it does not follow that they must be treated alike.[11] Recall that the question whether to conform to precedent arises only when a judge believes a prior decision was wrong. Treating litigants equally, therefore, means deliberately treating someone wrongly because someone else was wrongly treated in the past. In our view, this does nothing but compound the wrong. If anything, deciding wrongly now because others have suffered wrong decisions in the past denies the present litigants equal treatment with litigants who are treated in the way their judges believe is morally correct.[12]

Suppose, for example, that Lex or his judges have in prior cases allowed garage owners to maintain dangerously steep exit ramps without liability for customer injuries. Lex and his judges now believe that the decisions in those cases were morally wrong. Does "equality" now demand that garage owner Kent be allowed to endanger his customer Elaine? In other words, does "equality" require that *Elaine v. Kent* be decided in favor of Kent?

We are certain that "equality" does nothing of the sort. If a morally wrong decision in the past counted as a moral reason in favor of what would otherwise be a morally wrong decision in the present, then the more immorality in the past, the more *morality* would shift in direction toward what was formerly immorality. Two wrongs would tend to make a right. Moral principles would be moving targets, propelled in the direction of various immoral acts by "equality."[13]

Moreover, if there have been morally correct as well as morally incorrect past decisions, "equality" would point in opposite directions. Suppose, for example, that Blacks, Whites, and Reds are all morally entitled to equal concern from Lex. In prior cases, judges have wrongly allowed Lex to discriminate against Blacks in favor of Whites, but have correctly required Lex to treat Whites and Reds with equal concern. Now Browns arrive in the community and are also morally entitled to equal concern. Does the precedent of Lex's treatment of Blacks generate an equality reason in favor of discrimination against Browns? Or does equality require that Browns receive the same treatment that Whites and Reds have received? Clearly, the correct answer is for Lex to cease discriminating against anyone. But "equality" of the sort being considered here cannot tell us that. Indeed, it appears to require the coherence of morally correct decisions and morally incorrect ones—itself an incoherent directive.[14]

In the end, we need take no position on whether equality is an "empty" value, entirely derivative of other moral principles,[15] or whether instead equality of a certain kind is the value on which those principles are based.[16] All we need here is to argue that equality—as distinct from reliance—never requires abandoning correct moral principles and the decisions those principles dictate merely because past decisions were morally incorrect.[17]

Admittedly, the intuition that like cases should be treated alike is quite strong. This intuition, however, may be driven by considerations of reliance: it is important that official decision-makers be consistent because people order their lives in the shadow of past decisions. The intuition in favor of like treatment may also result from confusion between adjudication and allocation of scarce goods or necessary bads. If one believes that certain goods (or bads) should be distributed according to certain criteria, then equality may provide a reason why all who meet the criteria should share. But this reasoning does not extend to intertemporal equality among litigants. In the intertemporal situation, by hypothesis, the second judge believes that the criteria applied by the first judge were incorrect. In this context, we do not think equality provides an independent reason for conforming to precedent.

THE RULE MODEL

The second possible approach to precedent is what we call the rule model, in which judges are bound by rules announced in the opinions of prior judges.[18] Unlike the natural model, the rule model *is* a model of authoritative precedent. If a previously announced rule applies by its terms to the case at hand, then the present judge must follow it even if she believes, after taking account of the natural force of the precedent, that the balance of reasons favors a different decision. Thus, if prior judges have stated that a parking lot owner cannot be held liable for theft of a car when a car owner parks his car and keeps the keys, a judge presiding over a park-and-lock case must decide for the lot owner although she thinks the no-liability rule is wrong or should not apply to the case before her.

There are narrow and broad forms of the rule model of precedent.[19] In the narrow version, the binding force of prior judicial statements is limited to rules that are stated in canonical form and intended by the prior judge to operate as rules for future cases. In the broad version, implicit rules have binding force as well, as long as they are expressible in canonical form. The broad version entails a closer scrutiny of past opinions, including justificatory statements, references to ends or dangers that motivated the judge, emphasis laid on particular facts, or approving references to other cases. If these data imply that the prior judge was guided by a fairly determinate rule, that rule is authoritative even if it was not stated explicitly as a rule for the future.[20]

What the explicit and implicit forms of the rule model have in common is that they instruct the present judge to discover and conform to the intentions of past judges, who occupy for this purpose the position of Lex. Once a rule is found, the process of decision-making is deductive. The role of the present judge is only to determine whether the rule applies to the case at hand; if it does, she must treat it as a serious rule and follow it without further consideration of reasons for decision.

It should be noted that the rule model does not capture one fairly common judicial practice. Judges sometimes "distinguish" rules stated in prior cases by pointing out that the current case, while falling within the terms of the rule, presents a new fact that was absent in the prior case.[21] For example, suppose a judge is presiding over a case in which an owner parked his car in an enclosed, secured garage and took the keys away. A prior case held that parking lot owners who operate on a park-and-lock basis are not responsible for thefts of cars. The current judge might point out the prior case involved an open lot and proceed to hold for the car owner in the case before her. The result is a new rule: "Owners of park-and-lock businesses are not responsible for thefts from open, unsecured lots but may be responsible for thefts from enclosed, secured garages."

This manner of "distinguishing" a prior case should not be mistaken for an instance of the rule model of precedent coupled with a power to amend rules by distinguishing facts. What the judge has done is not to follow the rule, but to disregard it in a case she thinks is not justified by the reasons that motivated the original rule. At best, this is what we described in chapter 4 as rule-sensitive particularism, in which rule-subjects (in this case judges) act as they think best, with due consideration of the benefits of rules. And, as we explained in chapter 4, rule-sensitive particularism does not ensure that those benefits will be realized.[22]

THE RESULT MODEL

The third possibility is what we call the result model of precedent.[23] This term describes a family of approaches in which judges study the outcomes of past cases and infer from them how they ought to decide the cases before them. Like the rule model, this is a model of authoritative precedent: judges must decide in the manner dictated by past decisions, even if their own judgment supports a different result. Under the result model, however, what is binding is not the rules established by past judges but the past judges' actual decisions.[24]

The first question raised by the result model of precedent is how the outcomes of past cases, considered apart from the opinions of the judges who decided them, can dictate the outcome of later cases that are not identical in every respect. One possibility is an a fortiori approach: if a prior judge reached a certain result on a certain set of facts, then a later judge must do the same when the reasons for that result are stronger than they were in the prior case, or when the reasons for the opposite result are weaker.[25] If a prior judge held that there was no parking lot owner liability when a car owner parked in an enclosed garage and kept the keys, then there cannot be a liability in a later case in which the owner parked in an open lot and kept the keys. The later judge may think it best to hold the parking lot responsible, but she is bound by the earlier result because the case for liability in that case was stronger.

The difficulty with this approach is that something more must be going on than a simple counting of favorable and unfavorable facts. The conclusion that one case is stronger than another depends on a further, unstated metric or decisional principle that arranges the facts in relation to one another. A park-and-lock decision against the car owner in the case of an enclosed garage has a fortiori force in the case of an open parking lot only if it is assumed that the car owner's expectations of security are a factor on the car owner's side. Yet there is nothing in the notion of a fortiori decision-making to explain where the necessary metric or decisional principle is to be found. Moreover, we think there is a reason why the connecting principle or metric is obscure. There simply is no correct principle or metric that will produce order in a landscape that includes both correct and incorrect decisions.

This is easiest to see when the metric is defined at a high level of abstraction. Suppose, for example, that the relative strength of different fact patterns is determined by a criterion of utility, and that we have some means of measuring utiles. In case 1, which involved an enclosed, secured garage, a judge decided against the car owner and in favor of the garage. In case 2, a car owner has made a claim against the owner of an open parking lot. The judge believes the prior decision was wrong and calculates that it caused a net loss of five utiles in comparison with a decision for the car owner. The judge also calculates that a decision for the lot owner in case 2 will cause a loss of just three utiles because the car owner had less expectation of security. Case 1 now has a fortiori force in case 2. Absurdly, it also has a fortiori force for any result, in any case, that produces a net loss of five or fewer utiles. If a dispute arises over money found on the floor of a garage, and a decision in favor of the garage owner would cause a net loss of only four utiles, the earlier garage liability case qualifies as a precedent. Of course, this is nonsense, producing nothing but confusion.[26]

The impossibility of a correct metric for sorting correct and incorrect decisions leads to an alternative version of the result model, in which judges rely on the method of analogical reasoning to discover the authoritative force of prior decisions. As we explained in chapter 6, a judge reasoning by analogy abduces a decisional principle (or "analogy-warranting rule") from a set of examples provided by past decisions, then tests the principle against rationales and further examples. Under the result model of precedent, the examples of past decisions are binding, and the principle they yield determines the outcome of the present case, even if the judge believes the past decisions were wrong.

The best-known advocate of an analogy-based result model of

precedent is Ronald Dworkin. We take up Dworkin's approach to adjudication fully in chapter 8. Here we will provide only a sketch. Dworkin proposes that judges should decide cases that are not governed by legislative or constitutional rules by constructing the "best" legal principles that explain (or "fit") most existing decisions and then applying those principles to the facts before them.[27] The judge's moral and political convictions will determine which among eligible principles are "best"; but in Dworkin's view, the requirement of fit ensures that the "political history of the community" will act as a check on such personal moral convictions.[28] All legal decisions will be controlled by the principles immanent in precedent cases, and law will have the virtue of "integrity."[29]

Our judge, for example, might determine that various prior park-and-lock decisions suggest a principle, "Liability for theft depends on control over the operation of the car." She may believe that past cases undervalued the importance of the car owner's expectations of security; but if the pattern of results rules out an expectation-based principle, she must do the best she can against this background. At the same time, only the results reached by prior judges have authoritative force; she is not bound by the decisional principles prior judges relied on. Her task is to exercise her own judgment (including, presumably, her judgment about the possibility of reliance on past judges' statements) to construct the best principle that fits prior results.[30]

As we compare the various models of precedent in the discussion that follows, we shall assume that the most plausible version of the result model is the analogical version, with Dworkin's account as its paradigm. Conceived this way, the result model may look misleadingly like the implicit rule model of precedent we mentioned earlier. There is a critical difference, however, between these two approaches to precedent. Under the analogical version of the result model, the principle that decides a case is the work of the current judge. The judge abduces from prior decisions the best principle that is capable of explaining them. But abduction is not an inference about the motives or intent of prior judges; it is a creative process, representing the current judge's best moral and political judgment, limited only by the required assumption that most prior decisions were correct.[31] This assumption is required in order to give past decisions authoritative effect.

In contrast, under the implicit version of the rule model of precedent, the decisional principle is the rule that prior judges appear to have had in mind as they reached their conclusions. The task of the present judge is not to create a principle but to understand the intentions of other judges. If no such rule is reasonably inferable from prior decisions, those decisions have no precedential effect beyond their natural weight as historical facts.

Evaluating the Models

AUTHORITATIVE PRECEDENT: RULE MODEL VERSUS RESULT MODEL

The two models of authoritative precedent we have described—the rule model and the result model—have in common the problem of entrenched error. The result model, in its most plausible, analogical form, is subject to the criticism we outlined with respect to analogical reasoning in chapter 6. A judge reasoning by analogy begins with a set of decisions that serve as the data from which she draws a decisional principle. Some of those decisions inevitably are incorrect, and yet they shape the principle that will govern the judge's current decision. In this way, analogical reasoning incorporates past errors into the fabric of law. The same objection applies with special force to the result model of precedent because incorrect decisions are given authoritative effect: a judge who recognizes error in a past decision is not free to adjust her own conclusion accordingly.

The rule model also commits judges to tolerate errors of two kinds. Not only will some of the rules devised by prior judges be incorrect, but even correct rules will be incorrect in some of their applications because they are general rules.[32] In the last section of this chapter, we will discuss the possibility of combining the rule model of precedent with a judicial power to overrule unsatisfactory rules. Overruling, however, would at most reduce the errors due to unjustified rules; it would not solve the problem of incorrect results under justified rules.

A further danger of the rule model is that it effectively gives legislative power to judges.[33] The rule model allows judges to fashion authoritative general rules, both in a studied way, by explicit announcement, and more casually, if implicit rules are given precedential effect. Judges, however, are not ideal rule-makers. They lack Lex's investigative capacity, and they may be biased by the salience of a single set of facts seen in hindsight.[34] The result model avoids this problem by avoiding rules: each judge fashions a decisional principle, working from the particular decisions of others, but that principle will not bind future judges. Only outcomes bind.

As we compare the two models of authoritative precedent, we assume initially that the result model is exclusive of the rule model. In other words, we assume that construction of the best principles that can be made to fit the pattern of previous decisions entails disregarding rules stated or implicit in past opinions, or at least entails refusing to give such rules authoritative force.[35] Given this choice, we believe the rule model is much superior to the result model.

One point in favor of the rule model is that the errors it entails are likely to be more modest. The rule model adds the errors of blunt rules to the errors of incorrect past decisions, but its errors are confined to cases governed by explicit or implicit canonical rules. In the absence of such a rule, the judge is free to decide according to her best judgment. In contrast, under the Dworkinian result model, the outcome of every case is determined by principles drawn from prior cases, some of which are incorrect.[36]

The second comparative advantage of the rule model is that it offers far more justification for following erroneous precedent than does the result model. The most persuasive reason for honoring incorrect precedents is to protect those who have relied on official decisions and to encourage such reliance in the future. In other words, authoritative precedents, even when incorrect, provide coordination. The coordinating powers of rules, however, are much greater than those of principles drawn case by case from prior decisions. It is surely much easier for actors to interpret and apply canonical rules, even when the rules are merely implicit in prior opinions, than it is to anticipate which of the principles that might fit past decisions will be deemed morally best by individual judges. Moreover, once a rule assumes canonical form, it is stable, while the principles generated by the result model are remade in every case. Authoritative rules provide a more secure basis for prediction and therefore better protection for reliance. Put another way, the rule model produces authoritative settlements of moral controversies and the moral benefits of such settlements; the result model cannot do so because it produces no determinate outcomes and requires judges, in constructing their outcome-producing principles from prior decisions, to invoke the very moral principles that give rise to controversies in need of settlement. The result model builds in error without the settlement virtues of determinate rules.

The second reason sometimes given for respecting erroneous precedents is equality among litigants. For reasons explained earlier, we question whether equality in the sense of consistent treatment among litigants should count as a moral value; but if it does, we think the rule model offers a more reliable form of equality than the result model. Under the rule model, all those who fall within the terms of a rule are treated alike; the rule itself provides fixed criteria of likeness. Under the result model, criteria of likeness are supplied by prior judges' reports of facts—reports that are never complete and are filtered through the judges' decisional principles—and by the variable decisional principles developed by present judges. Therefore, we expect that litigants ultimately will be treated more consistently under the rule model than the result model.

A third reason to prefer the rule model over the result model is that the result model may be incoherent. It asks the same peculiar question we associated with analogical reasoning in chapter 6: "What would the morally correct result in this case be if the incorrect results in the earlier cases were in fact correct?"[37]

The rule model of precedent, when understood to include implicit as well as explicit rules, may also promote an epistemically superior process of decision-making. By its nature, the implicit version of the rule model requires judges to study the reasoning of a series of past judges. Judicial reasoning often does not take canonical form when it first appears in opinions. Instead, judges venturing into new areas of doctrine may hint at undeveloped reasons for decision or state rationales in very general terms. Under a rule model that recognizes the force of implicit rules, later judges will find these hints and vague statements as they search for rules, but will not yet be bound by them. If they approve, they will adopt and refine the same line of reasoning; if not, they can disregard the earlier statements. The rules that finally emerge from this process in canonical form have epistemic value because they have been tested over time and represent the collective efforts of a number of judges.[38] The result model, in which judges are bound by past outcomes but free to disregard the reasons given for past decisions, does not have the same capacity for cultivating insights over time.

Our conclusion in favor of the rule model of precedent is based on the assumption that the benefits we have cited—protecting and encouraging reliance, promoting evolutionary decision-making, and perhaps maintaining equality among litigants—justify treating precedents as authoritative. In other words, we are assuming that these benefits outweigh both the errors that result from incorrect judicial rules and the errors that result from the bluntness of rules. If this condition is met, there is reason for judges to announce authoritative rules. If the benefits of judicial rules do not outweigh the errors resulting from rules, we doubt that the weaker coordination and questionable equality produced by the result model can justify the errors that result from principles built on imperfect decisional data.

One more variant on authoritative precedent remains to be explored. We have assumed so far that the result model and the rule model are mutually exclusive. It is possible, however, that the two could be combined. Judges might give authoritative effect to canonical rules stated or implicit in prior cases, and also give authoritative effect to prior outcomes in cases not governed by rules through the method of analogy. The question raised by this variant is whether the result model or the natural model should be followed in those cases that are not governed by explicit or implicit rules.

As we have explained, the result model in its analogical version builds error into law because it accepts incorrect precedents as the data from which legal principles are drawn. The natural model, in contrast, calls for judges to exercise their moral judgment, taking into account incorrect past decisions and their effects as facts. There is no deliberate corruption of the judge's all-things-considered best judgment. So far, the natural model is clearly superior.

The next question is whether the result model, in its analogical form, has indirect benefits that make it preferable to the natural model in the absence of canonical rules. In chapter 6, we offered several tentative defenses of analogical reasoning as a method of judicial deliberation. If analogical reasoning is accepted as a professional custom, it may prompt judges to give attention they would not otherwise give to the examples of prior cases and so may be preferable to hasty decision-making. Analogical reasoning also may provide indirect protection for reliance. By forcing judges to take past decisions into account, it counteracts biases that might lead judges to undervalue reliance in the course of ordinary moral reasoning.

Although a practice of analogical reasoning may provide indirect benefits of this kind, we prefer not to incorporate analogical reasoning into a model of authoritative precedent. The benefits just cited—greater attention to the examples of past cases and greater protection for reliance—can be gained in large part through the rule model, at least in the version that requires judges to search for rules implicit in prior judicial opinions. When no rule applies, professional training and custom can secure the indirect benefits of analogical reasoning without the need to give authoritative status to the conclusions it yields. For these reasons, we omit the method of analogy from our preferred account of the binding force of precedent.

RULE MODEL VERSUS NATURAL MODEL

We have rejected the result model of precedent in favor of the rule model because the result model, even if it is coherent, entrenches incorrect decisions without providing indirect benefits that equal those of the rule model. But we have not yet compared the rule model to the natural model of precedent, under which prior decisions have no authoritative force at all. Our conclusion is that from Lex's point of view, the rule model is preferable; as we will explain below, it is preferable for reasons that follow from the natural model itself. From the point of view of a judge deciding a particular case, however, to accept the rule model is to commit a moral error. In other words, the choice between the rule model and natural model is a reprise of the problem of rules discussed in chapter 4.

To explain this, we begin with the implications of the natural model of precedent. The natural model takes account of past decisions as historical facts, although it does not treat them as authoritative. Rules announced in past decisions are important, within the natural model, primarily because they invite reliance. Reliance creates moral claims if there is reason to think the rule will be followed; further, the ability of actors to rely on announced rules contributes to general welfare. Judges operating under the natural model, however, may err in assessing both the extent of reliance on previously announced rules and the potential value of announced rules as sources of reliance. Moreover, the biases associated with adjudication make it likely that judges will systematically undervalue rather than overvalue the reliance generated by consistently applied rules. As a result of judicial error in assessing reliance, moral claims may be overlooked, and parties will be unable to act with confidence on the basis of announced rules. Under the natural model of precedent, these potential losses are cause for concern.

Of course, errors about the extent and value of reliance will not occur if, rather than assessing reliance under the natural model, judges treat rules announced in past cases as serious, authoritative rules. Authoritative judicial rules create errors of their own: some rules will be misconceived, and correct rules will sometimes give incorrect results in particular cases. Yet if the errors and lost opportunities that result from imperfect judicial assessment of reliance outweigh the errors that result from bad rules and blunt rules, judges will do better overall, by the moral standards of the natural model itself, if they treat rules announced in past cases as authoritative. In other words, the natural model of precedent, applied in the abstract, may require that judges follow a rule model of precedent.[39]

Thus, if the balance of error is favorable, Lex will prefer the rule model. At the same time, a judge deciding a particular case cannot share Lex's view. Recall that the choice between the rule model and the natural model is important only when the current judge believes that a previously announced rule is wrong, either generally or as it applies to her case. It follows that if the judge engages in moral deliberation, she cannot do as the rule model requires without committing what she believes to be a moral error. In other words, the rule model of precedent—like any practice involving rules—cannot be carried out in a completely self-conscious way.[40] It is rational for Lex to adopt the rule model, and it is rational for judges to endorse it in the abstract; but it is not rational for judges to practice it in particular cases. The rule model will succeed only to the extent that habit and training lead judges to apply the rules unreflectingly, without pausing to consider whether the results they require are morally sound, all things considered.

Overruling Precedents

We have concluded that if the balance of errors is favorable, Lex will prefer the rule model of precedent, in which judges treat canonical rules stated or implied in past opinions as serious rules, to the natural model, in which judges give past decisions their natural weight in moral reasoning. As with all rules, however, particular judicial rules may be wrongly conceived in the sense that they produce too many errors, or they may become obsolete. This leads to the problem of overruling.

Lex retains power to overrule the rules he issues, and can similarly overrule judge-made rules. When Lex considers whether to overrule or amend a rule, two considerations enter into his decision. The first is whether the rule is a justified rule. From Lex's perspective, rules are justified when there is a net benefit from full compliance—if obeyed by all, the rule will prevent more errors of individual judgment than it will produce by prescribing the wrong result in some of the cases it governs. If Lex concludes that full compliance with a particular rule will produce a net loss, he will naturally want to repeal the rule.

In addition to the desirability of the rule, however, Lex must also consider the impact of overruling it on the stability of the system of rules. Lex's subjects are likely to be both more productive and more content when they can rely on a fairly secure set of conduct rules. If the rules by which they live change too often, not only are these benefits lost, but rule-subjects may make costly errors as they attempt to anticipate change. Frequent change may also produce skepticism about rules and therefore could undermine habits of obedience that are necessary to counteract the gap we described in chapter 4.

With these difficulties in mind, Lex might take one of two approaches to overruling rules, including both his own rules and rules announced in judicial opinions. A quite confident Lex might assess the moral desirability of rules in a way that is sensitive to the question of stability but otherwise unconstrained. If he concludes that a particular rule carries a net compliance cost, and if that cost exceeds the costs of added instability that would result from overruling the rule, the rule should go; otherwise it should be left in place. A Lex who is particularly concerned with stability and is not confident that he can accurately assess the stability costs of overruling might prefer a self-inhibiting standard. For example, he might overrule only when the net costs of compliance are "substantial" or "conspicuously high."

Let us assume that Lex will overrule whenever he concludes that a rule is unjustified and that the net costs of compliance are greater than the instability costs of overruling. By accepting the rule model of precedent, Lex has effectively given judges the power to announce rules of their own as they decide cases. The question then arises whether judges should have the same or similar power to overrule judicial rules that Lex exercises over his own rules.

There are several differences between Lex and his judges that arise from the nature of adjudication and may bear on the problem of judicial overruling of judicial rules. One difference is that Lex acts prospectively on a field of potential controversies, while judges, whose primary task is to resolve particular disputes, normally make retroactive decisions. If judicial decisions to overrule are similarly retroactive, they may be unfair to those who relied on existing rules. Of course, retroactivity is an inescapable problem. Lex's decisions to enact or change rules have retroactive effects whenever actors plan for future activities or investments on the assumption that the present set of rules will remain in force. The effect of judicial overruling, however, is particularly harsh because acts that have already occurred will be judged under a new rule.

One solution to this problem is to adopt a practice of prospective judicial overruling: a judge could resolve the dispute before her according to previously established rules but at the same time announce a new rule for future cases.[41] Under a rule model of precedent, the objection that prospective overruling is essentially a legislative function does not carry much weight because judges have already assumed a legislative role.[42] Nevertheless, there are problems with prospective judicial overruling. Prospective application of new rules appears unfair to parties who have argued successfully that existing rules are defective, and it removes much of the incentive for advocating change.

A second and perhaps more important difference between Lex and his judges is that, unlike Lex, judges must apply rules to particular cases. As rule-appliers, judges directly confront the instances in which the bluntness of rules produces erroneous results. According to the rule model of precedent, it is best that judges treat rules announced in prior cases as serious rules. As we argued extensively in chapter 4, however, it will not always be rational to do so. We shall explain shortly how this comes to bear on the question of overruling.

Against this background, there are at least four positions Lex might take with respect to the power of judges to overrule judicial rules. The first and simplest is that judges may not overrule; once a rule is announced, only Lex can change or repeal it. This promotes settlement, but makes the system of rules unacceptably rigid. Lex cannot hope to review all judicial rules in a timely way without the help of judges, particularly if the rule model of precedent is understood to encompass rules that are implicit in prior opinions as well as explicit rules. As a result, rules may become seriously obsolete, not only causing errors, but also undermining from a different direction the general habit of obedience to rules. If rules are permitted to remain in place after their defects become evident, rule-subjects are much less likely follow rules without engaging in a moral analysis of their results. Moreover, we have already noted that judges, whose principal task is to resolve discrete disputes, are not ideal rule-makers; therefore, judicial rules may be particularly in need of review.

A second possibility, which we shall quickly set aside, is for Lex to issue a rule governing judicial overruling. He might, for example, fix criteria such as the age and level of acceptance of the rule ("Overrule precedents only when they have been cited fewer than ten times in five years"); or he might provide that judges should not overrule unless the reasons for overruling have a strength of at least X, or unless the reasons for doing so are at least twice as strong as the reasons for following the rule. In our view, however, rules for overruling can never be successful. Rules simplify moral principles in order to settle controversies about the application of those principles—that is their function. But questions about the justification of rules—whether the benefits of settlement exceed the errors of bluntness—cannot be successfully simplified in this way; they can only be answered through moral judgment. The rule "Overrule precedents only when they have been cited fewer than ten times in five years" is unworkable because the criterion for overruling—citation rate—is too loosely correlated with moral error. The rule "Overrule precedents only when the reasons for overruling exceed X" is unworkable because there is no metric, apart from morality itself, to give content to either the reasons for overruling or the value X.

A third possibility is to authorize judicial overruling on the same grounds that apply to overruling by Lex himself. If a judge concludes that a precedent rule is not, or is no longer, a justified rule, she should overrule it unless the instability costs of overruling exceed the net compliance costs of the rule.

It is important to distinguish this form of overruling from the natural model of precedent. Under the natural model of precedent, judges decline to follow a precedent rule whenever they believe the rule will produce a moral error if applied to the case before them. This model is equivalent to rule-sensitive particularism: it requires judges to engage in moral evaluation of rule violations, taking into the account the reliance on the rule and the effect of an unpunished violation on the value of the rule. It is not a form of overruling; it is simply an attitude toward rules that gives the rules no more than their natural weight in judicial decision-making.[43] As we argued earlier in this chapter, the value of settlement and the potential for judicial error in assessing reliance will lead Lex to reject the natural model in favor of a rule model of precedent that does not authorize rule-sensitive particularism.

In contrast to the natural model of precedent, the overruling power we are now considering is only a power to overrule *unjustified* rules. Judges must follow justified rules, but they can overrule when they believe the rules are not justified *as rules.* In other words, they can overrule if they conclude that the sum of moral errors that will follow from full compliance with the rule is greater than the sum of moral errors full compliance will avoid, and that this net compliance cost exceeds the cost of instability that would result from overruling the rule. This might be called a power of *rule assessment:* a power morally to assess the rules but not their results in particular cases.

It might be argued that rule assessment will quickly collapse into rule-sensitive particularism in the following way. Whenever a judge who possesses the power to assess and overrule rules believes that a rule will produce the wrong result in a particular case, she might simply overrule it and substitute a new rule that applies to all cases covered by the original rule, *except* her case. In other words, she might conclude that the new rule, "Follow rule R except in situation X," is a better rule than the original rule R, and use her overruling power to revise *R* accordingly.

This argument is not strictly correct, however, for it does not follow that because R yields the wrong result in situation X, the rule "Follow R except in situation X" is always a better rule than R. If rule R is the rule in place, replacing it with a new rule will have stability costs. Moreover, one aspect of the overall costs and benefits of any rule is its simplicity. Rules with multiple, fact-specific exceptions are difficult to comprehend and follow. Thus, as least in theory, rule assessment, meaning moral evaluation of rules *as rules,* is not coextensive with rule-sensitive particularism.

Nevertheless, the possibility that judges will slip from rule assessment into rule-sensitive particularism is a serious problem. Logically, overruling justified rules is distinct from declining to follow justified rules; but in practice, the distinction places a heavy burden on judges. Unlike Lex, who does not apply rules, judges must act simultaneously as rule-appliers and rule-assessors. As rule-assessors, judges are required to assess the moral justification for the rules, as rules. Yet Lex wants judges as rule-appliers to follow the terms of the rules because this will minimize error and achieve settlement. In other words, judges are required to take two different attitudes toward the same rules: they must engage in full moral evaluation for the purpose of assessing the overall justification of the rules; then they must eschew moral inquiry as they apply the rules. It may be psychologically impossible, if not conceptually impossible, for judges to separate these tasks. Not only must they shift from moral inquiry to moral abstention, but, from the vantage point of a single dispute, the most salient evidence that a rule is unjustified or obsolete is the incorrect result it requires in the case at hand.

Even if Lex were confident that judges could both assess the justification of precedent rules and follow those rules they found to be justified, he might fear that judges will undervalue the impact of overruling on the stability of the legal system. Lex himself faces this problem whenever he overrules, but the problem is exacerbated in the case of judges. Stability, like reliance, is an abstract consideration that may lack salience for a decision-maker whose primary task is to resolve a particular dispute.

This brings us then to the fourth alternative, a standard that allows judges to overrule, but presumptively favors retention of the rule. For example, Lex might impose the standard "Overrule only when the net costs of compliance with the rule are conspicuously high." This standard would be a standard of rule assessment, not one of rule application. Judges would be expected to follow justified rules, but to overrule when the rule, as a rule, was obviously unjustified.

A standard of this kind suffers from several difficulties. Because the standard is vague and dependent on moral judgment, judges will differ in their interpretations of when the moral costs of full compliance with the rule are conspicuously high, and they will sometimes err and overrule justified rules. Another problem is that judges must suspend rationality to apply the standard as Lex intends: from the point of view of the judge, it is not rational to follow a rule she believes to be unjustified but not conspicuously so.

Nevertheless, a presumptive overruling standard appears to be the best available alternative. Because judges must apply rules as well as assess them, and because judges are likely to undervalue the stability costs of overruling, some limit on judicial overruling is necessary. A rule for overruling is unworkable. A flat prohibition on judicial overruling of precedent rules is probably unacceptable because it will result in too much rigidity and error. This leaves only the rough solution of a presumptive standard.

A presumptive standard for overruling does not relieve the judge of the dual task of assessing the overall moral justification of rules and applying justified rules according to their terms. The presumption, however, provides some degree of insulation. Judges will not regularly evaluate the justification of rules; they will do so only when a rule is evidently mistaken or obsolete.[44]

EIGHT Reasoning from Legal Principles

In the previous chapter's discussion of the result model of precedent and analogical reasoning from past outcomes of cases, we alluded to Ronald Dworkin's account of "legal principles." Dworkinian legal principles are norms constructed from settled law—constitutional and legislative rules and judicial decisions—in light of the judge's view of moral principles.[1] They are not identical with moral principles because they must "fit" the settled law, some of which will be morally mistaken. And they are not posited rules, not so much because they are vague standards, but because they are not posited by Lex, Super Lex, or any judge. Even the judge who, in deciding a case not controlled by an existing rule, constructs a legal principle out of past settlements coupled with the judge's moral views is not positing a rule or standard to control future judges. The latter will be free to construct legal principles somewhat differently, merely adding the outcome of the first judge's case to the body of settlements that serves as legal principles' raw material.

One can see how legal principles are ideal norms for the result model of precedent. That model deems judges to be constrained by the decisions in prior cases, including morally mistaken ones, but

This chapter makes substantial use of material contained in Larry Alexander and Ken Kress, "Against Legal Principles," first published in *Law and Interpretation* (A. Marmor ed., 1995) and then republished at 82 *Iowa L. Rev.* 739 (1997). We want to thank Ken Kress, Oxford University Press, and the Iowa Law Review for kindly granting us permission to use this material.

not by any rules laid down in the judges' opinions in those cases. Legal principles—the morally best principles that can account for the past decisions—can provide the metric for determining whether an earlier case is "like" the present case and points to a similar decision. And legal principles can do so even if the earlier decision contains no authoritative rule, and even if the earlier decision was morally mistaken. In other words, legal principles provide the analogy-warranting norms necessary for reasoning analogically from case results, some of which were in error.

As we suggested in our discussions of analogical reasoning in chapter 6[2] and of the result model of precedent in chapter 7,[3] we do not believe that Dworkinian legal principles are normatively attractive or even coherent. Thus, we do not believe that they can support analogical reasoning or the result model of precedent. Because Dworkin is such a major figure in Anglo-American jurisprudence, and because so many lawyers and judges believe that analogical reasoning from sometimes morally mistaken results is both commonplace and coherent, we should set forth the case against Dworkinian legal principles more fully than we have in the previous chapters.

Legal Rules, Standards, and Principles

Legal norms can be divided up in two ways. First, there is the familiar dichotomy of rules and standards.[4] Rules are legal norms that are formal and mechanical. They are triggered by a few easily identified factual matters and are opaque in application to the values that they are designed to serve. Standards, on the other hand, are flexible, context-sensitive legal norms that require evaluative judgments in their application. A paradigmatic standard is "Drive safely." Most legal norms are hybrids, in that they have both rule-like and standard-like elements.

The second way that legal norms are divided up by some is into rules and principles. It is this categorization of legal norms that is the focus of this chapter.

The rule-principle dichotomy should be clearly distinguished from the rule-standard dichotomy. This distinction should be observed because the term "rule" appears in both but means something different in each, and because frequently the term "principle" is used in place of the term "standard" in discussions of the rule-standard dichotomy. For purposes of the rule-principle dichotomy, rules and principles are not distinguishable by how mechanical or flexible they are in form, nor by how factual or evaluative they are in content. Rather, they are distinguishable by whether they are posited in a canonical form by a specific institution at a particular time (e.g., by Lex, Super Lex, or judges), and by whether they are determinative of the outcomes of whatever transactions come within their terms. In the rule-principle dichotomy of legal norm-types, rules—which can include *both* rules *and* standards (the first dichotomy)—are identified by having been posited by a specific institution at a specific time and in a specific canonical form. Moreover, rules determine how transactions that fall within their terms are to be treated legally. Conversely, principles are not posited and have no canonical form, though they supposedly reflect and can be changed by changes in posited, canonical legal norms (rules). Moreover, principles do not determine legal outcomes in all cases in which they apply, though they can influence legal outcomes through adding normative *weight* to one outcome as opposed to another. Rules, which apply in an all-or-nothing way, are sometimes said to have no weight; but the more accurate way of characterizing rules is to say that, at least in the absence of conflict with other rules, their weight is infinite because they are determinative when applicable.

The leading theoretical expositor of the rule-principle distinction is Ronald Dworkin. He introduced the distinction in chapter 2 of *Taking Rights Seriously,* where he distinguished posited, canonical, applicable, all-or-nothing rules from legal norms that "operate . . . as principles, policies and other sorts of standards."[5] He gave as an example of a legal principle "no man may profit from his own wrong," the principle that Dworkin claimed was decisive in the case of *Riggs v. Palmer.*[6] Another example was the principle of freedom of contract, a principle that was operative in the case of *Henningsen v. Bloomfield Motors, Inc.*[7] but was nonetheless outweighed by the competing principles that "the courts must examine purchase agreements closely to see if consumer and public interests are treated fairly"[8] and that "courts will not permit themselves to be used as instruments of inequity and injustice" and "generally refuse to lend themselves to the enforcement of [unfair] bargains."[9]

The crucial distinction for our purposes is the one Dworkin draws between legal principles and legal rules:

> The difference between legal principles and legal rules is a logical distinction. Both sets of standards point to particular decisions about legal obligation in particular circumstances, but they differ in the character of the direction they give. Rules are applicable in all-or-nothing fashion. If the facts a rule stipulates are given, then either the rule is valid, in which case the answer it supplies must be accepted, or it is not, in which case it contributes nothing to the decision.
>
> This all-or-nothing [character] is seen most plainly if we look at the way rules operate, not in law, but in . . . a game, for example. In baseball, a rule provides that if the batter has three strikes, he is out. An official cannot consistently acknowledge that this is an accurate statement of a baseball rule, and decide that a batter who has had three strikes is not out. Of course, a rule may have exceptions (the batter who has had three strikes is not out if the catcher drops the third strike). However, an accurate statement of the rule would take this exception into account, and any that did not would be incomplete.[10]

Principles, on the other hand, do not operate like rules. There are many instances in the legal system where people are allowed to profit from their wrongs (for example, adverse possession). These are not repudiations of or exceptions to the principle that people should not profit from their wrongs. A principle is merely "a reason that argues in one direction but does not necessitate a particular decision."[11] It may compete with principles that argue in the opposite direction. "Principles have a dimension that rules do not—the dimension of weight or importance."[12]

What is crucial about Dworkin's theory of legal principles does not become fully apparent until chapter 4 of *Taking Rights Seriously.* Up to this point one might take Dworkin to be asserting that there are *moral* principles as well as *legal* rules, and that judges in our legal system frequently advert to those moral principles in deciding cases, even when a clear legal rule applies.

But in chapter 4 ("Hard Cases"), Dworkin makes clear that the principles he is concerned with are distinctly *legal* principles and not necessarily moral ones. In a mature, decent legal system, we should expect significant overlap between the classes of legal and moral principles, but neither identity between the classes nor subsumption of one class under the other.

In chapter 4 of *Taking Rights Seriously* and throughout his later writings Dworkin distinguishes legal from (mere) moral principles in two ways. First, legal principles must have institutional support in the legal system. That is, their influence must be reflected in constitutional, statutory, administrative, and decisional law.[13]

If institutional support were all that distinguished legal from moral principles, then legal principles might be merely a subset of moral principles, that subset which has been manifested in positive law. But what if, as is surely the case, positive law is not completely consistent with moral principles, or any subset of moral principles? In other words, what if no subset of moral principles, with appropriate moral weights, would have produced the existing legal rules? Or, to put it still differently, what if the existing legal rules cannot be perfectly reconciled with, and thus do not properly reflect, either the entire set of correct moral principles or any set of correct moral principles less than the entire set? Do we then say that there are no "principles" reflected in the legal system?

Dworkin's answer to this question is no, and it is his move to salvage *legal* principles in the face of the legal system's deviation from moral principles that is significant and the topic of this chapter. In essence, Dworkin's move is to divorce legal principles from moral principles to the following extent: legal principles are principles that would justify most of the extant positive law—that "fit" the positive law beyond a (vague) threshold level—and they are the morally best principles (as gauged by correct moral principles) among all possible principles that meet or exceed the threshold of "fit." In other words, legal principles are principles some or all of which may not be morally correct but that score highest on the "moral acceptability" axis while meeting the "fit" requirement.[14] This possibility of moral incorrectness is the second sense in which legal principles differ from moral principles for Dworkin.

Dworkin thus first, by means of the moral acceptability criterion, divorces legal principles from norms that fit the legal system perfectly, and secondly, by means of the threshold-of-fit criterion, differentiates legal principles from principles of pure moral-political theory. In doing so, he sabotages the obvious motivations and justifications for following legal principles: authority and certainty for theories dominated by fit; justice and moral correctness generally for theories following moral-political theory.

In what sense are legal principles "legal"? We know they are not necessarily moral principles because moral principles may not meet the requirement of "fit." That is, there may be an insufficient number of legal rules that are consistent with what moral principles would dictate. Moral principles play the background role of assessing the relative moral attractiveness of all the possible principles that fit the legal rules. But the principles that fit the legal rules and that are assessed for moral attractiveness are not themselves moral principles.

What makes the principles in question "legal" is the requirement of fit. Although legal principles are unlike legal rules in that they are not posited—they are not laid down by particular institutions at a particular time—and lack a canonical formulation, they arise from the body of posited, canonical legal rules. They are theoretical entities, like the ether once posited by physicists, in that they justify the bulk of the legal rules. And although in chapter 2 of *Taking Rights Seriously* ("The Model of Rules—I"), Dworkin could be read as requiring that legal principles be actually adverted to by judges in their opinions in order to "exist," Dworkin is quite clear in his subsequent writings that legal principles are the (morally) best principles among those that fit legal rules and decisions whether or not they are mentioned or even consciously adverted to by an official.[15]

Dworkin's Account of Legal Principles and the Standard Methodologies of Legal Analysis

On Dworkin's account, legal principles are distinguishable from legal rules in three respects: legal principles are not posited; they have no canonical formulations; and they have the characteristic of (finite) weight. They are connected to legal rules—those legal norms that are posited, do have canonical formulations, and have all-or-nothing application (infinite weight)—in that they are the morally best principles that would justify the promulgation of a high percentage of the extant legal rules and decisions. They are connected to moral principles in that moral principles determine which set of legal principles among those sets that "fit" the legal rules and decisions is the morally best set of principles. In other words, legal rules and decisions govern the "fit" axis, moral principles govern the "acceptability" axis, and the fit and acceptability axes determine the set of weighted principles that are legal principles. These legal principles are the theoretical entities that justify the legal rules and decisions, determine how they should be extended and modified, and resolve conflicts among them. Legal principles—the (morally) best (morally) incorrect principles that "fit"—ultimately determine all legal decisions, even those clearly covered by nonconflicting rules, since the decision to apply the rules rather than overrule or modify them is itself a product of the legal principles.[16]

Dworkin's account of legal principles is, of course, abstract and theoretical. But its force as an account comes from how well it tracks the standard methodologies of legal scholars, advocates, and judges. Anyone who has ever written legal briefs, legal opinions, or scholarly articles at the mid-level of doctrine will be familiar with the following procedure. One has a particular issue that one desires, as an academic or judge or advocate, to resolve. One first collects the cases in the particular area of law. One then casts about for an attractive principle or policy that, if consistently followed, would have generated most of the outcomes in those cases. In other words, one looks for a normatively attractive covering theory of the cases. The theory need not be morally correct, since correct moral principles might produce too many outcomes at odds with the existing outcomes in the area. The theory just has to be as morally attractive an incorrect theory as it can be and still account for the outcomes. Moreover, the theory need not account for all outcomes, though the more it accounts for, the better. Some outcomes may be deemed "mistakes" if the covering theory is otherwise sufficiently morally attractive. The theory just needs to account for most of the outcomes. We shall call this the reconstructive method.[17]

This method is so commonplace that it might be almost invisible to us. It is the dominant methodology both in the practice of law and in legal scholarship. "The (morally) best (morally) incorrect set of principles that 'fit' the legal rules"—legal principles—appears to be the theoretical foundation of legal practice.[18]

The Dworkinian judicial technique of surveying the past decisions in an area of law and distilling a legal principle from those decisions that is not (necessarily) the stated ground for any of them is so commonplace as to be the standard of orthodoxy. Indeed, a case that exemplifies this use of Dworkinian legal principles, *MacPherson v. Buick Motor Company,*[19] and the cases that it draws upon, are the cases selected by such expositors of common law methodology as Melvin Eisenberg, Edward Levi, and Henry Hart and Albert Saks to illustrate common law legal reasoning.[20]

In *MacPherson,* the defendant had manufactured an automobile that it sold to a retail dealer, who in turn sold it to the plaintiff. The car collapsed while being driven by the plaintiff, injuring him. The cause of the collapse was a defective wheel, which the defendant had purchased from another manufacturer and apparently failed to inspect adequately.

The difficulty in allowing recovery for the plaintiff stemmed from the fact that there was no privity of contract between plaintiff and defendant. The leading case in which the absence of privity was held not to bar recovery, *Thomas v. Winchester,*[21] a case involving the sale and resale of a falsely labeled poison, had been taken by subsequent courts to stand for a distinction between items inherently dangerous (such as poison) and items dangerous only if defective. Privity considerations were set aside only in cases involving the former. The opinion in *Thomas* appears explicitly to reject liability in cases like *MacPherson.*

Nonetheless, Justice Cardozo, writing for the majority of the New York Court of Appeals, held that a manufacturer owes a duty to inspect its goods for defects to anyone who might foreseeably be injured because of such defects regardless whether privity of contract exists between the manufacturer and the potential victims. Moreover, Cardozo purported to induce that principle from the prior case law, even though the prior cases had never announced so sweeping a principle. Cardozo admitted that some of the earlier cases following *Thomas* did not fit the principle he was announcing and that he found implicit in *Thomas:* "In application of . . . [the principle of *Thomas v. Winchester*] there may, at times, have been uncertainty or even error."[22] He went on to discuss some of these "erroneous" decisions, which he pointed out had been criticized by scholars,[23] as well as English cases, such as

Winterbottom v. Wright,[24] that also were inconsistent with the principle of negligence liability for all foreseeable injuries.[25]

Cardozo's method in *MacPherson*—the reconstructive method—fits perfectly Dworkin's account of how legal principles are derived. Cardozo purported to derive his principle from the extant law, not from morality. Moreover, he relied on what was decided in prior cases, not on the announced grounds of those decisions. (In other words, he did not just apply a previously posited canonical rule.) Finally, he was willing to settle for less than perfect fit with those past decisions. In other words, Cardozo's principle was a paradigmatic Dworkinian legal principle because, while Cardozo viewed it as morally more attractive than the stated grounds for earlier decisions, it was nonetheless derived from most (but not all) of these decisions and not directly from morality.

Levi asserts that Cardozo's method in *MacPherson* is paradigmatic of common law adjudication. We agree and will provide one additional illustration. In *Hannah v. Peel*,[26] the plaintiff, a British soldier, was staying in the defendant's house, the house having been requisitioned for use by military personnel. While adjusting the blackout curtains, the plaintiff discovered a valuable brooch in the crevice of a window frame. The plaintiff turned the brooch over to the police, who eventually gave it to the defendant. The plaintiff sued for the brooch. The King's Bench held in favor of the plaintiff on the basis of a principle favoring finders of personal property over landowners.

In fashioning its opinion, the King's Bench had to confront a number of troublesome authorities, particularly *South Staffordshire Water Company v. Sharman*.[27] In that case, a workman, who had been employed to drain a pool, discovered two gold rings at the pool's bottom. The court held that the rings should go to the landowners, notwithstanding their lack of knowledge of the rings. The court's expressed reason for so holding was that possession of land entails possession of what is attached to it. The King's Bench in *Hannah*, however, ignored the court's reasoning in *Sharman* and instead pointed out that the finder there, unlike plaintiff in *Hannah*, was in the landowner's employ.[28] (*Sharman* itself had "reinterpreted" an earlier case, *Bridges v. Hawkesworth*,[29] in which someone who found banknotes on a shop floor prevailed against the shop's owner.)

Hannah, like *MacPherson,* induced a covering principle for the previous cases that had not been announced in any of them and under which some previous cases were "mistakes." It thus supports the contention that Dworkin's account of legal principles reflects the dominant legal methodology.[30]

The doctrinal arguments of legal scholars lend further support for this contention. In article after article, treatise after treatise, legal scholars survey a doctrinal field and conclude that the legal materials in that field are best justified as expressions of this or that set of legal principles. Their arguments are not that such principles are moral principles, for they may not be morally ideal, and they owe their very existence to specific human decisions. Nor do their arguments depend upon these principles having been explicitly adopted by courts or legislatures, for frequently no court or legislature has done so. Rather, their arguments for these principles consist of showing that the principles are morally attractive even if not ideal, and that following these principles would have resulted in most of the legal decisions in the field, even if not their actual rationales. We shall illustrate this scholarly methodology with two examples.

In "The Right of Privacy,"[31] Brandeis and Warren argued that decisions by courts in a variety of doctrinal areas indicated the emergence of a new legal principle that they labeled "the right of privacy" or "the right to be let alone."[32] They regarded this principle as highly desirable, given the ever greater intrusiveness into private life that modern technology had made possible. However, it was not the principle's desirability that led Brandeis and Warren to assert its existence. Rather, the principle existed because it was implicit in numerous judicial decisions.

What is important to note is that the cases that Brandeis and Warren relied upon to establish the general right of privacy did not themselves assert such a general principle. The cases included those protecting artistic and intellectual property, those enforcing contractual and fiduciary relations, and those protecting trade secrets. What Brandeis and Warren said about the first set of cases extends to all the cases they discuss: "These considerations lead to the conclusion that the protection afforded to thoughts, sentiments, and emotions, expressed through the medium of writing or of the arts, so far as it consists in preventing publication, is merely an instance of the enforcement of the more general right to be left alone."[33]

Brandeis and Warren, like Dworkin's ideal judge Hercules and the common law courts in *MacPherson* and *Hannah,* thus discovered a principle that, unlike moral principles, arose from decisions in legal cases, but unlike the rules authored in those cases, was not itself an intentionally created norm and could extend beyond and revise the rules and decisions that were its source.[34] The Brandeis and Warren methodology, which is the dominant model of doctrinal legal scholarship, reflects perfectly Dworkin's reconstructive account of legal principles.

Our final example is a representative passage from *The Law of Torts* by William Prosser and Page Keeton.[35] In discussing the doctrine of "coming to a nuisance," Prosser and Keeton point out a decision by the Supreme Court of Wisconsin allowing a mink ranch to recover damages from the operation of a preexisting village dump. The court in that case had stated that "while coming to the nuisance may properly be entertained while weighing the equities in an abatement action, it is irrelevant in a damage suit."[36] Prosser and Keeton respond: "Such a general proposition would seem to be questionable. The result reached in the case can be justified because of other circumstances."[37]

What is notable about this response is that it invokes neither strictly moral considerations nor posited legal rules. A moral argument against the Supreme Court of Wisconsin's position would not have required "justifying" the result reached in the case. And there can be no gainsaying the Wisconsin Supreme Court on the question of what legal rule governs Wisconsin with respect to coming to a nuisance in a damage action. To reject the Wisconsin court's rule but accept the materiality of its result requires recourse to a principle that arises from such results rather than from morality standing alone but that is not itself posited by any court or lawmaker. In other words, the kind of principle Prosser and Keeton rely upon fits the reconstructive method and its legal principles: legal principles need not be any legal decision-maker's intended grounds for decision and need not be moral principles; they are influenced by both but not necessarily identical to either.

The Arguments against Legal Principles

Notwithstanding their dominance in legal practice, the case for legal principles fails. Our argument focuses on Dworkin's account of legal principles, which we believe to be the most careful account in the literature. Most other accounts of legal principles share the crucial flaw of Dworkin's, for they are based on the mistaken assumption that there can be norms that are not correct moral norms, that are not posited norms like legal rules but rather are norms that arise out of the posited legal rules.

THE NORMATIVE UNATTRACTIVENESS OF LEGAL PRINCIPLES

One of the earliest arguments against legal principles is found in Larry Alexander and Michael Bayles's criticism of *Taking Rights Seriously*.[38] Alexander and Bayles pointed out that moral principles are morally attractive because they *are* our moral ideals. They are the very standards of moral attractiveness. Moral principles are what ideally should govern our conduct in all instances, both within the legal system and without.[39]

Legal *rules* can be morally attractive because they can be formulated to give better guidance than the moral principles themselves.[40] As we pointed out in chapter 1, how moral principles apply to particular cases will frequently be controversial. Having everyone individually determine how the moral principles apply may lead to moral errors, lack of coordination, and other ills. Thus, the resulting state of affairs may, in light of the moral principles themselves, be morally inferior to the state of affairs emerging from clear, blunt, formal rules. This may be so even if the rules, because of their blunt, formal nature, produce morally incorrect results (in terms of the moral principles) in some particular cases.[41] Indeed, this may be so even if there are better rules available than those actually in place, for there may be higher-order rules that authorize the (nonideal) lower-order rules and which themselves are ideal (or as near ideal as can be agreed upon and morally preferable to anarchy).[42]

Moral principles have the virtue of moral correctness; legal rules have the virtues of being the creations of those with authority to make law and of giving clear guidance and settling moral controversy. Legal principles, however, have none of these virtues. They are neither morally correct nor uncontroversial in application. Nor have they been promulgated by authorities whose power to create norms is rule-based, for they are not posited norms. They represent the worst of all worlds. Alexander and Bayles concluded that Dworkin had made out no case for legal principles as appropriate norms.[43]

LEGAL PRINCIPLES AND THE SPURIOUS CLAIMS OF EQUALITY AND INTEGRITY

In *Law's Empire,* nine years after the publication of *Taking Rights Seriously,* Dworkin continued to press the case for legal principles derived from the axes of fit and moral acceptability, but he buttressed the case for such legal principles by arguments appealing to "integrity."[44] "Integrity" is Dworkin's name for a particular version of equality, namely, the equality that is manifested by acting in a "principled" way and applying the same legal principles to X that one has applied to Y. When one determines what are the most morally attractive principles that "fit" past legal decisions at the threshold level, and then applies those principles in the present, one is treating present litigants in a principled way and maintaining equality between them and past litigants. Dworkin also requires that the principles underlying various aspects of doctrine be consistently applied and fit coherently together in an overall scheme of principles expressing "a single and comprehensive vision of justice."[45]

Alexander, in commenting on *Law's Empire,* argued that Dworkin's support of legal principles by reference to equality was confused.[46] If "equality" is a value, it is not a freestanding one. Rather, it is theory-dependent. In other words, each moral theory—each set of moral principles—will generate its own conception of equality. Utilitarianism, for example, will require that everyone's utility be counted and given equal weight; egalitarianism will require equality of welfare or resources. And each moral theory will dictate the pursuit of equality through following the theory itself. Thus, there cannot be a coherent reason in terms of the true moral value of equality for ever departing from the requirements of the correct moral theory. The true moral value of equality is internal to the correct moral theory, not a reason to depart from it in favor of morally incorrect legal principles.

Although Dworkin is vague on this point, it appears that equality or integrity serves both as a constraining principle on other moral principles and (ambiguously) as simply one moral principle among equals. In its capacity as just one principle among others, it would presumably be theory-dependent, just as are "justice" and "due process." In its role as a constraining principle on others, it would serve as a test that the other principles must meet. Equality cannot coherently play both roles.[47]

Finally, recall our discussion of equality as a freestanding value in chapter 7. There we showed that freestanding equality would face problems of incoherence and of extending past evils into the future.

THE RETROACTIVITY OF LEGAL PRINCIPLES

In *Taking Rights Seriously* and thereafter, Dworkin argues that adjudicating by reference to legal principles protects legal rights against retroactive upsets.[48] Legal positivists, who argue that legal rules exhaust the legal norms available in adjudication, must decide cases on grounds other than legal grounds whenever those cases are not covered by legal rules. That, argues Dworkin, leads to applying new legal rules—those formulated in cases without preexisting legal rules—to transactions that arise before the legal rules are promulgated, which is akin to legislating retroactively. Legal principles, on the other hand, are already immanent in past decisions, define the legal rights to which those past decisions give rise, and can determine outcomes in cases not governed by legal rules.

Alexander and Bayles, along with others, argued that Dworkin's argument from retroactivity is both confused and question-begging.[49] It is confused because any moral arguments against retroactivity could be accommodated by judges through recourse to correct moral principles whenever the legal rules failed to resolve a case. In other words, among the factors that would have to be taken into account in making a legal decision based on correct moral principles are the parties' expectations, the extent of their reliance on those expectations, and the countervailing benefits of upsetting their expectations.[50] Dworkin's retroactivity argument is question-begging because it assumes that legal rights exist and thus could be retroactively upset in cases not covered by legal rules, a proposition legal positivists would dispute.

Perhaps the most interesting criticism of the argument from retroactivity is a *tu quoque* response by Kress.[51] Kress demonstrates that Dworkin's own theory of adjudication grounded in legal principles results in retroactive application of legal rights.

Kress's argument builds upon the role of authoritative institutional acts, such as constitutions, statutes, and judicial decisions, within Dworkin's theory. Legally authoritative principles and the rights that they describe are, for Dworkin, a function of institutional history and moral-political theory. Outcomes in concrete cases at law are in turn a function of the application and elaboration of legal principles (and rights). Thus, by transitivity, correct outcomes are a function of institutional history (along with moral-political theory). This much is obvious. Differences in constitutional and statutory provisions, precedents, and administrative rulings result in varying legal rights and principles, that is, in different law.

Suppose that, as a consequence of a judicial decision in another case, a change in legal rights occurs after the facts giving rise to a lawsuit but before the case is adjudicated. With only rare exceptions,[52] the case will be adjudicated on the basis of the legal rights existing at the time of adjudication and not on the basis of the legal rights that existed at the time of the events giving rise to the lawsuit. If one of the legal rights that changes in consequence of the intervening judicial decision is dispositive of the lawsuit, then the litigant who would have won (based upon the law existing at the time of the underlying events) will lose, and the litigant who would have lost will win. This is nothing less than retroactive application of law.

The same result can be established more elegantly by first noticing that, in Dworkin's theory, the legal principles—the morally best principles, P_1, that meet or exceed the threshold of fit—will always be precisely at the minimum threshold of fit. This can be demonstrated by reductio ad absurdum. Suppose the legal principles P_1 exceed the threshold of fit. P_1 could then be "transformed" into a morally more attractive set of principles P_2 by replacing one or more morally unattractive principles of P_1 that fit the institutional history well with morally more attractive principles P_2 that fit less well, yet still leave P_2 over the threshold of fit. But then P_2 is a better set of principles than P_1 because it is morally better than P_1 yet exceeds the threshold of fit. This contradicts the assumption that P_1 was the morally best set of principles exceeding the threshold of fit. QED.

That Dworkinian legal principles are always at the threshold of fit entails that principles are continuously changing. Applying these new principles to events arising before the new principles become legally authoritative amounts to retroactive application of law. We shall elaborate upon these claims.

Suppose that the minimum threshold of fit is 80 percent of judicial decisions. (Ignore, for simplicity, enactments, regulations, judicial hierarchies, and so on. The argument is sound even with these added complications.) Suppose that there have been 100 decisions to date, and that there is only one judge.

We have just seen that Dworkinian legal principles will just meet the threshold. Since the threshold is 80 percent, the set of Dworkinian legal principles P_1 will fit 80 percent of the cases. It will explain 80 and fail to explain 20 of the 100 cases.

Now suppose that 100 new decisions arise and the judge correctly applies the set of Dworkinian legal principles P_1 in resolving the cases. P_1 fits 100 of the new cases, since it was followed in deciding them. There are now 200 decisions. P_1 fits 80 of the first 100, and 100 of the second 100. Thus, P_1 fits $180/200 = 90$ percent of the cases. This exceeds the threshold of fit, 80 percent. Assuming that P_1 is a set of morally imperfect principles (as Dworkin's analysis necessarily implies), P_1 can no longer be the required set of Dworkinian legal principles since P_1 substantially exceeds the threshold of fit. We can construct a P_2 with 80 percent fit and morally better principles by trading off fit for moral appeal until we reach the threshold of fit.

For one or more principles, P_2 differs from P_1. This means that P_2 will decide some cases differently from how P_1 would. Litigants whose causes of action arise when P_1 is the set of legal principles will be subject to retroactive application of law whenever the differences between P_1 and P_2 are relevant to their lawsuit. If a changed principle is dispositive, the litigant who would have won loses, and vice versa.

THE ARGUMENT FROM WEIGHT

Legal principles, as we have said, are not the same as correct moral principles. They are, instead, incorrect moral principles, or just plain incorrect principles. But are there such things?

There are, of course, incorrect *rules,* norms posited by particular people at a particular time and with a particular canonical form and intentional structure that demarcates their extensions. Rules, correct or incorrect, are weightless. They either apply or don't apply, but they cannot be "weighed." More accurately, as we said earlier, rules are not weightless; rather, they claim to have *infinite* weight where they apply. Principles, however, are supposed to have (finite) weight. Indeed, weight is essential to their being principles, since they have neither canonical form nor dependence on particular persons' datable intentions to govern their application. Their application is a function of their weight.

An *incorrect* principle, insofar as it is a principle, must, therefore, have weight. How else can we determine in a particular case whether the incorrect principle outweighs competing principles? If incorrect principles never outweigh competing principles, correct and incorrect, then they can never determine the outcome of any case, since competing principles will always be available to govern the case. At a minimum, the entire set of morally correct principles will be available. But what weight will incorrect principles have, and how will such weight be determined? No set of past cases, no matter how large the set, can fix as a matter of logical entailment the weight in the context of a present case of any principle that would explain those past cases.

We can, of course, "assign" a weight to an incorrect principle by deciding a case in accord with it or against it. In doing so we are declaring that the incorrect principle P_1 shall outweigh correct principle P_C in case C. We are not *discovering* that it is the case, however, for there is nothing to discover. Our declaration that it is the case cannot be correct or incorrect. The weight of P_1 in case C does not determine the outcome in case C; rather, the outcome in case C determines the weight of P_1 in case C.

Suppose one were to argue that we induce the weight in the same way we induce the incorrect principle, by looking at past cases. Assume, for example, that there have been N cases in which plaintiffs named Green have won even though correct principles P_C would have dictated that they lose. Suppose we induce the existence of incorrect principle P_G, "Plaintiffs named Green should be preferred." Suppose we have a new case with a plaintiff named Green where P_C would dictate that Green lose. Does P_C outweigh P_G or does P_G outweigh P_C? All we know is that P_G outweighed P_C in past cases C_N. This does not tell us whether P_G outweighs P_C in the present case. What other arguments might determine P_G's weight in this case? Arguments about how this case ought (really) to come out? Those arguments will all be based on correct principles P_C. They will dictate that P_G be followed from now on only when it is consistent with P_C, which means P_G has no weight of its own, and which therefore means it does not exist. The argument for inducing the weight of incorrect principles mistakenly views the adjudicative enterprise as predictive, while in fact it is normative.

Suppose we do not induce the "correct" incorrect principle and its weight from past cases, but instead we rely on the incorrect principle's *promulgation*. Take freedom of speech, for example. Assume that there is no independent moral principle of freedom of speech. Rather, the freedom of speech we should endorse is the product of moral principles regarding liberty and antipaternalism.

Now suppose the constitutional framer, Super Lex, declares that "the principle of freedom of speech shall be recognized." There is no problem treating this as a *rule* (with infinite weight within the scope of its application). But suppose we try to take Super Lex at its word and treat free speech as a principle, albeit one with no counterpart among correct moral principles. What weight do we give it when it conflicts with P_C? Not its real weight (for, being other than morally correct, what would its *real* weight be?). Its promulgation cannot help us here, for unless Super Lex tells us how it is to be applied in each possible case—in which case Super Lex has made it into a *rule*—all we know from its promulgation is its promulgation. We do not know *it*. Nor can we. What is *there* to know?

Incorrect principles have a problematic metaphysical status. Our argument is that determining their weight may be like assigning a property to "the ether"; it cannot be done correctly or incorrectly, since there is nothing in the world that is "the ether" with (or without) the property.[53]

THE ARGUMENT FROM FIT

If there are legal principles that are morally incorrect principles, then Dworkin's account of them is the best there is. Namely, the incorrect principles (P_I) that exist are those principles that "fit" above some threshold with past governmental actions and that are the morally best such principles, "best" being measured by normative distance to correct principles (P_C). But in fact, $P_I = P_C$. Dworkin's case for legal principles is nothing more than a case for correct moral principles. Why?

Suppose there are in the past *N* cases, C_N, that have not been decided in accord with correct principles P_C. Of all the incorrect principles P_I that would "fit" the past cases, there is one principle that "fits" perfectly and is also morally best. That is the principle that is coextensive with P_C except for cases C_N (where it dictates the results reached in C_N). Let us call this principle $P_C - C_N$.

It is clear that no set of incorrect principles P_I fits better than $P_C - C_N$, since the latter exhibits 100 percent fit. Nor is any set morally better, since $P_C - C_N$ will dictate exactly the same results in all future cases and hypothetical cases as P_C. Therefore, Dworkin would have to urge that we decide based on incorrect principles $P_C - C_N$.

Is there anything wrong with this? Well, $P_C - C_N$ is not an *elegant* principle. But why should that disqualify it *normatively,* as opposed to aesthetically, given that it scores highest on both the fit and moral dimensions?

$P_C - C_N$ might be condemned as arbitrary and ad hoc. That is true. But if so, *all* incorrect principles are arbitrary and ad hoc, constructed to "justify" mistaken decisions.

$P_C - C_N$ might be condemned as failing to accord persons equal treatment in those future cases that are "like" cases C_N but in which $P_C - C_N$ will have a "different" outcome (one in accord with P_C not C_N). This objection is confused. Equality is in one sense completely dependent on substantive principles;[54] therefore, $P_C - C_N$ generates its own conception of equality. On the other hand, if the point is that true equality, that mandated by P_C, differs from $P_C - C_N$, the point is correct but supports $P_C - C_N$. The litigants in C_N and in $P_C - C_N$ are being treated equally in the sense that our best view of what is just at the time is being applied to each of them. C_N is in the past and cannot be undone. $P_C - C_N$ will produce all the true equality (P_C equality) one can now achieve.[55]

Thus, the objections based on inelegance, *ad hoc* principles, and equality all fail to dislodge $P_C - C_N$ as the preferred incorrect principle P_1.

Finally, since the past is past, and since $P_C - C_N$ dictates exactly the same results in the future as P_C does, there is no practical difference between $P_C - C_N$ and P_C. And since $P_C - C_N$ is the incorrect principle—P_I—that we are supposed to choose, $P_I = P_C$. There are no incorrect principles of any practical (what other?) consequence.

A MISLEADING ANALOGY: LEGAL PRINCIPLES & THE METHODOLOGY OF REFLECTIVE EQUILIBRIUM

Some might argue that the case for legal principles rests on the case for employing the methodology of reflective equilibrium. In the moral realm, reflective equilibrium is championed as the correct epistemological method for discovering (constructing?) correct moral principles.[56] One moves between one's considered moral judgments regarding particular cases and more general moral principles that would account for such judgments, adjusting the principles and reconsidering particular judgments until the principles and judgments reach an equilibrium state. Could we not say by analogy that legal principles are those principles that are in equilibrium with (most of) the cases?[57]

The answer is no. First, in moral reflective equilibrium, it is considered judgments that we have to bring into reflective equilibrium with our principles (and vice versa). In law, it is authoritative legal acts that must be brought into equilibrium with a theory of justice.[58]

Secondly, and relatedly, in the moral methodology of reflective equilibrium we consider everything that can possibly bear on our judgments (what we know about psychology, sociology, economics, and so forth).[59] In constructing legal principles, however, we are limited to primary legal materials (decisions, statutes, and so forth) and, importantly, cannot consider more than a certain percentage of those materials to be mistaken (the threshold of "fit"). There is no such limitation on moral reflective equilibrium.[60]

Finally, assume, as its proponents claim, that the method of reflective equilibrium does lead to correct moral principles. If so, the method would also lead to correct moral principles when applied to legal materials. For although those correct moral principles would not necessarily be consistent with any particular percentage of the primary legal materials—the method would presumably lead to dropping *all* morally misguided legal materials and supplanting them with morally correct notions that might have no legal pedigree—those moral principles *would* be consistent with our considered judgments *about* the primary legal materials.

LEGAL PRINCIPLES AND AGREEMENT AMONG COMPETENT PRACTITIONERS

One final objection to our case against legal principles goes as follows: Legal principles, like legal rules, are established through the practices and conventions of competent professionals. In cases where legal rules do not determine the results, those practices and conventions establish the governing legal principles and their weights. Legal principles and their weights are whatever competent practitioners would agree they were.[61]

We have several responses to this objection. First, the objection implies that when competent practitioners disagree about legal principles and their weights, there are no legal principles about which to agree or disagree. If legal principles and their weights are completely determined by professionals' conventions, then the absence of convention means the absence of legal principles. Professionals could never meaningfully disagree about what the legal principles are.

When professionals do agree, however, they could be agreeing about legal principles, as this argument we are constructing has it, or they could be agreeing about moral principles and establishing a higher-order legal rule to govern the case based on those moral principles. How would we tell whether, when professionals agree about a case not determined by legal rules, they are agreeing about legal principles or establishing a higher-order legal rule based on their moral principles? We submit that so long as agreement is what constitutes legal principles and their weights, we will never be able to distinguish legal principles from higher-order legal rules. The argument from convention does not support legal principles.[62]

The argument we have just made against agreement among competent practitioners as establishing legal principles assumes that what practitioners are agreeing about is how particular cases ought to be resolved. At that level, we have argued, legal principles cannot be distinguished from higher-order legal rules. Suppose, however, it is argued that the objects of these agreements are not particular outcomes but are legal principles themselves (and their weights). In other words, what establishes legal principles just *is* agreement among competent practitioners about what those legal principles are.

This position has two variants, neither of which is tenable. On one, the practitioners *posit* the legal principles through their agreement. As we have already noted, however, legal principles cannot be posited.

The alternative is to argue that it is the practitioners' agreement about what the legal principles *are* that establishes them. This alternative, however, involves fatal self-reference. If the practitioners' agreement *establishes* legal principles, how can the agreement be *about* preexisting legal principles? And if it is not an agreement about preexisting legal principles, we are back to posited rules.

Legal Principles as a Solution to the Dilemma of Rules

In chapter 4 we discussed the moral dilemma created by serious rules. The community may correctly believe that a mechanism for authoritatively settling questions about what ought to be done is morally preferable (on everyone's conception of morality) to leaving such questions unsettled, with resulting moral losses in terms of expertise, coordination, and efficiency. Establishing an authoritative decisionmaker, Lex, and having Lex promulgate serious rules that are more determinate than moral principles (at the level of abstractness at which moral principles are agreed upon) results in moral gains. Serious rules, however, require individual actors to adhere to their terms, even if the actors believe that, at least in certain circumstances, those terms dictate morally inferior courses of action to alternatives prohibited by the rules. The actors thus must acknowledge that there are overriding moral reasons to have rules prescribing courses of action that they have overriding moral reasons not to follow.

We examined several suggestions for ways out of or around the dilemma of rules, but we were doubtful that any of them succeeded. Dworkinian legal principles, however, might be thought to be capable of bridging this gap between morality and the rules morality sanctions. After all, the legal principles are constructed out of material from both sides of the gap. They must fit with existing legal materials—the rules—but they must be the most morally attractive principles that fit and thus must draw from morality as well.

Rather than giving us the best of both the worlds of moral principles and posited rules, however, legal principles give us the worst of both worlds. They do not close the gap. An actor faced with a legal principle that is nonetheless not equivalent to and thus morally inferior to a moral principle, will still see no moral reason to follow the legal principle rather than the moral one. On the other hand, legal principles do not provide the settlement benefits of serious rules. They can be no more determinate than the controversial moral principles that shape them. And indeed, the very controversies over the application of moral principles that give rise to the need for serious rules will be replicated in attempting to formulate, assign weight to, and apply legal principles.

In short, legal principles have neither the virtue of moral correctness nor the settlement virtues of serious rules. They can only worsen the normative situation and create a second gap. In the end, moral principles and posited rules are the only types of norms the community needs and should have in dealing with moral controversies.

PART FOUR

The Settlement Function and Jurisprudential Debates

NINE Legal Positivism and Natural Law

In the previous chapters we have shown that even in the very favorable circumstances of a small society whose members are motivated to do what is morally right, controversies and uncertainties about what ought to be done will be morally costly. The society can bring about moral improvement by accepting Lex (and perhaps Super Lex) as the authority regarding what ought to be done. And Lex will authoritatively settle moral controversies through promulgating determinate rules, as opposed to standards. Once he promulgates rules, his subjects will face dilemmas occasioned by the fact that they will have to interpret Lex's rules without reviving the moral controversies the rules were meant to settle, and by the fact that the rules often will require those subject to them to act against their perception of the balance of reasons. Finally, in the previous three chapters, we discussed the process of deciding specific cases not covered by Lex's rules, though perhaps covered by rules laid down by Lex's judges in previous cases.

In none of the previous chapters have we purported to define "law" or to make claims about what the concept of "law" entails. Nor have we described Lex and his rules as the society's "legal system," much less claimed that all legal systems must resemble Lex and his rules.

In this chapter and the next, however, we wish to map our account of the moral function of authoritative rules onto standard jurisprudential debates over the nature of law. We do so, not because we wish to put forward a competing concept of law, nor because we wish to endorse one of the contending concepts, but because we believe those debates can be substantially illuminated by our particular prism.

We have argued in previous chapters that Lex's rules are means to moral ends; yet, in order to serve those ends effectively, the rules must often be morally imperfect. In this chapter, we discuss the traditional natural law versus positivism debate and show how our story about the moral function of rules bears on that debate. Once the basic dilemma of rules is exposed, the difference between natural law and positivism becomes a difference in perspective, and the two leading approaches to legal theory emerge as more complementary than opposed. Natural law focuses on the moral aspirations and failures of law, while positivism focuses on legal rules as means for guidance. In chapter 10, we extend our analysis to such questions as whose point of view regarding law is primary for purposes of jurisprudence, whether several legal systems can simultaneously coexist within a given territory, what the legal effects of conquest and revolution are, whether law can be determinate and objective, and what the relation is between law and force.

Natural Law versus Positivism: Framing the Basic Debate

Those who take the natural law position in debates over the nature of law see as salient that law is normative, prescribing how we should act, and that it speaks in terms of "justice," "rights," and "obligations." Law appears to occupy the same ground as morality and to use the same terms. Therefore, they conclude, law must be essentially connected with morality. How, otherwise, could it purport to establish justice, protect rights, and prescribe what we are obligated to do?

The positivists, on the other hand, see as salient the "isness" of law: that law is a human artifact; that, unlike timeless and changeless moral principles, law's creation and extinction are datable events; and that, unlike morality's perfection, law is almost always morally imperfect and very often evil. For the positivist, although law usually appropriates moral terms, in the words of a wag, the "justice" of at least many legal regimes is to real justice as military music is to music. Although Nazi Germany and the Stalinist Soviet Union had "law," according to the positivist, their law was anything but moral.

Now there are several aspects of Lex and his rules that the natural lawyer will find congenial to her position about the nature of law. She will point out if we take Lex and his rules to count as a legal system, it is an important feature of our story that the system originates to settle a *moral* question (what ought to be done) for *moral* reasons (to gain the moral benefits of expertise, coordination, and efficient decision-making). Moreover, the members of the community accept the rule establishing Lex and Super Lex because the rule is, from the perspective of each, the morally best rule that all can accept, and acceptance of the rule by all is *morally* preferable to leaving moral controversies unsettled. And when Lex and Super Lex choose which rules to promulgate, they do so based upon their belief that the chosen rules are *morally* optimal. Finally, each person subject to the rules—including Lex's officials—must ultimately decide whether the balance of *moral* reasons supports following the rules in particular applications or instead supports violating the rules.

The positivist will also find various features of our account significant. He will point out that the master rules are accepted even though they are likely not morally optimal from anyone's perspective. Moreover, even if Lex and Super Lex are morally motivated, being human, they will inevitably promulgate rules that are morally flawed, and their rules must be interpreted in a way that reflects this inevitability. Finally, even if the rules are the morally best rules possible, they will inevitably be blunt and fail to capture precisely the results of particularistic moral reasoning; they will therefore require acts inconsistent with moral requirements.

We are tempted to conclude that what we have just said about the natural lawyer and the positivist fully exhausts the useful points that can be made about the nature of law. Law as authoritative rules is accepted and promulgated for moral reasons. However, both because authoritative rules are *rules,* and because they are promulgated by fallible beings, there will always be a gap between what the authoritative rules require and what moral reasons require (the subject of chapter 4). The natural lawyer's lens on legal rules is that of the moral reasons that the rules are meant to serve but will inevitably fail to serve in many instances. The positivist's lens is on the rules themselves, not their background moral reasons. And although there is, of course, a tension—indeed, an almost paradoxical relationship—between authoritative rules and the background moral reasons they are intended to serve, the natural lawyer's and positivist's points of view appear to be complementary rather than opposed.

Nevertheless, before concluding that the natural law–positivism debate reflects only perspectival or perhaps terminological differences but no true disagreement over the nature of law, we shall examine each of these positions in a bit more depth.

The Natural Law Position

The natural lawyer's question is a practical one: "What ought I, as an official or a citizen, to do in light of Lex's rule and the system of rules of which it is part?" If the natural lawyer is a citizen of Lex's community, she will be in one of the following postures depending upon her moral principles, her assessment of the facts, and the content of Lex's rules. First, she may accept Lex as a practical authority, such that if Lex's rule applies to her case, she will answer the question, "What ought I to do?" with "I ought to do what Lex's rule requires." The natural lawyer may accept Lex's authority either because she believes Lex is the best practical authority attainable in any world, or, what is more likely, because she believes Lex is the best practical authority attainable in the real world (most likely because so many others already accept Lex as a practical authority), and Lex is better than the complete absence of any practical authority.[1] Acceptance of Lex as a practical authority is subject, of course, to the dilemma discussed in chapter 4.

Second, if the natural lawyer does *not* (or cannot) accept Lex as a practical authority, she will act as a rule-sensitive particularist. When one of Lex's rules applies to her, whether she follows the rule will depend upon several considerations: her moral principles; the content of the rule, which may be morally compelling, morally obnoxious, or morally tolerable; and her perception of the facts, among which are that Lex is a practical authority for others, that practical authorities are valuable and should not ordinarily be undermined, that others will quite likely be doing what the rule requires and relying on others' obedience, and that noncompliance with the rule might be personally costly. Thus, the natural lawyer may decide that she ought to follow the rule despite the fact that she does not accept Lex as a practical authority.

If none of Lex's rules apply to her case, the natural lawyer will answer the question "What ought I to do?" by recourse to her moral principles and the facts she perceives, among which are the existence of Lex's rules and their acceptance as practically authoritative. Those rules are facts to be taken into account even when the rules do not purport to govern the case at hand, for they are part of the background environment that every moral decision must take into account. They will therefore bear on the natural lawyer's practical inquiry even when they do not apply to her case, and even when she rejects their practical authority.

Finally, if the natural lawyer is asking what *others* ought to do in light of Lex's rules, she will give the same answers that she would give if she were in their shoes. Thus, if she does not accept Lex as a practical authority—perhaps because she believes that Lex is worse than an available alternative, or worse than the complete absence of a practical authority—she will assess others' normative situations from the standpoint of Lex's lack of practical authority *for them,* even if they themselves actually accept Lex as a practical authority.

In sum, because Lex's rules claim to answer the question of what Lex's subjects ought to do, and because moral norms trump all competing practical norms, the natural lawyer concludes that Lex's rules can be normative in the way they claim only if they are consistent with moral norms. And because we associate "law" with norms that claim to trump all competing norms, Lex's rules can be "law" only insofar as they are consistent with moral norms.

We have presented the natural law position as if it were monolithic, but there are various possible distinctions within the natural law camp that might be jurisprudentially significant. One such distinction is between those natural lawyers who equate "law" with morality—that an act is morally required or forbidden is for them both necessary and sufficient for deeming it to be legally required or forbidden—and those natural lawyers who make consistency with morality a necessary but not sufficient condition for a norm's being "law." The latter might maintain that Lex's rules are "law" to the extent that their dictates are what moral principles, in light of the rules, themselves dictate, but that what moral principles dictate is not "law" if not also dictated by Lex's rules. "Law" for this kind of natural lawyer then is but a subset of moral requirements and a subset of what Lex's rules require. It represents the area where the two sets of requirements overlap. For the simpler version of natural lawyer, "law" and morality are completely coextensive, though Lex's rules may affect "law's" content by affecting the circumstances in which moral norms apply.[2]

The Positivist Position

IN GENERAL

The positivists are those legal theorists who contend that Lex's community has a legal system, and that the ingredients of that legal system, its "laws," are the various orders, rules, and other norms that represent decisions about what ought to be done by actual human beings—either Lex himself or subordinate officials in pursuance of rules issued by Lex. Moreover, the positivists contend that Lex's rules and orders are the laws of the community even if those rules and orders are terribly immoral and should not in fact be obeyed. The positivists' perspective is the perspective of those who do not necessarily accept Lex's practical authority, but who note that a sufficient number of people do accept it, so that Lex's decisions are generally efficacious in ordering the lives of Lex's subjects. The positivists' view is an uncommitted view of others' commitments, an external point of view on others' internal point of view.[3] The positivists accept the following propositions: law is a human artifact, a set of norms posited by human beings as the result of actual decisions; law claims practical authority; law's claim to practical authority must be accepted by a sufficient number of its subjects to be generally efficacious in ordering their practical affairs; and law may not—and for some positivists, at least, cannot—have the authority it claims.[4]

The positivists recognize, at least implicitly, that there are two modes in which the statement "X is the law" might function. The statement might be uttered in the committed mode, that is, as a statement implying the commitment of the speaker to the practical authority of X's author. Alternatively, the statement might be uttered in the uncommitted mode, that is, as a statement that does not imply any such commitment on the part of the speaker, though it does imply that others do have such a commitment (otherwise X could not be a law). The positivists *qua positivists* speak about law in the latter mode only, recognizing that their statements are parasitic on others' speaking in the committed mode.

Thus, positivists, speaking as positivists, can question whether law has the practical authority it claims while asserting (uncommittedly) that it is law nonetheless because its claim to authority is accepted by others. At the same time, the claim to practical authority by those who issue rules is essential for positivists to recognize the rules as "law." Otherwise, a legal system could not be distinguished from coercive orders established by thugs who make no claim that their rules are practically authoritative for those subject to them in the sense of settling what morally ought to be done. A practical authority may have had its origin in raw coercion. And coercion may produce the efficaciousness and hence the confidence in others' compliance that leads to general acceptance of the coercer as a practical authority.[5] But coercion cannot supplant the claim to practical authoritativeness as the positivists' hallmark of a legal system.

Further, although positivists may deny that law has the practical authority it claims and still accord it the status of "law," this does not mean that positivists deny the moral value of practical authorities.[6] Positivists deny only that the statement "X is the law" entails *their* commitment to X's author's being a practical authority *for them.*

Some final implications of legal positivism. First, for the positivists, the existence of a legal system can be a matter of degree. If Lex and his officials cease to be generally obeyed—that is, if Lex's rules cease to be efficacious in securing compliance—some positivists might deny that Lex's rules constitute a legal system, while others might claim that those rules were still a legal system, though one in a pathological rather than normal state.[7] And second, it is possible on the positivists' account of law that competing legal systems can and perhaps often do coexist within a given territory.[8]

EXCLUSIVE VERSUS INCLUSIVE POSITIVISM

We have thus far painted the natural law and positivist positions with a very broad brush, neglecting the many subtle and sometimes not so subtle points that distinguish some natural lawyers and positivists from other natural lawyers and positivists. We have glossed over multitudes of distinctions within the broad positions because however important those distinctions might be for certain purposes, they are not important for ours. Nonetheless, we do wish to draw attention to one such division within the positivist camp because our account of Lex and his rules can shed light on what is (and is not) at stake. We refer to the debate between exclusive legal positivists and inclusive legal positivists.

Exclusive Legal Positivists. Exclusive legal positivists take a jurisprudential position that is 180 degrees from the natural law position. The exclusive legal positivist believes that the existence of "law" can never be determined by moral considerations. Rather, law's existence is exclusively a matter of "hard" (nonevaluative) facts, such as what rules the community has accepted and what rules Lex has promulgated. Moreover, if the content of those rules refers to moral considerations, only the nonmoral portion of the rules is "law."

The exclusive legal positivist's rejection of morality as a basis for identifying the content of the law is based on a theoretical position about law's moral function. This is most evident in the work of Joseph Raz, perhaps the most careful and most influential of the exclusive legal positivists.

In his book *The Authority of Law,*[9] Raz states that in order for a legal system to exist, it must satisfy the following three conditions: (1) it must be efficacious;[10] (2) it must be institutionalized, a system of guidance and adjudication that claims supreme authority;[11] and (3) its identity and content must be determined by social facts—that is, moral principles are not law even if they are referred to by law.[12] According to Raz, the function of law is to provide publicly ascertainable standards by which people are bound, so they cannot excuse disobedience by challenging the justification of the standards.[13] Thus, the authority of law requires law to exclude consideration of the background moral principles on which it is based.

In a subsequent article, Raz further elaborates his version of legal positivism.[14] First, he defends the third condition above, what he calls the "sources thesis." He says the following: "A law is source-based if its existence and content can be identified by reference to social facts alone, without resort to any evaluative argument."[15]

Raz defends the "sources thesis" by reference to the features of practical authorities. A practical authority is one whose decision about what ought to be done has a certain peremptory status.[16] It is not enough that one has a reason to obey an authority—after all, one may have reasons to obey people who are not authorities. In the case of an authority, the authority's decision has a special status in the actor's process of deliberation.

Raz explains the special status of an authority's directives by describing the situation of an arbitrator. For two disputants who have turned their dispute over to an arbitrator, the arbitrator's decision is a reason for their obedience: they should do what he orders, simply because he has so ordered. But this reason is a special kind of reason; it is not just another reason that is added to the reasons they already had for doing what he says. The arbitrator's decision is supposedly based upon those other reasons and is a reflection or summing up of them. But once the arbitrator issues his decision, his decision is supposed to supplant the reasons for his decision and operate as a totally independent and "preemptive" reason for those who have submitted their dispute to him. Reasons the actor might have relied on before the arbitrator reached his decision are no longer available.[17]

Raz summarizes his discussion of practical authority by setting forth three more theses.[18] The first thesis he calls the "dependence thesis." The dependence thesis holds that authoritative rules should be based primarily on reasons for action that otherwise would apply to the subjects of the rules. The second thesis is the "normal justification thesis," which holds that the "normal and primary" reason why one person has authority over another is that the other will conform better to applicable reasons for action if he follows the authority's directives than if he refers directly to the reasons for action the directives supplant. The third thesis is the "preemption thesis," which holds, as we have already described, that authoritative directives create reasons to obey that are not simply added to relevant reasons for action, but instead supplant at least some of those reasons.

Raz goes on to discuss practical authority in legal systems, and he argues that all legal systems, as such, must claim to possess legitimate practical authority. They may not *have* legitimate practical authority; but they must *claim* such authority, and most subjects must accept the claim of authority.[19] Based on this assertion—the assertion that all law must claim authority—Raz argues that law must be "a system of a kind that is capable in principle of possessing the moral properties of authority, even if it turns out that, in fact, the legal system does not possess authority."[20]

Raz describes two properties that are essential to authority. First, an authority's directives must purport to be statements of right action, "someone's view of how its subjects ought to behave."[21] Second, subjects must be able to identify the directive "without relying on reasons or considerations [it] purports to adjudicate."[22]

These two necessary features of authority are tied to what Raz calls the "mediating role of authority."[23] The first requirement is fairly obvious and straightforward; a directive cannot have practical authority unless it presents a view of what its subjects should do.[24] To explain the second requirement, Raz again invokes the example of an arbitrator:

> Suppose that an arbitrator, asked to decide what is fair in a situation, has given a correct decision. That is, suppose there is only one fair outcome, and it was picked out by the arbitrator. Suppose further that the parties to the dispute are told only that about his decision, i.e., that the arbitrator gave the only correct decision. They will feel that they know no more what the decision is than they did before. They were given a uniquely identifying description of the decision, and yet it is an entirely unhelpful description. If they could agree on what was fair they would not have needed the arbitrator in the first place. A decision is serviceable only if it can be identified by means other than the considerations the weight and outcome of which it was meant to settle.[25]

In other words, the existence and content of any authoritative directive must depend on conditions that are separate from the underlying reasons on which it depends.[26]

Legal sources are sources that conform to the two conditions for practical authority.[27] Law's claim to authority, says Raz, supports the sources thesis: to mediate between reasons for action and people's decisions about what to do, law must purport to express the view of some person or institution about what its subjects should do. Therefore, identification of a rule as law "consists in attributing it to the relevant persons or institutions as representing their decisions and expressing their judgments. . . . Such attribution can only be based on factual considerations. Moral argument can establish what legal institutions *should* have said or *should* have held, but not what they *did* say or hold."[28]

There are strong affinities between Raz's exclusive legal positivism and our account of Lex and his rules. For Raz, law has a moral function, one that it can fulfill only if it has certain characteristics. Those characteristics become definitive of law on his account.

We argue in parallel fashion that Lex's rules have a moral function, one that they can fulfill only if they possess certain characteristics. There is at least one significant way in which we depart from Raz's analysis, however. Whereas Raz argues that the content of law must rest exclusively on social facts, we emphasize determinateness as the essential requirement for Lex's rules if they are going to serve their moral function. As we pointed out in chapter 2, some factual matters might be so difficult to resolve, because of vagueness or complexity, that rules referring to such matters might fail to settle the moral disputes they were meant to settle.[29] On the other hand, some evaluative matters might be quite determinate within the community and could usefully be referenced by Lex's rules.[30] More generally, our interest in authority derives from our concern with settlement of moral controversies, and thus our account of authority is less theoretical and more instrumental than Raz's account.

What Raz and we agree on is that authoritative norms cannot fulfill their function of settling moral controversies if they merely direct people to the very moral considerations that are in dispute. Aside, then, from some minor points of difference, exclusive legal positivism as exemplified in Raz's jurisprudence maps quite nicely onto our account of Lex and his rules. However, Raz claims that a system and its norms such as we describe are definitive of law, whereas we make no such claim.

INCLUSIVE LEGAL POSITIVISM

The inclusive legal positivist, in contradistinction to Raz and exclusive legal positivists, claims that law is only contingently rather than necessarily distinct from morality. The dispute is not over the banal point that Lex's rules might turn out to be morally nonoptimal or even morally pernicious. No one denies that. Nor is it over the equally banal point that Lex's rules might turn out to be morally superb. No one denies that either. What the exclusive legal positivist claims and the inclusive legal positivist denies is that law's content must be identifiable without invoking moral notions, or at least moral notions the application of which is controverted.[31] The inclusive legal positivist is a positivist by virtue of his position that the content of law turns at least in part on some social fact, such as the acceptance by the community of Lex's authority.[32] But the inclusive legal positivist parts company with the exclusive legal positivist by contending that law's identity and content can turn on moral considerations in addition to social facts. For the inclusive legal positivist, if the community accepts the rule "Lex's rules shall be authoritative insofar as they are consistent with morality," then the "laws" of the community are Lex's rules only insofar as they meet the moral condition. Or if the community accepts all of Lex's rules as authoritative, but Lex's rules themselves incorporate moral principles, then the "law" includes those moral principles. If Lex requires business partners to deal "fairly" with each other, moral notions of fairness are part of the law.

The exclusive legal positivist would claim that in those examples, the only "law" was that portion of the community's accepted rule that makes Lex the authority, and that Lex's rules are "law" only in the respects that they settle the moral disputes they purport to cover. The inclusive legal positivist rejoins that the exclusive legal positivist's restrictive view results in vast numbers of norms commonly referred to as "laws" being deemed "not law," included in which are many provisions of the United States Constitution and state constitutions, as well as countless statutory, administrative, and judicial promulgations.

The inclusive legal positivist, insofar as he is, as a positivist, taking a theoretical attitude toward law, may appear to have the upper hand vis-à-vis the exclusive legal positivist. After all, as he points out, countless norms that are referred to as "laws" do refer to moral concepts, many of which are quite controversial. If a theory of law is to be judged by how well it accounts for the phenomena generally associated with it, then a theory that deems, say, the Fourteenth Amendment of the United States Constitution to be every bit as much "law" as those portions of the Constitution setting forth the age requirement for the presidency or the requirement that each state have two seats in the Senate would appear to be superior to any theory that deemed the latter portions of the Constitution but not the Fourteenth Amendment to be "law."[33]

The exclusive legal positivist has a rejoinder. It is at the core of the concept of law, he will argue, that law be capable of making a practical difference.[34] A "law" that simply tells people to "do what's right" makes no practical difference. For it to do so we would have to imagine someone to whom moral obligations did not matter but who took his legal obligations quite seriously, even when he had no fear that his legal violations would be detected or punished. That is, we would have to imagine someone who could say, "I don't know why I should be just and respect others' moral rights, that is, unless you tell me that I'm legally required to do so." Or we would have to imagine someone who did not know that moral norms were obligatory until he was told that they were also his legal obligations. Here, the imaginary subject might say, "I know what morality entails, but I am not sure I should comply unless I am legally required to do so." In contrast, the normal person knows that he should do what is morally required; he needs law to help him epistemically toward that end. "Laws" that incorporate disputed moral notions cannot do this, and so cannot make the practical difference law is meant to make.[35]

Moreover, the exclusive legal positivist can give an account of why a norm like the Fourteenth Amendment is regarded as "law" without conceding to the inclusive positivist that it is law merely by virtue of its pedigree and irrespective of its content. The Fourteenth Amendment is law, according to the exclusive legal positivist, because, although it does not clarify the moral duties of state governments, its primary addressees, it does lay down a *rule* authorizing federal (and state) courts and Congress to enforce those moral obligations. It does make an important practical difference to that extent. And this account of how the Fourteenth Amendment can be "law" for the exclusive legal positivist can be extended to other legal norms that incorporate controversial moral concepts. Frequently, these norms will operate as determinate rules effecting delegations of decision-making authority to courts or administrators, thus making a practical difference.

So whereas the inclusive legal positivist assesses Lex's "rule" "Be moral" as incorporating morality into the law as an ontological matter, the exclusive legal positivist assesses it perhaps as a rule that delegates to courts or administrators the authority to settle what is morally required and to enforce that settlement. For the exclusive legal positivist, Lex's "rule" is law only to the extent that it has a practical effect, whereas for the inclusive legal positivist, law's practicality and ontology are separate matters.[36]

Natural Law versus Positivism: A Final Assessment

Let us recap the major jurisprudential positions. The natural lawyer is someone whose concerns are ultimately moral: she wants to know what she and others are obligated to do. Her question may arise in deciding whether to accept Lex or Super Lex as a practical authority. Or it may arise if she occupies the role of Lex or Super Lex (or their delegate) and wants to know what rules she should promulgate. And, of course, the question may arise in her role as a subject of Lex's rules, the topic of chapter 4. Moreover, because law purports to occupy the same territory as morality—it speaks in terms of obligations, rights, and justice—the natural lawyer concludes that her normative concerns are at the heart of what law is. For her, rules cannot be law if they do not correctly answer her questions about what to do.

The positivist is someone whose concern is theoretical, who takes an external, uncommitted point of view on others' practical commitments. Given that a society has accepted Lex and his rules as practically authoritative—regardless whether they should have done so—how does the concept of law map onto these phenomena? The inclusive legal positivist will regard the rule establishing Lex and the rules Lex promulgates under that rule as laws regardless of their content. The exclusive legal positivist would agree with the inclusive legal positivist that those rules could have morally pernicious content and yet be "laws" for all that, in opposition to the natural lawyer. On the other hand, the exclusive legal positivist would part company with the inclusive legal positivist and deny that those rules could refer to controverted moral concepts. For the exclusive legal positivist, the relation between law and morality must always be a contingent one. For the inclusive legal positivist, that relation may or may not be contingent, depending on whether the basic rule incorporates moral terms. What for the inclusive legal positivist is a matter of law's *effi-*

cacy in fulfilling its moral function, namely, its separation from and hence its epistemic improvement over disputed moral notions, is for the exclusive legal positivist a key to law's *identity*.

There are points of view on "law" other than the committed view of insiders, who accept Lex's rules as authoritative, and the detached, descriptive view of the positivists. The most notable is that of the naturalist, who focuses not on norms that claim to guide official decisions but on what officials do in fact and what causes them to act as they do.[37] The naturalist, represented in jurisprudential debates by the "legal realists," may find that factors other than Lex and his rules best explain and predict the behavior of various actors. Yet even the naturalist, if she wishes to say something about "law" and "judges," will at some point need to pick out these phenomena by recourse to the concepts provided by the positivists.[38]

Other points of view—for example, that of a citizen seeking advice on how to comply with law, that of a schemer wishing to avoid legal sanctions, or that of a law professor attempting to describe the "law"—ultimately must assume one or another of the basic jurisprudential stances. Some directly assume the internal, committed position. Some take the postivist's perspective, which is parasitic on the internal point of view. Some assume the naturalist's predictive position, which is parasitic on positivism for an account of "law," and thereby parasitic as well on the internal point of view.

We ultimately take no position on either the natural law–positivism debate or the debate between exclusive and inclusive legal positivism. With respect to the latter, whether a moralized standard promulgated by Lex is a practically inefficacious "law" or no law at all, or whether moral limitations can be part of the basic rule for what counts as "law," are for us ultimately terminological matters on which nothing of jurisprudential importance turns.

With respect to the larger debate, we do not see natural law and positivism as antithetical theories of law but as different perspectives on the problems of law. The natural lawyer, as natural lawyer, displays a practical attitude toward Lex and his rules, whereas the positivist, as positivist, displays a theoretical attitude toward them. More accurately, the positivist displays a theoretical attitude toward others'—and possibly his own—practical attitudes. Both the positivist and the natural lawyer are affected by the dilemma of chapter 4—the dilemma of morally imperfect rules as means to moral ends; the natural lawyer faces that dilemma directly, while the positivist faces it indirectly, as a problem in practical attitudes toward legal rules.

Thus, if the positivist and natural lawyer share the same moral and empirical beliefs, they will answer any practical question concerning "law" the same way. And if they share the same terminology, they will answer any theoretical question concerning "law" the same way. The positivists' theoretical attitude is dependent upon the natural lawyers' practical attitude in the sense that the former is "about" the latter. But that does not mean the natural law position in legal theory is superior to the positivist position. They are not two opposed positions about the same thing but complementary positions about different aspects of the same thing.

Once the difference between the practical and theoretical perspectives is exposed, nothing further turns on whether Lex's rules or the rule establishing Lex are "laws" properly so called if one concludes they diverge from what is morally proper. Of course, those who accept Lex as authoritative will believe that their acceptance of Lex and his rules is morally warranted, and for them, Lex's rules will be law. Whether the jurisprude who disagrees morally with their acceptance of Lex should join the natural lawyer and deny that Lex's rules are law, or should join the positivists and deny only that Lex's laws are morally binding, is in the end unimportant, so long as terminological clarity and consistency are preserved.

It may be helpful to end this discussion of the natural law–positivism debate by focusing on some recent examples of it. M. J. Detmold is a modern natural lawyer in that he argues for the primacy of the practical point of view regarding legal statements.[39] When someone says "X is the law" in a practical context—a context in which the utterer is attempting to influence conduct—then, according to Detmold, he is asserting the moral bindingness of X.[40] When the positivist from his theoretical perspective makes the same statement, it translates into "X is regarded by people in the society in question as morally binding."[41] Obviously, the positivist's perspective depends upon there being someone who takes the practical perspective and regards X as morally binding, hence making the natural law position primary and the positivist position secondary and derivative.

Detmold is not a natural lawyer who simply equates law with

morality. Rather, he is a natural lawyer who makes moral bindingness a necessary but not sufficient condition for law's existence. For a norm to be legal it must also be valid under the society's "rule of recognition"—the basic social rule that serves as a test of the validity of all other rules within the system. (In our scheme, the analogue to the rule of recognition is the rule "Let Lex decide.")

According to Detmold, the existence of a legal system depends on two assumptions made by those who act within the system. Those who assert that a rule identified by the rule of recognition as law should be obeyed are assuming, first, that the rule of recognition is morally binding, and second, that the audience of the assertion also accepts the rule of recognition as binding. A legal system, says Detmold, is an "ongoing conversation constituted by" these two assumptions. When either assumption is missing, there is no law, and officials of the system are no different from a gang of robbers, who exercise coercive power without legitimate authority. It is still possible to assert that the rules of the system should be obeyed, but the assertion is now an external statement. Even a gang of robbers might issue orders that ought to be obeyed for moral reasons, but the reasons would not be that the gang of robbers constituted a legitimate authority. The reasons would have to be something like, "If we abide by their commands, lives will be saved and other morally good things will be accomplished." According to Detmold, the external statement, that one *ought* to obey the rule of recognition and the rules valid under it, is not itself a legal statement. Only when the rule of recognition and rules under it are accepted internally is the statement that one ought to obey a statement of law.[42]

Detmold's otherwise clear distinction between internal and external statements begins to collapse in light of our analysis in chapters 3 and 4. In chapter 3 we pointed out that the basic rule establishing a practical authority may be accepted by everyone, not because it is anyone's ideal moral rule, but because it is from everyone's perspective the morally best rule establishing a practical authority that everyone can accept and that is morally preferable to the absence of practical authority.[43] Moreover, the rules promulgated by Lex under the basic rule may be less than morally ideal, and even morally ideal rules will have morally problematic applications (this is the dilemma of chapter 4). Is that rule then accepted internally as morally binding in Detmold's sense, or is it accepted only externally, as might be the commands of a gang of robbers? Those who are clearheaded about the predicament will accept the basic rule in a way that effaces Detmold's neat distinction.

Ronald Dworkin, although not a pure natural lawyer,[44] is, like Detmold, a critic of positivism. Dworkin criticizes H. L. A. Hart's position in *The Concept of Law* on the source of a judge's duty to enforce Lex's rules. Hart says the source of judicial obligation is the rule of recognition (the analogue of our basic rule, "Let Lex decide").[45] For Hart, this basic rule is a convention, a norm that exists by virtue of its acceptance.[46]

Dworkin, however, asserts that the basic rule must be an example of concurrent rather than conventional morality.[47] As Dworkin puts it,

> A community displays a concurrent morality when its members are agreed in asserting the same, or much the same, normative morality, but they do not count the fact of that agreement as an essential part of their grounds for asserting that rule. It displays a conventional morality when they do. If . . . churchgoers believe that each man has a duty to take off his hat in church, but would not have such a duty but for some social practice to that general effect, then this is a case of conventional morality. If they also believe that each man has a duty not to lie, and would have this duty even if most other men did, then this would be a case of concurrent morality.[48]

If the basic rule is only a matter of convention, then disagreement about its meaning would be impossible. For if there is disagreement, there is, to that extent, no convention. Dworkin maintains that there can be and frequently is disagreement about judicial duties, an impossibility on the view that the basic legal rule is a matter of convention.[49] Dworkin argues, moreover, that the mere practice of judges following Lex does not *justify* their doing so; yet judges do believe that they are justified in following Lex and therefore must base that belief on reasons beyond the mere existence of the convention.[50]

Hart is a positivist, and Dworkin is attempting to undermine positivism by attacking Hart's claim that law consists of a hierarchical system of conventional rules. Dworkin's intention is to show that law must at bottom rest on moral reasons rather than conventional rules. But Dworkin's attack can be parried by recalling our account in chapter 3. There we pointed out that each member of society could accept the same basic rule—"Let Lex decide"—even though some believed some other rule would be morally preferable, if each believed that "Let Lex decide" was the morally best rule that everyone would accept, and that having that rule accepted by everyone was morally preferable to not having any rule accepted by everyone.[51] In essence, "Let Lex decide" is a purely conventional rule that constitutes the source of legal duties, but it itself is, in Dworkinian terms, the product of concurrent moral reasons.[52]

Moreover, as we also pointed out, if disagreement breaks out over the content of the basic rule, then to that extent no basic rule can exist. All argument at that point would be over what the basic rule should be and not over what it is. Nevertheless, the moral impetus to have some basic rule for authoritative settlement of moral disputes will frequently bring about agreement fixing a new convention.[53] (In the United States, with over a quarter billion people and a complex and contentious constitutional practice, most people accept as part of the basic rule "Whatever the Supreme Court, by majority vote, in good faith decides, the Constitution means"; only the Supreme Court itself requires some different basic rule.)[54]

Now Dworkin wants to say that because the basic rule itself is justified by moral reasons, and because moral reasons must be resorted to whenever conventions are disputed (and hence cannot be conventions), the boundary between "law" and "morality" is effaced. But neither Hart nor any other positivist need agree with this conclusion. If the positivist wishes to restrict the concept of law to rules accepted by the community or posited by authorities constituted by accepted rules, the fact that such rules are meant to serve moral ends and are truly justified only insofar as they do so does not undermine the positivists' theoretical, detached account.

Moreover, the positivist can explain how it is that people can claim to be disagreeing about "the law." Dworkin cites such disagreements as evidence that law cannot be conventional.[55] Disagreements about what Lex's rules require are no problem for the positivists. Lex's rules may give rise to interpretive difficulties of the sort we explored in chapter 5.[56] Or Lex may have posited unhelpful standards. With respect to these, inclusive legal positivists will claim that disagreements about their content will be legal disagreements, while exclusive legal positivists will maintain that the disagreements are moral rather than legal. Disagreements about the basic rule will ordinarily have to be relegated by all positivists to the moral column rather than the legal column.

Dworkin anticipates this move and ridicules it: "I hope no one will want to say that in this sort of case [disagreements over the basic rule] judges are disagreeing about their political or moral duty as judges, but not about their legal duty. The only ground for this distinction is one which . . . plainly begs the question."[57] We do not find Dworkin's response to be telling, however, because he too is begging the question. A positivist can respond to Dworkin by pointing out that law can be a means to a moral end without being reducible to morality. Indeed, claims the positivist—or at least the exclusive legal positivist—law can only serve its moral end if it is *not* reducible to morality. Dworkin, taking the natural lawyer's committed stance, is focused on the moral ends. The positivist, taking the theoretical, detached stance, is focused on the nonmoral means. For the former, whether the moral ends *are* being served is paramount. For the latter, what matters is whether members of a society have systems of authoritative guidance to settle what ought to be done, whether or not the settlements effected are morally correct or should be accepted as authoritative.

It is thus permissible for positivists like Hart to emphasize the conventionality of the legal system's basic rule and to claim that disagreements about its content, being inconsistent with the existence of a convention, must be moral and not legal disagreements. And it is likewise permissible for Dworkin to point to the moral reasons that justify the basic rule. Here, as elsewhere, the natural lawyer and the positivist are not disagreeing, once different stances (practical, committed versus theoretical, detached) and different terminologies are taken into account.

Roger Shiner's account of the debate between natural lawyers and positivists is akin to ours in that he sees a place for both in legal theory.

Shiner rejects the "compatibilist" view that natural law and positivism can be combined within a single theory of law, but proposes a "dynamic" view of law in which natural law and positivism interact with each other dialectally.[58]

> Positivism is the prime theory of those aspects of a legal system in virtue of which it is the repository of certainty and procedure. Anti-positivism [natural law] is the prime theory of those aspects of a legal system in virtue of which it is the repository of flexibility and substance. The good legal theorist, therefore, is the one who is able to keep the right balance between the claims of the theory of certainty and procedure, and the claims of the theory of flexibility and substance. The balance between certainty and procedure at the level of actual legal practice is achievable only in history as a continuous process of adjustment. The legal system in operation moves dialectically between the pole of certainty/procedure and the pole of flexibility/substance. This salient and crucial fact about law can be perspicuously represented only in a theory of law which represents law as thus in dialectical motion. Such a theory, however, will not be a theory of law of the conventional kind. It can only be a meta-theory of legal theories, which shows how legal theory itself is similarly in a constant process of movement and adjustment between theories which glorify certainty/procedure and theories which glorify flexibility/substance.[59]

We believe, however, that "dialectical" misdescribes the relationship between positivism and natural law. Instead, we view positivism and natural law as responding, from different angles, to the tension between rules and the moral reasons that motivate them. Within the committed, natural law, perspective, there is a relationship between rules and background moral reasons that is best described as dilemmatic rather than dialectical. Those who accept Lex and his rules as practical authorities do so for moral reasons, yet those reasons often conflict with the rules.[60] Meanwhile, the positivist observes the rules from a detached perspective, but this perspective is dependent on at least some people taking the committed perspective on Lex and his rules. Thus, the relationship between positivism and natural law is again not a dialectical one, any more than the relationship between an anthropologist and the native practices she investigates is dialectical. Both positions reflect and are affected by the unavoidable conflict between rules and reasons.[61]

Lex and His Rules as an Account of Law

To this point, we have been careful to avoid taking a stand in the debate between positivists and natural lawyers about the nature of law. We believe an account of Lex and his rules provides a useful prism through which to view that debate; however, a claim about the identity of "law" is not necessary to our analysis, which concerns the manner in which law can bring about settlement of moral controversies.

We could, however, recast the points we have made in previous chapters as a theory of "law." We could maintain that authoritative settlement is the essential function of law, and that our account of Lex and his rules is an account of the nature of law.[62] Where might such a claim place us on the jurisprudential map? Practically speaking, it would bring us very close to such exclusive legal positivists as Joseph Raz, with his emphasis on law's claim to *authority,*[63] Frederick Schauer, with his emphasis on *rules,*[64] and Thomas Campbell, with his emphasis on the *moral function of settlement.*[65] And it would place us in one line of descent from the major positivist forebears Austin,[66] Kelsen,[67] and Hart.[68]

For the balance of this chapter, we shall tentatively drop our position of jurisprudential agnosticism and declare ourselves positivists who believe that the basic rules establishing Lex's authority and the rules Lex issues comprise "law." On that assumption—which remains tentative—we shall first address the question of methodology and then return briefly to the debate between internal and external positivists.

METHODOLOGY: DESCRIPTIVE JURISPRUDENCE

As positivists, we would present a descriptive rather than a normative jurisprudence; that is, our methodology would entail an external view of others' internal, normative commitments. In our role as theorists, we would bracket our own acceptance or nonacceptance of Lex and his rules as authoritative and merely point out that for those who did so accept Lex and his rules, Lex and his rules would constitute a legal system. Of course, there would be no "law" for us to consider unless some people accepted Lex and his rules as authoritative. Thus, in one sense, the internal, committed view would have jurisprudential primacy. However, our jurisprudence itself would remain detached and uncommitted with respect to any particular Lex and his rules.

Recently some have issued a challenge to the positivist of the following sort: The positivist's detached point of view on Lex and his rules cannot ultimately be maintained because it cannot be disengaged from the normative questions faced by the insider. Not only is the insider's point of view primary in the way we have already conceded, namely, that it must be presupposed in the positivist's account of law. It is also primary in the sense that it must be fully engaged by the positivist, thus bringing the positivist inside the normative enterprise and undermining his detached observer's stance.

Consider, for example, the following passage by Stephen Perry:

> A philosophically satisfactory analysis of the concept of legal authority, and hence a philosophically satisfactory analysis of the concept of law that takes the law's claim to authority seriously . . . must be offered from the internal point of view. Such a theory will try to make sense of law to *us*—that is, to those who engage in or are subject to law—by offering an account of whether and how the law's claim to authority over us might be justified. It will do this by attributing a point or function to law and showing how law's serving that function either does give us, or could under certain conditions give us, reasons for action of a specified type. In specifying one type of reason for action over another the theory will attempt to refine our initial, rough, and partially unclear conceptualization of our own practice. In Hart's terms, "the framework of legal thought" will thereby be clarified or elucidated. It is only in this way—looking at the practice from the participants' point of view, and employing normative argument—that conceptual clarification can take place.[69]

Perry concludes this particular article with this statement about jurisprudential debates:

> Deciding among . . . various [jurisprudential] theories is not just a matter of determining which succeeds in better describing a pre-

existing but partially implicit conceptualization of a social practice. There is no such conceptualization that . . . can simply be described. This is philosophically contested ground, and the disagreement must ultimately be settled by moral and political argument intended to show which theory makes the best moral sense of the social practice we call law. In this way legal theory inevitably incorporates political philosophy.[70]

Gerald Postema has made a similar and perhaps even stronger claim than Perry's:

> The recognition of a practice as normative arises from observation of a people engaging in a living, functional practice, not of participants' *beliefs about it.* The practical normative character of familiar practices will be immediately apparent to us. . . . Surely the natural way for inquiries about such practices to proceed is in the language and framework of practical inquiry. What reason do I, or they, have to do this or that? Of course, if the practice is unfamiliar, one may have no choice but to seek the help of participants, if one wants to understand it. But even in this case, the route to understanding is surely not . . . to simulate the reasoning of participants, for that reasoning is not likely to be available. Rather, one must learn how to participate in the practice. With the help of native participants one learns *the practice* first of all, not what they *believe* about it.

It is true that law exists only insofar as it is in force or practiced in a community, that is, only insofar as it takes shape in and guides the behavior of (a substantial number of) members of that community. We can conclude from this that we can fully understand law only if we can explain how it figures in the practical reasoning of participants. It might be thought that it follows from this that any explanation of the normative character of law can only be in terms of the beliefs and attitudes of participants. This argument, however, does not show that hermeneutic observer theory provides the only appropriate methodology for philosophical jurisprudence. On the contrary, because explanations of how legal norms figure in practical reasoning of participants presuppose an account of the norms as action-guiding reasons, these explanations presuppose, rather than supplant, a practical inquiry into legal norms.

> . . . Law and other similar social practices present those who encounter them, whether in practice or in thought, with meaningful, rule-governed behavior. If we are sensitive to the cues we can recognize that such practices claim to give guiding reasons to those who fall within their jurisdiction. If we seek to understand this claim we must address the practical issues and questions it poses. The natural form of inquiry is practical, not theoretical, but it is practical with regard to the practice we have encountered, and not some ideal according to which we would like to invent a practice. It is natural because it poses the following question: In virtue of what is this practice's claim to offer reasons for action plausible, warranted, true?[71]

The position taken by Perry and Postema is much too strong if it is meant to collapse the positivist's detached stance into the participant's committed stance. We concede (although some do not)[72] that positivists must pick out some value that it is law's primary function to serve, in order to give shape to an account of law and legal systems. For Raz[73] and Shapiro,[74] that value is rule guidance; for Schauer[75] and us,[76] it is authoritative settlement. There is a normative aspect to the selection of a function of law to be given theoretical primacy. Nonetheless, attributing a moral function to law does not collapse the distinction between the positivist's detached, descriptive jurisprudence and the natural lawyer's internal, committed jurisprudence.[77] The normativity involved in selecting a function to be given theoretical primacy in a jurisprudential theory is not moral but invokes norms of adequacy in concept explication.[78]

A second point at which positivism might be thought to take a normative turn is in showing how insiders can assume a committed attitude toward law. Can the positivist make intelligible that people can accept Lex and his rules as authoritative settlements of moral controversies without himself morally endorsing Lex and his rules? This appears to be the problem that Perry and Postema have in mind.

We agree with Joseph Raz that although any explanation of law must make it intelligible that subjects can regard their law as morally good, it is not necessary to assume or show that the subjects' beliefs are correct—that the law they accept *is* good.[79] Of course, as Raz goes on to say, "one's view of morality colors what one finds morally intelligible."[80] One's own morality may limit what can be intelligible, but morality and intelligibility are not coextensive. Therefore, the distinction between the positivist's stance and that of the natural lawyer does not collapse.

Consider our account of Lex and his rules, taken as an account of the nature of law. We do assume certain things about the nature of morality, namely, that it consists of principles that may be controversial in content and application, that it can conceivably be realized better through authoritative rules of settlement than without such rules,[81] and that human beings can be motivated to comply with its principles. Surely these minimal assumptions about morality and human nature do not embroil us in substantive moral disputes. Yet armed only with these assumptions, we can make intelligible the proposition that people would accept Lex and his rules, without ourselves endorsing any set of rules. First, we, as detached observers, can understand that insiders could accept imperfect rules for moral reasons. As we have demonstrated, there may be moral reasons to accept a rule with morally nonideal applications; there may be moral reasons to accept morally nonideal rules if they are "applications" of an ideal higher-level rule (such as "Let Lex decide"); and there may be moral reasons to accept a non-ideal basic rule if it is the morally best basic rule that others will also accept and is morally superior to the absence of authority. In all these cases, we—the detached observers—may be unable to suspend rationality in a way that permits us to accept the nonideal applications of any rules, no matter how ideal. Yet even if we cannot do so, we can recognize the moral reasons for doing so, and this makes the committed attitude of insiders intelligible. Second, we, as detached observers, can understand that others make moral errors. Even if we disagree that there are good moral reasons for accepting a particular basic rule or set of rules, it is surely intelligible that others would accept it if they believed, incorrectly, that there were no morally superior alternatives and thus that the rules were morally justified in one of the senses mentioned above.

In chapter 4, we raised the question whether following serious rules as serious rules can ever be fully rational, and suggested that it cannot.[82] The fact that there are moral reasons for adopting morally nonideal rules does not make it rational to accept their nonideal applications in particular cases. This may prevent the theorist, as theorist, from taking a committed view of Lex and his rules. Yet it does not undermine the *intelligibility* of others' acceptance of and obedience to the rules. Rationality and intelligibility are separate phenomena. And given that it can be quite rational to render oneself or others irrational, it perforce must be intelligible.[83]

We believe, therefore, that a positivist, detached jurisprudence is possible, and that our account of Lex and his rules, if taken as such a jurisprudence, does not collapse into the committed insiders' normative debates about what should be done. To make law intelligible, jurisprudence need not make law as morally attractive as it can be, any more than a descriptive sociology of Nazism must make its subject the best it can be.[84]

INCLUSIVE AND EXCLUSIVE POSITIVISM REVISITED

If we take our account of Lex and his rules to be an account of "law," we find not only that our methodology is parallel to that of the legal positivists but that our conclusions about effective law have a close affinity to the conclusions of legal positivists about the identity of law. However, our conclusions do not perfectly track either the inclusive or the exclusive positivist position on what should count as law.

Central to our account is a moral purpose served by Lex's rules—the settlement function set forth in chapter 1. Our account also shows that members of a society can accept the basic rule establishing Lex and his rules as authoritative for background moral reasons though none of them considers it morally ideal. In other words, it may be for everyone the best rule that all will accept and preferable to no rule at all, and still be a serious rule that is overinclusive and underinclusive with respect to each person's background moral reasons.[85] Thus, from within the committed stance—the perspective of those who accept Lex and his rules as authorities—Lex's rules serve moral purposes, although from the detached perspective of those who reject or for theoretical purposes bracket off Lex's authority, there may appear to be no reason to endorse these particular rules.

The moral function of settlement is served by rules that refer to facts rather than values, for normally facts will be more determinate—less controversial—than values. We do not reject inclusive positivism, but we note that inclusion of *controversial* moral norms within legal rules to that extent deprives the rules of their raison d'être, their ability to settle moral controversies. For us, however, nothing turns on whether such moral norms are deemed "law."

At the same time, because we are interested primarily in settlement rather than the concept of "authority," efficacy matters more to us than to Raz.[86] Thus, we say that facts "normally" are more determinate, to emphasize again that some questions of value may be quite settled in the community, and some questions of fact may be quite unsettled. On our account, the desideratum for rules is capacity to settle controverted matters, not facticity for its own sake.[87] If a moral predicate is uncontroversial within a community but a factual predicate is highly controversial, then a rule that incorporates the former can more easily perform the settlement function than one that incorporates the latter. So we do not reject inclusive legal positivism on Razian grounds.[88]

With these points in mind, consider the following hypothetical basic rules:

1. Do what Lex decides ought to be done unless it is morally wrong.
2. Do what Lex decides ought to be done unless it is egregiously morally wrong.
3. Do what Lex decides ought to be done unless it violates moral principle P.
    a. The meaning of P is settled.
    b. The meaning of P is controversial, but P does not implicate the whole of morality, and the boundary of P is settled.
    c. The meaning of P is controversial, P does not implicate the whole of morality, but the boundary of P is controversial.
    d. The meaning of P is controversial, and P implicates the whole of morality.
4. Do what Lex decides ought to be done unless the weight in angstroms of the ink used in the statute books is the square of a prime number.

The exclusive legal positivist would accept only (4) as wholly "law." The inclusive legal positivist would accept all of these basic rules as "law." From our perspective, (1), (3)(c), (3)(d), and (4) are completely ineffective in settling what ought to be done. (3)(a), however, produces complete settlement. And the other possible basic rules will settle some controversies and fail to settle others. Therefore, if one places the settlement function at the core of the concept of "law," then some of the inclusive legal positivist's "laws"—(1), (3)(c), and (3)(d)—would not identify laws, and neither would the exclusive legal positivist's (4). Rules promulgated under the other basic rules would be more or less "laws."

TEN Lex, Rules, and Some Miscellaneous Problems of Jurisprudence

In the last chapter, we took up the debate between positivists and natural lawyers. Although we did not take a firm position on the nature of law, we suggested that our account of Lex and his rules can help to clarify the debate. In this chapter we explore the connections between our account of Lex's rules and some other stock issues of jurisprudence: the effect of revolution, conquest, and loss of general obedience on legal systems; the obligation to obey the law; the relation between law and coercion; and the objectivity and determinateness of law.

Lex and Pathological Legal Systems

Can two or more legal systems exist within a given territory, each claiming exclusive authority to settle what ought to be done? What should we say about an amendment to a community's basic legal rule that does not comply with that rule's specified amendment procedures but is nonetheless accepted by the community? And how efficacious must a legal system be, and in what sense, in order to be a legal system properly so called?

Conquest, dissent, revolution, and widespread disobedience raise basic jurisprudential questions regarding the existence and identity of legal systems. We believe that our account of Lex and his rules—and particularly our discussion in chapter 3—if taken as an account of "law," can shed light on these matters.

CONQUEST AND DISSENT

Suppose Lex's community is conquered by Tex. Immediately following the conquest, attitudes toward Tex and Lex are mixed. Tex is accepted as the legitimate authority by his occupying army and his puppet officials. Most of the original community, however, continues to look to Lex and his rules and to regard them, and not Tex and his rules, as authoritatively settling what ought to be done. These members of the community might generally comply with Tex's rules for various reasons, including because Lex's rules so dictate, but they do not regard Tex's rules as authoritative. The question then is, is it Tex and Tex's rules or Lex and Lex's rules that is *the* legal system, or are there two legal systems within the territory?

We see no reason not to say that there are two legal systems, and that it is theoretically possible for there to be many legal systems within a territory, each claiming to govern the entire population. As we pointed out in chapter 3,[1] there will be powerful reasons to agree on a single authoritative system, even if it is far from ideal from anyone's perspective. And if one "Lex" has more coercive power than competing Lexes, there will be good reasons for those who follow the latter to treat the former's rules as though they regarded those rules as authoritative. These two sets of reasons will go far toward securing general coordination of conduct even in pathological situations such as that of hostile occupation. And the more Tex succeeds in coordinating conduct, the greater the reasons to follow his rules will be. Thus, unless he is quite iniquitous, Tex may come to be accepted as the authority by the occupied population.

The same point just made about conquest applies more generally to dissenters within a legal system. Alexander and Sherwin may believe that their constitution of the United States, one that they have drafted in light of the best moral theory and social science, is quite superior in every way to the antiquated document in the National Archives. They may even choose to recognize their constitution, and laws passed in pursuance thereof, as authoritative for the United States. From a positivist's detached perspective, then, there will be two legal systems operating in the United States. But notice that the moral values attached to authoritative settlement will incline Alexander and Sherwin both to comply with the laws passed under the 1787 document and ultimately to accept its authority and abandon their constitution.

Thus, we are content to say that in situations of transition or dissent, more than one legal system can be in effect. Most theorists find such a position unsatisfactory, either because they take it as axiomatic that only one legal system can exist in a given territory, or because they prefer, for pragmatic reasons, to recognize just one system. For we are accustomed to speaking of *the* law of France and *the* law of South Carolina, and it is understandable why one would expect a sound jurisprudential theory to vindicate that usage.

The alternatives to our position, however, have serious problems of their own. In cases of divided loyalty or dissent, the percentage of the population that accepts Lex as authoritative and the level of obedience to his rules will be matters of degree. Those who insist that there can be only one legal system in effect must therefore either deem Lex and his rules to be a legal system only if Lex's acceptance and the level of obedience to his rules meet a stipulated threshold, or they must deem Lex and his rules to be a legal system only to a certain degree. The first of these is unsatisfactory because the choice of threshold must be arbitrary. The second possibility—that legal systems have degrees of existence—is surely as unpalatable as our position that conceivably many legal systems can coexist in a single territory. We see no other possibilities.

REVOLUTIONARY CHANGE

The case of revolutionary constitutional change is an easy one, we believe, although perhaps disturbing. Suppose the basic rule declares that Lex may not prohibit any speech because of its content. Suppose further that the basic rule specifies the procedure by which it can be amended. Finally, suppose that Lex promulgates a rule proscribing speech that is disrespectful of racial minorities, and that the officials and citizens accept this rule as authoritative, even though it contravenes the free speech rule and was not promulgated in accordance with the amendment procedures.

We believe it is correct to characterize these events as having effected a revolutionary constitutional change. One basic rule has been replaced by another. And because the second was not "adopted" in pursuance of the terms of the first, the replacement of the first by the second represents a revolutionary break with the first, no matter how peaceful and even unnoticed this revolution was.

Revolutionary changes of legal systems such as the one described may be occurring all the time.[2] The existence of the basic rule of authority depends from moment to moment on its acceptance as such. If we were to all awake tomorrow morning no longer accepting the Constitution in the National Archives as the fundamental law of the United States, it would no longer be so, despite its bootstrapping declaration to the contrary.[3] Its status would fall to beneath that of the aforementioned Alexander/Sherwin constitution, which would at least have two adherents.

If such utter contingency of all legal systems seems to render them evanescent and deprive them of the hardiness we want them to possess, we should remember several points. First, as we pointed out in chapter 3, there will be powerful reasons for people of divergent moral views to accept a basic authority-conferring rule that is from no one's perspective an ideal one.[4] Again, so long as the basic rule all can accept is, from each person's point of view, the best such rule all can accept and preferable to the absence of any basic rule, each will have an on-balance moral reason to accept it.

Further, as we pointed out in chapter 4, acceptance of the basic rule means acceptance of particular applications of that rule, even when they are less than morally ideal.[5] The moral reasons that support acceptance of the basic rule support accepting it as a *serious rule.* Any inclination to reject the basic rule's applications but not the rule itself is simply inconsistent with acceptance of the basic rule as a rule.

The moral benefits of accepting a basic rule will give the basic rule a certain durability. In addition, as we pointed out in chapter 7, frequent overturning of rules undermines the stability and predictability that are part of the raison d'être of serious rules.[6] Therefore, even if all agree that a new basic rule would be slightly better than the present one, it does not follow that they should agree to replacing the latter with the former.

These points go a long way toward establishing the solidity and durability of a community's basic rule, notwithstanding the radical contingency of a basic rule's existence. Even if a basic rule exists only so long as it is accepted, there will be reasons to expect continuity of acceptance of basic rules that are perceived to be morally adequate, even if not morally ideal.

LOSS OF EFFICACY

Suppose that Lex's rules are widely disobeyed. Perhaps some disobey the rules because they do not accept Lex as the authority for what they ought to do; perhaps they accept Rex, or perhaps they accept no one, despite the moral reasons that should incline them to accept a single authority within their community. Or perhaps they disobey Lex, not so much because they do not accept Lex as the moral authority, but because they are not motivated to do what they morally ought to do and the threat of sanctions does not alter their behavior. If this combination of dissenters and miscreants results in widespread disobedience because Lex and his adherents are not sufficiently powerful to coerce the miscreants and dissenters into obedience, can Lex and his rules still be deemed a legal system?

Our response to loss of efficacy is the same as our response to the problems of conquest and dissent. Lex and his rules constitute a legal system for those who accept his authority, even if that means there are other and perhaps many legal systems within the same territory.[7] The only alternatives are an arbitrary threshold requirement or the disconcerting notion that the one true legal system is only a legal system to some partial degree.

H. L. A. Hart's jurisprudence is quite instructive here. For Hart, a legal system exists if officials internally accept a basic authoritative rule and the rules it authorizes, and if the rest of the citizenry generally obey the authorized rules.[8] But the line between officials and citizens will not bear the weight that Hart places on it. For example, what if an all-powerful despot, Lex, is the only person who accepts his own authority, and his "officials" enforce his rules out of fear of Lex personally? Moreover, obedience by "citizens" will never be total—if we are trying to be realistic and accept ordinary usages regarding what is "law" and a "legal system."

Moreover, one of the points we made in chapter 4 was that, in a community of morally motivated people, sanctions are not a reliable means for bringing about obedience to law. Actors who believe that they ought not obey Lex's rules in a particular case will expect judges to be reluctant to punish their disobedience, and may even be willing to accept punishment rather than follow a rule when they believe they ought not. If this is correct, then it is important that citizens, as well as officials, accept the authority of Lex and his rules. Thus, in the absence of full acceptance of Lex's authority by officials, and probably by citizens as well, Hart would either have to say that legal systems have degrees of existence, or else stipulate an arbitrary level of citizen compliance as the necessary threshold for a system of rules to be a legal system.

The Obligation to Obey the Law

One of the perennial topics of jurisprudence is whether, and under what conditions, there exists an obligation to obey the law. We believe that our analysis explains the controversy.

Natural lawyers who identify "law" with what we are morally obligated to do will, of course, deem it true by definition that there is an obligation to obey the law. Other, "weak" natural lawyers accept positivistic criteria for identifying law and then add to the equation a moral principle that one should obey "law," positivistically defined, if it is "sufficiently just" and perhaps democratically enacted.[9] These hybrid natural lawyers affirm the obligation to obey the law, but only as a prima facie obligation.

Positivists generally deny any obligation to obey the law, even a prima facie one.[10] Given the positivist's detached point of view, this position is what one would expect. After all, a legal system might be quite morally invidious, even if the insiders, from their committed perspective, view it otherwise.[11]

We believe that our discussion in chapters 3 and 4 illuminates this issue. First, for those who do not accept the authority of Lex and his rules, even given the strong moral reasons to accept an authority, Lex's rules will not be morally obligatory, at least from their perspective. The positivists are surely correct to that extent.

More important, however, as we emphasized at length in chapter 4, even for those who accept Lex as authoritative, there remains a question about the obligation to obey. For in that chapter, we illustrated the dilemma faced by those subject to Lex's rules whether to obey the rules in all circumstances—as the rules demand—or to disobey them whenever disobedience is morally preferable. The latter position is inconsistent with having serious rules, and having such rules seems required by morality. But the former position looks to be inconsistent with acting morally. Thus, the dilemma of rules.

It is that dilemma which we believe the controversy over the obligation to obey the law reflects. We appear to have a moral obligation to have serious rules. And yet serious rules, even morally ideal ones,[12] appear to contravene morality in some of their applications. We believe that nothing more can or need be said on the putative obligation to obey the law than we have said in chapter 4, other than to repudiate the dilemma of rules as we have portrayed it or to solve it.

Law and Coercion

It may seem strange that in all of our discussion of the nature of law in this and the preceding chapters, we have paid almost no attention to the relation between law and coercion. For to many, law's essential function is to coerce those who would otherwise breach their moral duties into compliance with those duties. Law is the Hobbesian sovereign, whose coercive power is what rescues its subjects from their nasty, brutish, and short life in the lawless state of nature.

We have acknowledged that Lex's efficacy in coercing miscreants will be a factor in deciding whether to accept Lex as the authority regarding what ought to be done. Beyond that, however, our tack has been diametrically opposite from the Hobbesian picture of law's function. We have assumed a community of morally motivated people whose problem is that they are uncertain or disagree about what morality dictates in a host of concrete cases. Uncertainty and disagreement generate the moral costs of lack of coordination, lack of expertise, and inefficiency. Rules both constituting and promulgated by authorities can reduce or eliminate these moral costs if they are more determinate for members of the community than the moral principles the applications of which they are meant to resolve. Law as determinate rules is a solution to the problem of the limits of moral knowledge.

To see why it is lack of information, not immoral motivation, that gives rise to the need for law as determinate rules, imagine a different hypothetical community. In this one, everyone *can* apply moral principles unerringly in concrete cases. Its problem is that some members are not motivated to comply with those moral principles.

In this community, there would be no need for posited norms. Morality would be self-sufficient. For if some members violated their moral obligations, morality itself would instruct the remaining members how they should investigate, try, and punish the offenders. Remember, everyone can apply the moral principles correctly in concrete cases. And there is no reason that morality does not extend beyond its first-order requirements and speak to how to treat miscreants. Instead, moral theory regarding crime and punishment, and moral theory regarding adjudication, are just such aspects of moral theory generally.[13]

Thus, if people were gods—morally omniscient—but not angels, morality would be an adequate guide to behavior and posited norms would be unnecessary. If, however, people were angels but not gods, then posited norms in the form of determinate rules would be necessary to implement morality. Law as determinate rules is a solution to a cognitive, not a motivational, problem.[14]

The Objectivity and Determinateness of Law

A final pair of jurisprudential issues that we believe can be illuminated by our project are whether propositions of law are "objective" and whether they are "determinate." We shall take up the questions of objectivity and determinateness in turn.

Recent analysis by Jules Coleman and Brian Leiter is useful in framing the problems of objectivity and determinacy. In Coleman and Leiter's taxonomy, a proposition is *subjective* if its truth is fixed by the beliefs of a particular person.[15] Thus, if X says "Chocolate ice cream tastes good," the truth of that proposition depends entirely on X's believing it. There is no deeper truth of the matter of how ice cream tastes than how it tastes to particular people.

A proposition is "objective" if its truth is independent of beliefs about it.[16] Coleman and Leiter distinguish three degrees of objectivity from each other and from subjectivity. A proposition is *minimally objective* if its truth is fixed by the beliefs of a community.[17] Fashion is a good example. Propositions about what is fashionable depend for their truth on the beliefs of a particular community. Thus, any one person may be mistaken in believing that something is or is not fashionable—which distinguishes fashion from the taste of ice cream—but the entire community cannot be.[18] Whenever a discourse refers to conventions, whether they be the conventions of fashion or, more important for law, the conventions of language, that discourse is minimally objective in Coleman and Leiter's terms.

In contrast, a proposition is *strongly objective* if its truth is independent of anyone's beliefs.[19] Propositions about the height of Mount Everest or the volume of the Atlantic Ocean are strongly objective. Propositions about what another person believes, intends, or perceives also can be strongly objective, although in one obvious sense they depend on subjective states of mind. The proposition "Brian liked chocolate ice cream when he was a child" is a statement about Brian's beliefs, but its truth is independent of whether anyone, including Brian, now believes that Brian once liked chocolate ice cream.

Coleman and Leiter also identify an intermediate form of objectivity, which they call modest objectivity. A proposition is *modestly objective* if its truth is fixed by the beliefs of an "ideal observer," one who forms her beliefs about the matter under certain specified conditions.[20] Propositions about an object's color are examples of modestly objective propositions. The truth of "The car is red" depends upon how the car would appear to an observer who viewed it in proper light and was not color blind. Coleman himself believes that propositions of law are modestly objective, a position with which we disagree.[21] For Coleman, a legal proposition is true if a judge operating under ideal conditions (full information, rationality, impartiality, maximum empathy, and cultural expertise) would believe it to be true.[22]

Questions about the determinateness of propositions of law, as opposed to their objectivity, ask to what extent legal sources uniquely warrant particular legal outcomes.[23] If the set of legal reasons does not yield an outcome, or yields more than one outcome, the law is indeterminate. Given our concern with law's practical function, what is important for us is not whether law is determinate as a metaphysical matter but whether it is determinate as an epistemological matter.[24]

Let us now step back and look at the issues of objectivity and determinateness from the vantage point of Lex and his rules. We shall distinguish two questions that someone in our hypothetical community might ask, and then examine the objectivity and determinateness of the answers. The first question we label the *moral question:* "What am I, as a judge or a subject, morally obligated to do, all things considered?" The second question we label the *legal question:*[25] "What has been authoritatively determined that I, as a judge or a subject, ought to do?"

Now with regard to the *moral question,* we need take no stand on either moral ontology or moral epistemology. We surely need not declare morality to be strongly objective or to be determinate. The assumptions we make about morality are quite modest. To make sense of Lex and his rules, we assume only that (1) people deem meaningful questions about what they ought to do; (2) people can disagree about what they ought to do; (3) people can believe that they ought to seek to minimize the moral costs of their disagreements; and (4) people can agree that some methods of authoritative settlement are morally preferable to others and to none.

These assumptions seem to us quite compatible with a wide variety of positions about moral ontology and epistemology. Obviously, they are not compatible with any metaphysical or epistemological position that cannot account for moral disagreement, or that makes the truth of all moral propositions radically inaccessible. The story we have told of Lex and his rules would lose its point if moral disagreement were impossible, or if people were always radically uncertain whether "Let Lex decide" represents moral improvement. Nonetheless, our commitments regarding the nature of morality and moral knowledge—or, rather, the commitments we must assume for Lex and his rules to have a point—are extremely modest ones.[26]

Turning to what we have called the *legal question,* what can be said about the objectivity and determinateness of Lex's rules and of the basic rule that makes Lex the authority? As we argued in chapter 5, the meaning of Lex's rules is a function of Lex's intentions—what sounds or marks Lex intended to make, what language he intended to communicate in, what Lex intended his words to mean, and so forth—and of various conventions, both linguistic conventions and conventions governing Lex's authority. Propositions referring to conventions are in Coleman and Leiter's schema *minimally objective.* Propositions about Lex's intentions, though they refer in part to subjective states that are properly regarded as *strongly objective*—as objective as propositions about the freezing point of water or the atomic weight of iron—are not completely reducible to strongly objective matters of fact. Yet they are objective in the sense that they invoke a set of skills that are learned as part of a form of life and that permit determinate communication and rule-following.

Our conclusion in chapter 5 was that it is possible for Lex to promulgate rules whose meaning within a range of cases is objective, accessible, and determinate.[27] And, of course, there are multitudes of rule-governed domains—mathematics and games, for example—where although controversies do arise, no one doubts either the objectivity or the determinateness of the rules as a general matter.

We suspect that questions about the objectivity and determinateness of law arise for the following reasons. First, if Lex issues *standards* rather than rules, their meaning will be a function of the meaning of moral terms. To the extent, therefore, that moral terms are regarded as nonobjective or indeterminate, their incorporation will undermine the objectivity or determinateness, or both, of the incorporating norms. Second, if legal reasoning relies on the method of analogical reasoning or reasoning on the basis of "legal principles," then, as we argued in chapters 6, 7, and 8, those attempting to apply the law will have to ask such things as what prior case is most "like" their own, or what is the morally best account of past moral error. We doubt if these questions are fully coherent, which might explain why any legal method dependent upon them will appear nonobjective and indeterminate.

The meaning of rules, however, rests on facts that are not necessarily ontologically mysterious or epistemically inaccessible. Law in the form of rules, like chess, can be objective and determinate.

Conclusion

As we have stressed throughout, we have not purported to offer a theory of what law is. Our aim, rather, has been to illuminate issues surrounding law, issues having to do with the moral function of authoritative rules and rule-defined institutions, the interpretation of authoritative rules, the morality and rationality of rule-following, and reasoning in cases not covered by rules (and why "reasoning by analogy," the result model of precedent, and "legal principles," which are interrelated, lack rational force). Our account has had the form of a hypothetical moral imperative: given a relatively uncontroversial picture of morality and moral reasoning, and a realistic portrait of the difficulties faced by ordinary humans in achieving moral coordination unaided by authoritative rules, even a community of morally motivated people will require authoritative rules to achieve maximum realization of their moral principles. We ourselves have taken no particular moral position, although we have raised the possibility that authoritative rules are in tension with some deontological theories. On the other hand, we have criticized, or at least questioned, some existing practices, such as reasoning by analogy, the result model of precedent, and the invocation of legal principles. And we have given an account (in chapter 4) of why we should expect such phenomena as the synchronic and diachronic tensions between law and equity, between substance and procedure, and between rules and standards. We have also given accounts of the debate between natural law and positivism, the debate over the obligation to obey the law, and how peaceful revolutions occur.

Rules are a response to our imperfections as moral reasoners. But the very imperfections that lead us to establish authoritative rule-promulgators confront us at the point of applying those rules. The rules, because they have been promulgated by imperfect beings, may appear to us to be less than morally ideal. More important, even if they are the morally best rules we can imagine, they will have immoral applications. The very imperfections that require us to have rules will require that the rules themselves be blunt and thus at least occasionally immoral in application. And therein lies the dilemma of rules and, we believe, the dilemma of law itself, and the key to many puzzles of jurisprudence.

NOTES

Introduction

1 See chapter 4, for further discussion of the moral costs of rule-making within a deontological theory of morality.

2 H. L. A. Hart, *The Concept of Law* (1961).

3 See Gregory Kavka, "The Toxin Puzzle," 43 *Analysis* 33 (1983); Gregory Kavka, "Some Paradoxes of Deterrence," 75 *J. Phil.* 283 (1978).

4 See Saul A. Kripke, *Wittgenstein on Rules and Private Language: An Elementary Exposition* (1982).

5 See Ronald Dworkin, *Taking Rights Seriously* 110–23, 340–41 (rev. ed. 1978).

6 See Roger A. Shiner, *Norm and Nature* (1992).

7 See Dworkin, supra note 5, at 46–80.

8 See Jules J. Coleman and Brian Leiter, "Determinacy, Objectivity, and Authority," in *Law and Interpretation* 203 (A. Marmor ed., 1995).

Chapter 1. Disagreement, Uncertainty, and Authoritative Settlement

1 Of course, in real communities, people often agree about what ought to be done in concrete cases even though they disagree about abstract principles. See, e.g., Cass R. Sunstein, "Incompletely Theorized Agreements," 108 *Harv. L. Rev.* 1733 (1995). When there *is* such concrete agreement, the community does not require authoritative rules.

2 See Joseph Raz, *The Authority of Law* 24–25, 30–33 (1979); Joseph Raz, "Authority and Justification," 14 *Phil. and Pub. Aff.* 3 (1985); Joseph Raz, "Authority, Law and Morality," 68 *Monist* 295 (1985).

3 It should be apparent—and so we will not argue for it—that these coordination, expertise, and efficiency problems will arise even in a society all of whose members accept the same basic social morality, and even if that social morality is extremely libertarian. Even in a Nozickian utopia, where everyone accepts Nozick's libertarian principles and desires to comply with them, human fallibility regarding knowledge of the world together with differing reasonable interpretations of Nozick's abstract principles would give rise to coordination and expertise problems under the best of realistic assumptions, as Nozick himself recognized. See Robert Nozick, *Anarchy, State, and Utopia* 96–108 (1974). See also Jonathan Wolff, "Anarchism and Skepticism," in *For and against the State* 99, 111–14 (J. Sanders and J. Narveson eds., 1996).

4 See Heidi M. Hurd, *Moral Combat* (1999).

5 Sometimes it is said that authoritative settlement is necessary for solving prisoners' dilemmas. There are two points we want to make about prisoners' dilemmas. First, they do not require narrowly self-interested actors. Perfect altruists

can face prisoners' dilemmas. For example, suppose altruist 1 is faced with the choice whether to take a shortcut across the grass. If he takes the shortcut, he can spend five more minutes with his sick aunt, which will bring her pleasure. He also knows, however, that altruists 2 and 3 face the same choice, and that if two cross the grass to spend more time with their sick aunts, the grass will be killed, which will be a greater loss to others than the aunts' gain. If only one crosses the grass, however, the grass will not be killed. Altruists 1 through 3 face an "altruist's dilemma" that is parallel to standard prisoners' dilemmas. See Frederic Schick, *Making Choices* 96 (1997); Wayne Eastman, "Telling Alternative Stories: Heterodox Versions of the Prisoners' Dilemma, the Coase Theorem, and Supply-Demand Equilibrium," 29 *Conn. L. Rev.* 727, 766–67 (1997).

Second, the problem in both types of dilemmas is coordination. In this respect, however, prisoners' and altruists' dilemmas are no different from the coordination problem faced by Agnes and Ben. Therefore, we shall not treat these dilemmas separately from the general topic of solving coordination problems.

6 Many writers have emphasized the coordination function of authoritative rules. See Tom Campbell, *The Legal Theory of Ethical Positivism* 6, 50, 53, 58 (1996); Frederick Schauer, *Playing by the Rules* 137–45 (reliance), 162–66 (1991); Jules Coleman, "Authority and Reason," in *The Autonomy of Law* 287, 304–5 (R. George ed., 1996); Neil MacCormick, "The Concept of Law and *The Concept of Law*," in George, *The Autonomy of Law,* supra at 162, 182, 190; Mark C. Murphy, "Surrender of Judgment and the Consent Theory of Political Authority," 16 *Law and Phil.* 115, 125–27 (1997); Gerald J. Postema, "Law's Autonomy and Public Practical Reason," in George, *The Autonomy of Law,* supra at 79, 89–93; Gerald J. Postema, "Coordination and Convention at the Foundation of Law," 11 *J. Legal Stud.* 165 (1982); Raz, "Authority and Justification," supra note 2, at 17. Many have also pointed out the expertise function that makes the choice *of* the authority, in addition to the choice that there *be* an authority, important. See, e.g., Campbell, supra at 51, 58; Schauer, supra at 150–52, 158–59; Coleman, supra at 305.

7 See Campbell, supra note 6, at 58; Schauer, supra note 6, at 145–49.

8 A good analogy would be to an army attempting to operate with no chain of command. An army requires coordination to execute battle plans. And because not every battle plan is equally good, it requires expertise in selecting among them. That is why armies have chains of command and why they attempt in choosing generals to find people with strategic expertise.

9 This acceptance by society of the rule "Let Lex decide" can obviously vanish at any moment. In other words, Lex's status as the authoritative settler of moral controversies and queries depends from moment to moment on his being regarded as such. There is no privileged moment of such acceptance; therefore, if Lex at any time ceases to be *regarded* as authoritative, he will cease to *be* authoritative. The fact that he *was* authoritative at one time will make no difference to his present authority. We take up some of the implications of this point in chapter 3, where we discuss constitutions and preconstitutional rules.

10 See, e.g., Amos Twersky and Daniel Kahneman, "Availability: A Heuristic

for Judging Frequency and Probability," in *Judgment under Uncertainty* 163–78 (D. Kahneman, P. Slovic, and A. Twersky eds., 1982).

11 For a thoughtful discussion of the problem of establishing authoritative institutions in the face of moral uncertainty and disagreement, see Thomas B. McAffee, "Substance above All: The Utopian Views of Modern Natural Law Constitutionalists," 4 *S. Cal. Interdisciplinary L.J.* 501, 516–21 (1995).

12 We have used the terms "moral authority," "moral controversy," and "moral query" rather than "practical authority," "practical controversy," and "practical query" only to emphasize that our interest is primarily with those disputes and uncertainties about what ought to be done that are couched in the language of interpersonal moral rights and obligations rather than in the language of personal prudence.

13 An exception is a rule that solves a coordination problem by selecting one of several equally attractive options. We discuss this further in chapter 4.

14 The continuity from the most general moral questions, such as, "What moral principle governs risk imposition?," to the most specific, such as, "May Alex dump the substance here now?," is well known to American constitutional lawyers, who must grapple with how specific a question must be to be deemed a question of adjudicative fact as opposed to a question of legislative fact. The former must be determined in adjudicatory proceedings, whereas the latter need not be. See Bi-Metallic Investment Co. v. State Board of Equalization, 239 U.S. 441 (1915); Londoner v. City and County of Denver, 210 U.S. 373 (1908). Lex might decide that certain persons and procedures work best for totally factual questions, whereas others are best for devising more general rules, which are less dependent on specific factual knowledge and more dependent on moral norms and general factual knowledge.

Finally, Lex may devise rules about to what degree these various rules should be entrenched against future change. He might decide that he should be minimally restrained in changing the most general rules, but that he should never change—or rarely change—specific adjudications.

15 H. L. A. Hart, *The Concept of Law* (1961).

16 Id. at 89.

17 Id. at 89–90.

18 Id. at 90 (emphases in original).

19 Id. at 90–91.

20 See, e.g., Larry Alexander, "Are Procedural Rights Derivative Substantive Rights?," 17 *Law and Phil.* 19 (1998).

21 Hart, supra note 15, at 91–94.

22 Id. at 91.

Chapter 2. Settlement Requisites and the Nature of Authoritative Rules

1 See Frederick Schauer, *Playing by The Rules* 18–19 (1991).

2 See id. at 4–5, 104–5; John Rawls, "Two Concepts of Rules," 64 *Phil. Rev.* 3 (1955).

3 See Schauer, supra note 1, at 23.
4 See John Rawls, *A Theory of Justice* 60 (1971).
5 See Robert Nozick, *Anarchy, State, and Utopia* 150–53 (1974).
6 See Bernard Gert, *The Moral Rules* 125 (1966).
7 See Schauer, supra note 1, at 77–78.
8 See id. at 19–21.
9 See Cass R. Sunstein, *Legal Reasoning and Political Conflict* 27–28 (1996). See also Larry Alexander, "Incomplete Theorizing," 72 *Notre Dame L. Rev.* 531, 541–44 (1997).
10 See Tom D. Campbell, *The Legal Theory of Ethical Positivism* 118 (1996).
11 Hart calls this rule-making difficulty "indeterminacy of aim." H. L. A. Hart, *The Concept of Law* 125 (1961).
12 This is an important qualification. If it were not meant to settle some moral controversy other than how the reasonable farmer should behave, the rule would be incapable of making a practical difference. The members of the community would be left in the same position epistemically that they occupied in the absence of the rule. See Scott J. Shapiro, "On Hart's Way Out," 4 *Legal Theory* 469, 489–97 (1998); Anthony J. Sebok, *Legal Positivism in American Jurisprudence* 256–66, 307–12 (1998).
13 See Campbell, supra note 10, at 119.
14 See Gerald J. Postema, "Law's Autonomy and Public Practical Reasoning," in *The Autonomy of Law* 79, 115–16 n.38 (R. George ed., 1996).
15 But see the qualification of this point in the text with respect to standards whose vague terms can be more satisfactorily translated in application by the subjects than eliminated in advance by the positing authority.
16 See Schauer, supra note 1, at 31–35 (over- and underinclusion), 38–39 (entrenchment), 42–45 (entrenchment), 49–50 (entrenchment and over- and underinclusion), 84 (entrenchment), 87 (entrenchment).

Chapter 3. Hierarchies of Rules

1 We shall continue to refer to "agreement" among the members of the community to the terms of rules, but frequently such agreement will consist merely of each member's *accepting* those terms as authoritative.
2 Some democratic theorists argue that there is no defensible reason to make Super Lex supermajoritarian or nonmajoritarian in character. See, e.g., Jeremy Waldron, *Law and Disagreement* chaps. 14, 15 (1999); Jeremy Waldron, "Precommitment and Disagreement," in *Constitutionalism: Philosophical Foundations* 271–99 (L. Alexander ed., 1998). For a response to Waldron's position, see Larry Alexander, "Introduction," in id. at 1, 11–13; Larry Alexander, "Are Procedural Rights Derivative Substantive Rights?," 17 *Law and Phil.* 19, 36–42 (1998).
3 Although this point is frequently denied, at least by implication, with respect to constitutional rules, constitutional rules are no different from other rules in terms of their function—to settle matters of moral controversy—and in terms of the determinateness required to fulfill that function. See, e.g., Larry

Alexander, "With Me, It's All er Nuthin': Formalism in Law and Morality," 66 *U. Chi. L. Rev.* 530, 550–51 (1999); Larry Alexander, "Constitutional Tragedies and Giving Refuge to the Devil," in *Constitutional Stupidities, Constitutional Tragedies* 115 (W. N. Eskridge and S. Levinson eds., 1998); Larry Alexander, "The Constitution as Law," 6 *Const. Commentary* 103, 106–10 (1989); Larry A. Alexander, "Painting without the Numbers," 8 *U. Dayton L. Rev.* 447, 460–62 (1983); Thomas B. McAffee, "Substance above All: The Utopian Vision of Modern Natural Law Constitutionalists," 4 *S. Cal. Interdisciplinary L.J.* 501, 516–21, 527–30 (1995).

4 In chapter 4 we introduce the rule-sensitive particularist, one who takes account of the benefits of rules and the effects of rules on others' behavior in deciding what she ought to do, all things considered, but who does not regard the rules as authoritative on that question. We ask whether such a stance is rationally compelled, and whether, if it is, rationality undermines authoritative rules and hence the rule-sensitive particularist position itself, which is dependent on authoritative rules.

5 See Mark C. Murphy, "Surrender of Judgment and the Consent Theory of Political Authority," 16 *Law and Phil.* 115, 126–27 (1997); David A. Strauss, "Common Law Constitutional Interpretation," 63 *U. Chi. L. Rev.* 877, 907–8 (1996).

6 Our account of how the community comes to accept as authoritative a set of basic rules that is perhaps no member's preferred set is consistent with Andrei Marmor's recent explanation of how a legal rule of recognition can be accepted for reasons but also be thoroughly conventional. See Andrei Marmor, "Legal Conventionalism," 4 *Legal Theory* 509 (1998). We agree with Coleman, however, when he claims that the foundational rule is a coordination convention, though we view it as such in the sense described above, namely, as the morally best rule that all can accept and that all view as morally superior to the absence of such a rule. See Jules L. Coleman, "Incorporationism, Conventionality, and the Practical Difference Thesis," 4 *Legal Theory* 381, 397–402 (1998).

7 We take up the general topic of courts' being bound to follow their precedents in chapter 7.

8 See Larry Alexander and Frederick Schauer, "On Extrajudicial Constitutional Interpretation," 110 *Harv. L. Rev.* 1359, 1377–81 (1997); Emily Sherwin, "Ducking *Dred Scott:* A Response to Alexander and Schauer," 15 *Const. Commentary* 65 (1998).

9 Super Lex's superiority to the supreme court as a promulgator of constitutional rules implies, however, that the community is unlikely to accept a preconstitutional rule making the court's interpretations binding even if mistaken, unless the preconstitutional rules also require the court to attempt to discern Super Lex's meaning rather than impose constitutional rules of its own creation. See Ara Lovitt, Book Note, "Constitutional Confusion?," 50 *Stan. L. Rev.* 565, 593 (1998).

10 When officials contravene rules that are authoritative by virtue of tracing their pedigree to the preconstitutional rules, the officials are acting without authority, given that all authority derives from the preconstitutional rules.

11 Someone might object that those who have agreed to the preconstitutional rules

cannot unilaterally cease recognizing those rules and the rules derived from them. If they have agreed to certain authoritative rules, they are morally bound to continue accepting the rules as authoritative.

In some cases—for example, when rules are agreed to in a way that constitutes a promise to regard the rules as authoritative, or that causes others to rely on the agreement to their detriment—it may be immoral to cease recognizing the authority of the rules. See Murphy, supra note 5, at 137. The matter is complex, and we touch on it briefly in chapter 4 when we ask whether one can promise to abide by rules in the sense of morally binding oneself to so abide when one knows that some of the rules' prescriptions in particular circumstances will be morally wrong.

Even if some repudiations of the agreement on preconstitutional rules are immoral, however, those who so repudiate will not necessarily believe that they are acting immorally. They may be violating the basic agreement for moral reasons, even if those reasons are mistaken. Or they may be doing so inadvertently, believing that they are actually adhering to the original agreement. Moreover, as people are born into the community and come of age, or immigrate into the community, their acceptance of the basic agreement may not involve any express or implied promise to accept the preconstitutional rules as authoritative. (Indeed, although we have generally described our community as having agreed to the preconstitutional rules, we could have just as accurately described them—and in the case of a larger society, more accurately described them—as having *accepted* those rules inwardly as opposed to *agreed* to them through some outward manifestation thereof.)

12 See Michael C. Dorf, "Integrating Normative and Descriptive Constitutional Theory: The Case of Original Meaning," 85 *Georgetown L.J.* 1765, 1772 (1997); Frederick Schauer, "Amending the Presuppositions of a Constitution," in *Responding to Imperfection* 145–61 (S. Levinson ed., 1995); Richard S. Kay, Book Review, 7 *Const. Commentary* 434, 437–41 (1990).

13 See Neil MacCormick, "Institutional Normative Order: A Conception of Law," 82 *Corn. L. Rev.* 1051, 1058–60 (1997).

14 See Murphy, supra note 5, at 138; David A. Strauss, "Common Law Constitutional Interpretation," 63 *U. Chi. L. Rev.* 877, 910–11 (1996).

15 Some suggest that the people of the United States have acquiesced in several constitutional amendments effected by the U.S. Supreme Court and not by the methods prescribed in the Constitution itself. See Sanford Levinson, "How Many Times Has the Constitution Been Amended? (A) <26; (B) 26; (C) 27; (D) >27: Accounting for Constitutional Change," in *Responding to Imperfection* 13–36 (S. Levinson ed., 1995); Schauer, supra note 12, at 156–57.

Moreover, it is widely accepted that the U.S. Constitution itself represented a revolution in which the established foundational rules gave way to a new set. The framers of the Constitution went well beyond the authority granted them under the existing rules. The Constitution they wrote, with its provision declaring how it would become the supreme law (ratification by three-fourths of the states), was not provided for in the rules accepted up to that point. See Richard S. Kay, "The Illegality of the Constitution," 4 *Const. Commentary* 57 (1987). Yet when the Constitution was ratified according to its terms, even those who voted against it accepted it as supreme law. Likewise, if the two of us were to draft our ideal constitution and declare that it supplants the U.S. Constitution as the supreme law of the United States on January 1, 2001, the Alexander/Sherwin constitution would indeed be supreme law on that date if—but only if—it were almost universally accepted as such. See Schauer, supra note 12, at 152–53 (similar example); Dorf, supra note 12, at 1776.

Finally, the mechanism by which millions of citizens can acquiesce in informal constitutional revolutions is not in the least mysterious. Most citizens accept as *their* basic authoritative rule whatever officials acting in good faith take the Constitution to mean. And officials accept good faith constitutional interpretations by the Supreme Court as supremely authoritative. If the Supreme Court coordinates around a new interpretive methodology, this constitutional change will be authoritative for lower officials and thus for ordinary citizens as well, even if the latter know little or nothing about the Constitution.

16 Likewise, if one system of rules—say, that of a conqueror—is more efficacious than competing systems in the sense that people generally comply with it regardless of their objections to it, that fact in itself generates a moral argument for accepting it. Even if the conqueror is believed to lack moral expertise, the conqueror's rules do facilitate coordination. Of course, if the conqueror's rules are perceived as sufficiently unjust, then even if they are generally complied with out of fear of sanctions, they will not be deemed authoritative by the conquered people. The moral benefits of coordination that they provide will be deemed outweighed by their substantive immorality.

17 See Larry Alexander, "Originalism, or Who Is Fred?," 19 *Harv. J.L. and Pub. Pol'y* 321, 326 n.17 (1996); Schauer, supra note 12; Richard S. Kay, "Preconstitutional Rules," 42 *Ohio St. L.J.* 187 (1981).

18 See Richard S. Kay, "American Constitutionalism," in *Constitutionalism: Philosophical Foundations* 16, 33–35 (L. Alexander ed., 1998).

Chapter 4. The Problem of Rules

1 See Frederick Schauer, *Playing by the Rules: A Philosophical Examination of Rule-Based Decision-Making in Law and in Life* 31–34, 555, 100–102 (1991). As Donald Regan has pointed out, the rule itself has no moral importance. Donald H. Regan, "Authority and Value: Reflections on Raz's *Morality of Freedom*," 62 *S. Cal. L. Rev.* 995, 1006–10 (1989).

2 We use the term "rational" to refer to action in accordance with the balance of reasons accessible to the actor. The choice of one action over another is rational if the first action is better according to all the reasons the actor perceives as relevant. Without taking a position on whether this is a satisfactory definition of rationality, we believe it is the way people ordinarily address problems of how to act. At the least, it is all that Lex can expect from his subjects.

3 See Larry Alexander, "The Gap," 14 *Harv. J.L. and Publ. Pol'y* 695 (1991); Larry Alexander and Emily Sherwin, "The Deceptive Nature of Rules," 142 *U. Penn. L. Rev.* 1191, 1194–99 (1994). Fred Schauer refers to this situation as the "asymmetry of authority." Schauer, supra note 1, at 128–34.

4 We are assuming a community of morally motivated people whose problem is that they are uncertain or disagree about what morality dictates in a host of concrete cases. Uncertainty and disagreement generate the moral costs of lack of coordination, lack of expertise, and inefficiency. Rules both constituting and promulgated by authorities can reduce or eliminate these moral costs if they are more determinate for members of the community than the moral principles the applications of which they are meant to resolve. Law as formal rules is a solution to the problem of the limits of moral knowledge.

To see why it is lack of information, not immoral motivation, that gives rise to the need for formalistic law, imagine a different hypothetical community. In this one, everyone *can* apply moral principles unerringly in concrete cases. Its problem is that some members are not motivated to comply with those moral principles.

In this community, there would be no need for posited norms. Morality would be self-sufficient. For if some members violated their moral obligations, morality itself would instruct the remaining members how they should investigate, try, and punish the offenders. Remember, everyone can apply the moral principles correctly in concrete cases. And there is no reason that morality does not extend beyond its first-order requirements and speak to how to treat miscreants. Indeed, moral theory regarding crime and punishment, and moral theory regarding adjudication, are just such aspects of moral theory generally. See, e.g., Larry Alexander, "Are Procedural Rights Derivative Substantive Rights?," 17 *Law and Phil.* 19 (1998).

Thus, if men were gods—morally omniscient—but not angels, morality would be an adequate guide to behavior and posited norms would be unnecessary. If, however, men were angels but not gods, then posited norms in the form of determinate rules would be necessary to implement morality. Formalistic law is a solution to a cognitive, not a motivational, problem. See Gregory S. Kavka, "Why Even Morally Perfect People Would Need Government," 12 *Soc. Phil. and Pol'y* 1 (1995).

5 The rule in our example is at least in part a paternalistic one. Yet the argument we make applies equally to rules that protect the interests of persons other than the rule subject. We need not take a stand on the legitimacy of paternalistic rules. See generally, Joel Feinberg, *Harm to Self* (1986).

6 Occasionally, Lex can combine his own expertise with special information available to individual actors. For example, he might issue a mixed rule, such as "Salt to taste." Salt is the correct ingredient, but individuals know better than Lex how much salt they will enjoy.

7 See Joseph Raz, *The Morality of Freedom,* 49–50 (1986); Schauer, supra note 1, at 163–66; Gerald J. Postema, "Coordination and Convention at the Foundations

of Law," 11 *J. Legal Stud.* 165, 172–86 (1982); Regan, "Authority and Value," supra note 1, at 1019–31.

8 For a discussion of procrastination and act consequentialism, see Richard A. Fumerton, *Reason and Morality: A Defense of the Egocentric Perspective* 178–88 (1990). See also Scott J. Shapiro, "Rules and Practical Reasoning" 138–206 (1996) (unpublished Ph.D. dissertation, Columbia University).

9 An altruist's dilemma is structurally identical to a prisoner's dilemma. For a more complete description, see chapter 1, note 5. The altruist's dilemma may be more relevant to our project, given our assumption that members of the community are morally motivated.

10 See Mark V. Tushnet, "The Hardest Question in Constitutional Law," 81 *Mich. L. Rev.* 1, 16–19 (1996) (pointing out the advantages of serious rules over particularistic, case-by-case reasoning and also the irrationality of forgoing particularistic reasoning if rules are underinclusive and overinclusive); Gerald J. Postema, "Law's Autonomy and Public Practical Reason," in *The Autonomy of Law* 79, 106–10 (Robert P. George ed., 1996) (pointing out reasons for rule-subjects to doubt the expertise of rule-makers).

11 See, e.g., Donald A. Dripps, "Beyond Rape: An Essay on the Difference between the Presence of Force and the Absence of Consent," 92 *Colum. L. Rev.* 1780 (1992); Douglas N. Husak and George C. Thomas III, "Date Rape, Social Convention, and Reasonable Mistakes," 11 *Law and Phil.* 95 (1992); Joan MacGregor, "Force, Consent, and the Reasonable Woman," in *In Harm's Way: Essays in Honor of Joel Feinberg* 231 (Jules L. Coleman and Allen Buchanan eds., 1994); Robin L. West, "Legitimating the Illegitimate: A Comment on Beyond Rape," 93 *Colum. L. Rev.* 1442 (1993); Symposium on Sex and Consent, Parts I and II, 2 *Legal Theory* 87 (1996).

12 Schauer, supra note 1, at 94–100. Schauer describes rule-sensitive particularism this way: "Given that result *a* is indicated by rule *R,* you (the rule subject) shall reach result *a* unless there are reasons for not following rule *R* in this case that outweigh the sum of the reasons underlying *R* and the reasons for setting forth those underlying reasons in the form of a rule." Frederick Schauer, "Rules and the Rule of Law," 14 *Harv. J.L. and Pub. Pol'y.* 645, 676 n.66 (1991).

13 If Leo knows that his swimming in defiance of Lex's rule will set an example that less competent swimmers will follow, he will have an additional reason to comply with the rule. His swimming will have this effect, however, only if others are not already disposed to violate the rule whenever they believe a violation is justified. Of course, rule-sensitive particularists *are* so disposed. Further, the exemplary effect of Leo's violation on others does not serve as a reason why Leo should not swim if he expects that other competent swimmers will also violate the rule. In that case, his own example will add little or nothing to the example set by others.

14 See Regan, supra note 1, at 1025–26.

15 See id. at 1026–27.

16 Assume that ant season lasts exactly 100 days. Extermination has a negative

value for Brian of 1,000, representing monetary costs and inconvenience. If Brian sprays on May 1, ants will never enter his house. If he does not spray on May 1, there is a probability of .01 that ants will enter the house on any given day, and a probability of .634 that they will enter sometime during the ant season of 100 days. The expected cost of failing to spray on any one day is 10 (.01 x 1000), and the expected cost of failing to spray throughout the summer is 634 (.634 x 1000).

Thus, on May 1, Brian might assign a value of 634 to the coordinating benefits of the rule. (More likely, he will assign a somewhat lower value to the rule because he discounts future losses. For discussion of variations in preferences over time, see Shapiro, supra note 8.) At the same time, he will know that postponing the ant spray from May 1 until May 2 has an expected cost of just 10 (the risk that ants will enter the house on the intervening day). If his interest in doing something else on May 1 has a value greater than 10, it looks rational for Brian to postpone. If the same is true on May 2, it is rational to postpone again, and so on until the ants arrive (or his opportunity costs drop below 10).

(Calculations might change if the probability of ants increases throughout the summer [they are multiplying]. As time passes and the expected cost of delay rises, Brian is more likely to spray. But this is not a function of the rule; it reflects change in Brian's natural balance of reasons.)

17 Not quite. The present Brian may discount the expected value of following the rule (634) because he assigns a lower value to future costs than to present costs. Yet Brian-over-time, and certainly Brian-when-the-event-occurs, would give the rule its full value of 634.

18 Further, on the facts we have assumed, the value of the rule decreases as time goes on because the chance that ants will arrive at some point during the remainder of the season is steadily decreasing. Therefore, the longer Brian goes without spraying—thinking that another day will be more auspicious—the less value compliance has in his balance of reasons. Another point is that Brian ought to discount the value of the rule at the outset to reflect this and other weaknesses we have described. As a result, the opportunity cost necessary to outweigh the cumulative value of the rule may be less than 634. If the lowest opportunity cost is less than this revised value, then Brian will never comply.

19 This might be viewed as a form of rule-sensitive particularism, but it comes closer to the category of equivocation than to the category of coordination involving conflicting interests or beliefs. If in fact we do not think deliberation can yield much benefit, then within the range we have in mind, one rule is as good as another, and the rule "7:00" simply provides salience.

20 A rule-sensitive particularist might say that the salience of May 1, together with awareness of the potential benefits of the rule, has at least some impact on the subject's reasoning, because it initiates a comparison of opportunity costs over a period of time. Brian will assess the various conflicting plans he is likely to have on May 1 and each day thereafter until the ants arrive. But, particularly

when the date of future catastrophe is unknown, this calculation involves too many uncertainties to advance Brian's position in any significant way.

21 On tipping points in compliance with norms, see Robert D. Cooter, "Decentralized Law for a Complex Economy: The Structural Approach to Adjudicating the New Law Merchant," 144 *U. Pa. L. Rev.* 1643, 1669–75 (1996).

22 Schauer, supra note 1, at 202–5; Schauer, supra note 12, at 674–79. See Regan, supra note 1, at 1003–13 (indicator rules); Stephen R. Perry, "Second-Order Reasons, Uncertainty and Legal Theory," 62 *S. Cal. L. Rev.* 913, 966 (1989) (reweighting reasons). For criticism, see Gerald J. Postema, "Positivism, I Presume? . . . Comments on Schauer's 'Rules and the Rule of Law,'" 14 *Harv. J.L. and Pub. Pol'y* 797, 809–22 (1991).

23 Schauer, supra note 1, at 204.

24 Id. at 205.

25 Regan, supra note 1, at 1010.

26 Perry, supra note 22, at 966; Stephen R. Perry, "Judicial Obligation, Precedent and the Common Law," 7 *Oxford J. Legal Stud.* 215, 239–43 (1987).

27 Schauer, supra note 12, at 677.

28 Regan, supra note 1, at 1011. In the example Regan provides, his normal rule is to trust Jones's arithmetic, but when he happens to notice that Jones's total for a column of even numbers is odd, he abandons the rule.

29 How to determine a unit of strength is an obvious problem.

30 We are assuming here that the threshold operates as a "standard" and is not a determinate qualification or exception to the rule. That is, the threshold is not itself a rule. To the extent that the threshold is simply a determinate exception to the rule, it cannot be a strategy for closing the gap between what rules require and what reason dictates. Further, specifying the content "10" in rule-like, determinate fashion would require a recipe for the threshold's application to every application of the primary rules. The complexity of such a threshold rule would deprive it of the simplicity necessary to bring about effective settlement. See chapter 2, section "Norm Types: Characteristics of Serious Rules."

31 We are ignoring the problem of risk. If the danger in question is that Leo will drown, the actual strength of reasons not to dive in is either zero or incalculably high, depending on whether he drowns. But ex ante, it makes more sense to speak of danger in terms of probabilities, and in any event, the hypothetical can be altered so that the consequence is a certainty (unknown to Leo) that a lifeguard will spend time and energy rescuing him.

32 See Postema, supra note 22, at 815–16 ("Surely it is not enough to defeat a rule that there is a reason of *great strength* against following it, *if* the reasons for following are even stronger").

33 For each potential violation of the rule, the reasons for following the rule must be revised downward, because the practice is less pervasive and a single violation causes less harm that would not otherwise occur and less incremental harm to confidence in the rule. At this point, less is necessary to outweigh the reasons

for following the rule. A violation is now easier to justify and therefore easier to believe justified, and therefore more likely. Depending on the distribution of reasons or perceived reasons to violate, a recursive downward revision may follow until the rule has no potential value at all.

In a mixed community of blind rule-followers, presumptive rule-followers, and rule-sensitive particularists, we might add another set of reasons for compliance. Now, any presumptive rule-follower's violation may move the general level of compliance toward the tipping point at which blind rule-followers will cease to comply. It might decrease a particularist's (or a presumptive rule-follower's) assessment of how many blind rule-followers exist, and therefore what effect his own violation might have on blind rule-following. This fortifies the strength of the presumption. On the other hand, the existence (and perhaps encouragement) of an option of presumptive rule-following is likely to mean there will be fewer blind rule-followers than there would be in a community made up only of blind rule-followers and particularists.

34 Joseph Raz, *The Authority of Law,* 16–19, 22–23, 30–33 (1979); Raz, supra note 7, at 57–62. For a comprehensive argument that legal rules cannot have exclusionary effect, see Heidi M. Hurd, "Challenging Authority," 100 *Yale L.J.* 1011 (1991).

35 Raz, supra note 34, at 17–18.

36 Raz speaks at times of the law's "claim" to exclusionary authority. Id. at 28, 30. But he also suggests that one can have second-order reasons for actions and therefore be "justified in not doing what ought to be done on the balance of first-order reasons." Id. at 27.

37 Even if the average addressee of the rules does better by following them, the rules themselves can never be more than reasons to believe compliance is more likely to be the correct action (based on expertise and coordination). The actual reasons for compliance—the rule *is* expert, the right mix of acts *will* result—are still reasons that predated the rules. They have been neither excluded nor added to by the rules. See Larry Alexander, "Law and Exclusionary Reasons," 18 *Phil. Topics* 5, 7–9 (1990) (arguing that law can affect our first-order reasons for action and our beliefs but it cannot be a reason for action, first-order or otherwise).

38 See Mark C. Murphy, "Surrender of Judgment and the Consent Theory of Political Authority," 16 *Law and Phil.* 115 (1997).

39 Scott Shapiro argues that rule-subjects can constrain their later deliberations by committing to follow rules. See Shapiro, supra note 8, at 124–33, 301–4. See also note 40 infra. Joseph Raz suggests that consent to be governed by law, or an undertaking to obey legal rules, can increase the scope of legitimate political authority and create an obligation to obey, provided that the governing authority is reasonably just. See Raz, supra note 7, at 88–99.

40 Regan, supra note 1, at 1037. See also Gregory Kavka, "The Toxin Puzzle," 43 *Analysis* 33 (1983), and Gregory Kavka, "Some Paradoxes of Deterrence," 75 *J. Phil.* 285 (1978) (describing conditions in which it may be rational but impossible to form certain intentions).

For an attempt to overcome this logic, see Shapiro, supra note 8, at 111–16, 124–33. Shapiro first describes situations in which the best course of action would be to follow a rule, although if the actor cannot be sure that he will follow the rule over time, it would be better for him to acknowledge this and revise his plans accordingly. Shapiro then reasons that when people set out to follow rules—as they often do—they must be committed in a meaningful way to follow them, because adopting a rule without binding commitment would be irrational. See also Richard Holton, "Intention and Weakness of Will," 96 *J. Phil.* 241 (1999) (examining the reconsideration of intentions); Joe Mintoff, "Rational Cooperation, Intention, and Reconsideration," 107 *Ethics* 612 (1997) (exploring cultivation of dispositions not to reconsider commitments as a way out of dilemmas similar to those posed by rules); Murphy, supra note 38 (arguing that accepting a rule is accepting another's judgment as one's own).

How does Shapiro deal with the problem that at the point of decision whether to comply with the rule, the actor may correctly believe that the reasons for violation outweigh the reasons for compliance? His response is that if one has accepted a rule—committed himself to follow it—then that commitment *causes* him to follow it and renders intentional rule-violation *infeasible.* The actor is not caused to comply with the rule because reason favors compliance. Rather, the rule is the dominant reason to comply because *it* causes compliance. See Scott J. Shapiro, "The Difference That Rules Make," in *Analyzing Law* 47–54 (B. Bix ed., 1998) (describing how commitment to rules—by repressing reasons to violate them—makes violations for reasons infeasible); Edward F. McClennen and Scott Shapiro, "Rule-Based Behavior," in *The New Palgrave Dictionary of Economics and the Law* 3 (P–Z) (P. Newman ed., 1998); Edward F. McClennen, "Pragmatic Rationality and Rules," 26 *Phil. and Pub. Aff.* 210 (1997); David Gauthier, "Commitment and Choice: An Essay on the Rationality of Plans," in *Ethics, Rationality, and Economic Behavior* 217 (F. Farina, F. Hahn, and S. Vannucci eds., 1996). On Shapiro's analysis, if the actor weighs the reasons for and against compliance with the rule and acts according to the balance of reasons, he really has not accepted the rule.

Our question then becomes, Given that Lex's subjects realize that Lex's rules may compel some actions against the balance of reasons, can they "accept" those rules in the sense Shapiro describes, namely, in the sense that would render them unable intentionally to violate those rules because reason so dictated? Are Lex's subjects not in a situation analogous to Kavka's potential toxin drinker, who wishes to be able to intend an irrational action? See Kavka, "The Toxin Puzzle," supra. See also Michael E. Bratman, "Following Through with One's Plans: Reply to David Gauthier," in *Modeling Rationality, Morality, and Evolution* 55 (P. Danielson ed., 1998); David Gauthier, "Intention and Deliberation," in *Modeling Rationality, Morality and Evolution* 41 (P. Danielson ed., 1998); Michael H. Robins, "Is It Rational to Carry Out Strategic Intentions?," 25 *Philosophia* 191 (1997).

41 Regan, supra note 1, at 1074–75.

42 See id. at 1036.

43 See Raz, supra note 7, at 90–94, 97–98.

44 For an analysis of optimal sanctions, see Richard A. Posner, *Economic Analysis of Law* 217–31 (4th ed. 1992).

45 Of course there are many occasions for adjudication to which no canonical rule applies. The facts that bring parties before a judge may not fall within any known rule, or the applicable rule or norm may be too indeterminate to function as a serious rule. Because we are interested in adjudicative sanctions as a strategy for narrowing the gap associated with serious rules, our discussion is limited to those cases that fall within the terms of an existing canonical rule.

46 See Hurd, supra note 34, at 1646–66; Heidi M. Hurd, "Justifiably Punishing the Justified," 90 *Mich. L. Rev.* 2203, 2279–334 (1992) (defending the correspondence thesis). Rolf Sartorius labels the moral principle that punishment and blame should only reflect culpable wrongdoing the "reflection principle." Rolf E. Sartorius, *Individual Conduct and Social Norms* 56–57 (1975).

47 This third approach is intended to mimic standards of criminal culpability under a retributivist theory of punishment. See generally, Michael Moore, "The Moral Worth of Retribution," in *Responsibility, Character, and the Emotions* 179, 179–82 (Ferdinand Schoeman ed., 1987).

48 In this case, it is possible that Leo was negligent, as that term in commonly used. But this does not alter our conclusion that he is not culpable. If he had acted in conscious disregard of risk, he would indeed have been culpable; but under the assumption we have made that Leo and other members of the community are morally motivated, he would not have done this. If, on the other hand, he was merely mistaken in his assessment of risk, or merely failed to avert to a risk, punishment is not justified from a retributivist point of view. See Larry Alexander, "Reconsidering the Relationship among Voluntary Acts, Strict Liability, and Negligence in Criminal Law," 7 *Soc. Phil. and Pol'y* 84 (1990); Ishtiyaque Haji, "An Epistemic Dimension of Blameworthiness," 57 *Phil. and Phenom. Research* 523 (1997); Steven Sverdlik, "Pure Negligence," 30 *Am. Phil. Q.* 137 (1993); Michael J. Zimmerman, "Moral Responsibility and Ignorance," 107 *Ethics* 410 (1997).

49 Moreover, if one obeys a rule when one believes one could do better morally by violating it, is one's obedience really nonculpable?

50 See Larry Alexander, "Can Law Survive the Asymmetry of Authority?," in *Rules and Reasoning* 39, 45 n.23 (L. Meyer ed., 1999) (arguing that punishing unjustified rule-followers is a logical corollary of not punishing justified rule-violators).

51 For analysis of the effect of example on justification, see Hurd, supra note 46, at 2293–301.

52 Amos Tversky and Daniel Kahneman, "Availability: A Heuristic for Judging Frequency and Probability," in *Judgment under Uncertainty: Heuristics and Biases* (Daniel Kahneman, Paul Slovic, and Amos Tversky eds., 1982).

53 See Hurd, supra note 46, at 2295–301.

54 Assume that Stephen's act causes eight units of direct harm and one unit of harm through example. His reasons for violating the rule have ten units of value

(marking in the book preserves an important thought). So far, his act is justified (a net value of one). If Heidi declines to impose sanctions, her decision will cause three units of harm through its effect on other actors and judges. This means Stephen's act is not justified (twelve units of harm, ten units of value, net harm of two). Heidi should punish Stephen.

But suppose that Heidi's public decision to impose sanctions on Stephen will deter ten others from engaging in similar violations that would be justified if punished. Now Heidi must consider that if she declines to punish, these ten acts, undeterred, will produce twenty units of value if punished but could cause twenty units of harm if not punished. What should she do?

55 See Alexander, supra note 50, at 51–53 (on the consequentialist character of rules).

56 As Gerald Postema has put it, sanctions work by "*corruption* of the decision-making process." Postema, supra note 22, at 819, 822. See also Ronald Dworkin, "Foundations of Liberal Equality," in *The Tanner Lectures on Human Value XI* 50 (Grethe B. Peterson ed., 1990) (on the value of "constitutive" rather than "additive" choices).

57 Only if sanctions were sufficiently draconian that they changed the actor's balance of *moral* reasons, and not just his prudential reasons, would sanctions work without corrupting. But in that case, judges would have to treat consent as a moral permission weighty enough to justify draconian punishment.

58 See Gerald J. Postema, *Bentham and the Common Law Tradition* 403–8, 448–52 (1986) (on Bentham's proposal to separate adjudication from laws governing conduct); Meir Dan-Cohen, "Decision Rules and Conduct Rules: On Acoustic Separation in Criminal Law," 97 *Harv. L. Rev.* 625, 630–36 (1984) (on "selective transmission" of conduct rules and decision rules, made possible by conditions of "acoustic separation").

59 Dan-Cohen, supra note 58.

60 See id. at 636–64.

61 In traditional doctrine, "legal" damage remedies for wrongs such as breach of contract were subject only to fairly determinate defenses such as fraud and duress. This reinforced a well-understood conduct rule, "Perform your contracts." Yet the remedies available for breach of contract did not always carry out this rule. Damage remedies were affected by obscure requirements such as foreseeability and certainty of proof. As a result, they might fail to give the promisor the full benefit of his bargain. Meanwhile, the "equitable" remedy of specific performance—a decree requiring the promisor to perform what was promised—traditionally was subject to even more obscure "equitable defenses," which allowed the courts to excuse foolish and unsophisticated promisors from harsh bargains. For a more detailed description, see Emily L. Sherwin, "Law and Equity in Contract Enforcement," 50 *Md. L. Rev.* 253, 263–64 (1991).

62 Thus, the sardonic term "government-house utilitarianism," referring hypothetically to colonial governments' encouraging primitive subjects to believe in the rectitude of their traditional mores, but only because the government

secretly believes that the correct morality—utilitarianism—cannot be applied by the subjects and that therefore the traditional mores are utilitarian-warranted.

63 See R. M. Hare, *Moral Thinking* 44–64 (1981) (describing a two-level process of moral reasoning, in which people usually reason like "proles" and follow rules unthinkingly, but sometimes reason like "archangels" and reflect upon the rules); Bernard Williams, "A Critique of Utilitarianism," in J. J. C. Smart and Bernard Williams, *Utilitarianism: For and Against* 134–135 (1973) (criticizing utilitarianism as a criterion of act evaluation divorced from anyone's decision procedure).

64 See Sissela Bok, *Lying: Moral Choice in Public and Private Life* 18–22 (1978); Gerald Dworkin, *The Theory and Practice of Autonomy* 14, 104 (1988); Charles Fried, *Right and Wrong* 62–69 (1978); Immanuel Kant, "On a Supposed Right to Lie from Altruistic Motives," in *A Critique of Practical Reason and Other Philosophical Writings* 346–50 (Lewis W. Beck trans., 1949).

65 See generally Larry Alexander, "Pursuing the Good—Indirectly," 95 *Ethics* 315, 325–29 (1985). John Rawls argues that valid principles of justice must meet the test of the "publicity principle," namely, that they be capable of being generally publicized without being undermined. John Rawls, *A Theory of Justice* 133 (1971). What such a principle, if it exists, implies about serious rules and their deceptive implicit claims is uncertain. See Larry Alexander and Emily Sherwin, "The Deceptive Nature of Rules," 142 *U. Pa. L. Rev.* 1191, 1211–22; Alexander, supra.

66 For an argument along these lines, see Dan-Cohen, supra note 58, at 671.

67 The literature is replete with hypothetical examples of moral choices to become an immoral person, or rational choices to become irrational. See, e.g., Thomas Schelling, *The Strategy of Conflict* (1969); Eugene Mills, "The Unity of Justification," 58 *Phil. and Phenomenological Res.* 27, 35 n.16 (1998); Kavka, "Some Paradoxes of Deterrence," supra note 40.

68 See Robert Nozick, *Anarchy, State, and Utopia* 32 (1974); Michael Clark, "Euthanasia and the Slippery Slope," 15 *J. Applied Phil.* 251 (1998). See also Andrew von Hirsch, "Extending the Harm Principle: 'Remote' Harms and Fair Imputation," in *Harm and Culpability* 259 (A. P. Simester and A. T. H. Smith eds., 1996).

69 "Saints" are those who never put prudential reasons ahead of moral reasons. On some theories of morality, saints must weigh their personal interests along with everyone else's, in which case their suffering punishment counts against the morality of their act. On other theories, they are permitted to be completely self-sacrificing, in which case they will consider only the effects of their punishment on others.

70 A similar device historically has been swearing an oath to abide by the rules on pain of divine punishment. Assuming that God would in fact punish those who swear such an oath and then violate the rules for moral reasons, the oath gives the same assurance of compliance as an ARD, at least if we also assume the oath swearer believes in a god who punishes oath violations. It has been recently argued that this function of oaths and its dependence on sincere religious belief explains demands for religious orthodoxy within a nation. See Mariam Thalos,

"The Economy of Belief, or Explaining Cooperation among the Prudent," 35 *Amer. Phil. Q.* 349 (1998).

71 Postema, supra note 22, at 819, 822. See also note 56 supra.

72 Rule violations that are *not* morally motivated will not trigger the ARD. And the morally motivated will not violate the rule because of effects on the innocent "hostages." (Of course, if the effects of the ARD are taken into account, someone who violated a rule for moral reasons would be immoral and thus would not trigger the ARD, which would make his act moral, which would trigger the ARD, . . . ad infinitum. To avoid this paradox, the ARD would have to be triggered by acts motivated by moral considerations independent of the ARD itself.)

If such an ARD were available, then based on an argument in favor of Lex and his rules, it would be morally right for Lex to install it. Of course, such an ARD fix would be dangerous. Once in place, the ARD produces perfect compliance. But Lex is fallible, and one of his rules might produce great evil, much worse evil than undermining serious rules would produce. Perhaps this is just another way of arguing that, like deception and other methods of giving up moral autonomy in return for moral benefits, automatic draconian punishments dangerously lock us into the rules we have and ask us to have faith that all will turn out for the best.

73 For example, even in the classic case of a rule, "Drive on the right," the presence of a boulder in the right lane would be a reason to violate the rule.

74 See H. L. A. Hart, *The Concept of Law* 127–30 (1961) (discussing the use of vague standards and custom in cases of uncertainty). Sexual conduct may be an area in which the costs of uniformity outweigh the benefits of settlement. See generally Emily Sherwin, "Infelicitous Sex," 2 *Legal Theory* 220–30 (1996).

75 Kavka, "The Toxin Puzzle," supra note 40. For recent commentary on Kavka's puzzle and its implications, see David Gauthier, "Rethinking the Toxin Puzzle," in *Rational Commitment and Social Justice* 47–58 (J. Coleman and C. Morris eds., 1998); Michael E. Bratman, "Toxin, Temptation, and The Stability of Intention," in *Coleman and Morris,* supra, 84–89; Gilbert Harman, "The Toxin Puzzle," in *Coleman and Morris,* supra, 59–83. See also Bratman, "Following Through with One's Plans: Reply to Gauthier," supra note 40; Gauthier, "Intention and Deliberation," supra note 40; Roy Sorenson, "Rewarding Regret," 108 *Ethics* 528 (1998); Robins, "Is It Rational to Carry Out Strategic Intentions?," supra note 40.

Chapter 5. Interpretation of Rules

1 Nor is disagreement about the meaning of rules a problem that can be solved by issuing more rules. A rule governing the meaning of rules must itself be a prospective rule stated in general terms, and therefore questions about *its* meaning will arise as it is applied. For example, if Lex provides that the words used in rules should be given their dictionary meaning, disputes can develop: "Which dictionary?" "Which edition?" "What if the dictionary meaning pro-

duces a ridiculous result?" Indeed, even if these questions do not arise, there is still the question of what language Lex is using in formulating his rules. If he were to issue a rule, "All my rules shall be interpreted as if they were in English," that rule would provide guidance only if we took *it* to be written in English. Any attempt to answer these questions by means of rules will lead to infinite regress.

2 In this chapter, we are consciously glossing over a number of very difficult issues affecting interpretation of rules. Our objective is simply to outline our position and relate it to the theme of authoritative settlement that runs throughout this book. For a fuller treatment of interpretive issues, see Larry Alexander, "All or Nothing at All?: The Intentions of Authorities and the Authority of Intentions," in *Law and Interpretation: Essays in Legal Philosophy* (Andrei Marmor ed., 1995). For other comprehensive discussions of the problems of interpretation, see Kent Greenawalt, *Statutory Interpretation: 20 Questions* (1999); *Law and Interpretation: Essays in Legal Philosophy,* supra; Keith E. Whittington, *Constitutional Interpretation: Textual Meaning, Original Intent, and Judicial Review* (1999). And for a very insightful treatment of many of the problems we take up in this chapter, see Kent Greenawalt, "From the Bottom Up," 82 *Corn. L. Rev.* 994 (1997).

3 For a good account of "semantic skepticism" and possible responses to it, see Jules L. Coleman and Brian Leiter, "Determinacy, Objectivity, and Authority," 142 *U. Pa. L. Rev.* 549, 568–72 (1993) (discussing Saul Kripke's interpretation of Wittgenstein in Saul A. Kripke, *Wittgenstein on Rules and Private Language* (1982)). See also Tomogi Shogenji, "The Problem of the Criterion in Rule-Following," 60 *Phil. & Phenomenological Res.* 501 (2000).

4 See, e.g., Frederick Schauer, *Playing by the Rules: A Philosophical Examination of Rule-Based Decision-Making in Law and Life* 54–68 (1991) (words have "semantic autonomy" independent of the "unformulated purposes for which a speaker employs that language" and the "particular context in which that language is used"); Coleman and Leiter, supra note 3, at 71–72 (there is a "public meaning" given to words through public behavior and understandings). Schauer appears to equate the meaning of rules with the conventional (dictionary) meaning of the words used, saying that this is necessary to preserve the "extensional divergence between instantiation and justification" that is essential to governance by rule. Schauer, supra, at 54–55. In contrast, we equate the meaning of rules with the rule-maker's intended meaning in issuing the rules. We believe intended meaning can be understood in a way that preserves the necessary divergence between rules and the purposes they serve.

5 Michael S. Moore, "A Natural Law Theory of Interpretation," 58 *S. Cal. L. Rev.* 277 (1985).

6 See generally Whittington, supra note 2.

7 See Ronald Dworkin, *Law's Empire* 176–224 (1986) ("integrity").

8 See, e.g., Jeffrey Goldsworthy, "Marmor on Meaning, Interpretation, and Legislative Intention," 1 *Legal Theory* 439, 454–56, 460–63 (1995) (showing the impoverished nature of literal meaning and the dependence of sentence meaning

on context and background assumptions); John R. Searle, "Literal Meaning," in *Expression and Meaning* (J. Searle ed., 1979) 117, 127 (same); John R. Searle, *The Construction of Social Reality* 129–37 (1995) (same); Whittington, supra note 2, at 95–96 (same); Greenawalt, supra note 2, at 38–39 (same, and illustrating by comparing "Keep off the grass" uttered by a park custodian and with the same command uttered by a drug counselor); Abner S. Greene, "The Work of Knowledge," 72 *Notre Dame L. Rev.* 1479, 1486–89 (1997) (arguing that meaning depends on authorial intent); Alexander, supra note 2, at 361–62 (pointing out that ambiguities in "text" produced by the proverbial thousand monkeys are in principle unresolvable).

9 See, e.g., Timothy A. O. Endicott, "Linguistic Indeterminacy," 16 *Oxford J. Legal Stud.* 667, 682–85 (1996) (demonstrating the semantic meaninglessness of unauthored "signs"); Whittington, supra note 2, at 94–99 (asserting the ontological identity of text and authorial intent and the semantic meaninglessness of unauthored "signs"); Laurence H. Tribe, "Comment," in *Antonin Scalia, A Matter of Interpretation* 65, 76–77 (1997) (pointing out that even "this text is to be read with the aid of the Oxford English Dictionary" may not mean what we think it does if *it* is not intended to be in English); Alexander, supra note 2, at 361–62 (arguing that the meaningfulness of a text requires an author who intends to communicate meaning in a particular language); Steven Knapp and Walter Benn Michaels, "Intention, Identity, and the Constitution," in *Legal Hermeneutics* (G. Leyh ed., 1992), 187, 190 (same); Steven Knapp and Walter Benn Michaels, "Against Theory," 8 *Critical Theory* 723, 725–30 (1982) (same); Steven Knapp and Walter Benn Michaels, "Against Theory 2: Hermeneutics and Deconstruction," 14 *Critical Theory* 49, 54, 60 (1987) (same); Richard S. Kay, "Original Intentions, Standard Meanings, and the Legal Character of the Constitution," 6 *Const. Commentary* 39, 40–45 (1989) (same); E. D. Hirsch Jr., "Counterfactuals in Interpretation," in *Interpreting Law and Literature* 57 (S. Levinson and S. Mailloux eds., 1988) (same); Stanley Fish, "Play of Surfaces: Theory and the Law," in *Legal Hermeneutics,* supra at 297, 299–300 (endorsing authorial intention as central to interpretation); Paul Campos, "Against Constitutional Theory," 4 *Yale J. Law and Hum.* 279, 301–02 (1992) (same); Jorge J. E. Garcia, "Can There Be Texts without Historical Authors?," 31 *Amer. Phil. Q.* 245, 251–52 (1994) (same).

10 See authorities cited in note 8 supra.

11 See Goldsworthy, supra note 8, at 448.

12 See, e.g., Whittington, supra note 2, at 60 (pointing out that all communication occurs within a context that provides information for deciphering authorial intent); Searle, *The Construction of Social Reality,* supra note 8, at 129–37 (same); Goldsworthy, supra note 8, at 456–58 (arguing that speaker's meaning is partially inferred from contextual implications); Peter Jeremy Smith, "Commas, Constitutional Grammar, and the Straight-Face Test: What If Conan the Grammarian Were a Strict Textualist?," 16 *Const. Commentary* 7 (1999) (demonstrating that we frequently disregard some evidence of speaker's meaning—such as the rules of grammar and punctuation and dictionary definitions—whenever the

contextual evidence of grammatical, punctuation, or diction errors outweighs it); Alexander, supra note 2, at 364, 403–4 (discussing nonstandard or idiosyncratic meanings and malapropisms); Hirsch, supra note 9, at 66–67 (discussing slips of the tongue); Greenawalt, supra note 2, at 46–49, 51–54, 57, 66 n.82, 93, 162–66 (discussing slips, unintended meanings, etc.).

13 See, e.g., Gary Lawson, "On Reading Recipes . . . and Constitutions," 85 *Georgetown L.J.* 1823 (1997) (analogizing constitutional interpretation to the reading of a recipe); Saikrishna B. Prakash, "Unoriginalism's Law without Meaning," 15 *Const. Commentary* 529, 541–46 (1998) (arguing that because the author of a legal text is the lawmaker—the person with authority to prescribe what ought to be done—we will want to know what he intended by his words, and that when we accept a text as law, we accept the meaning that the lawmaker intended it to carry).

14 See, e.g., Lawson, supra note 13 (analogizing legal rules to recipes).

15 See, e.g., Whittington, supra note 2, at 59 (adopting a Gricean analysis of textual meaning, that is, that the meaning of a text is what the author intended the audience to take the author as intending); Anita Avramides, "Intention and Convention," in *A Companion to the Philosophy of Language* 60, 71–75, 78–80 (Bob Hale and Crispin Wright eds., 1997) (setting forth the Gricean view of the meaning of a communication); H. P. Grice, *Study in the Way of Words,* essays 5, 6, and 14 (1989) (setting forth analysis of utterance meaning as turning on response that utterer intends an audience to make in light of audience's understanding of utterer's intent); Tom D. Campbell, *The Legal Theory of Ethical Positivism* 140–41 (1996) (giving Gricean analysis of legislative meaning); Joseph Raz, "Intention in Interpretation," in *The Autonomy of Law* 249, 259, 266 (Robert P. George ed., 1996) (relying on Gricean analysis of legislative meaning); Alexander, supra note 2, at 365–66 (arguing that legal texts mean what their authors intend their audience to take them to mean); Steven D. Smith, "Believing Like a Lawyer," 40 *Boston Coll. L. Rev. 1041* 1056–57 (1999) (same); Richard S. Kay, "American Constitutionalism," in *Constitutionalism: Philosophical Foundations* 16, 29–30 (L. Alexander ed., 1998) (same); Antonin Scalia, "Response," in Tribe, *Antonin Scalia,* supra note 9, at 144 (noting the relation between what a text is understood to mean and what it was intended to mean).

16 See, e.g., Greenawalt, supra note 2, at 103–4, 162–66 (arguing that legislature's expertise, but not coordination, gives interpreter reason to seek the legislature's intended meaning); Andrei Marmor, *Interpretation and Legal Theory* 156, 179 (1992) (same).

17 But see Hirsch, supra note 9, at 55, 62–67.

18 The text from this point through the paragraph after note 54 is taken substantially from Alexander, supra note 2, at 367–75.

19 Gregory Bassham, *Original Intent and the Constitution* 28–34, 69–71 (1992).

20 Bassham calls these latter intentions nonbinding intentions and includes among them such things as the authorities' intentions regarding their own authority. Id.

21 Id. at 29.

22 Id.

23 Id.

24 Id.

25 Id.

26 Id. at 32.

27 Id.

28 Id. at 79. They may not have always been rich, however. Bassham gives the example of a question that can arise under the Twenty-fifth Amendment, namely, whether a president who has suffered cessation of brain activity but not respiration or circulation is "dead." Here, the framers arguably intended their realist intentions to trump their conventionalist intentions. Id. at 82.

There are indications that on the question which semantic intentions should dominate—rich or spare—Bassham would follow the framers' own intentions. If a legislature discovered that its definition of toxicity was inconsistent with toxicity's true nature, it presumably would want true toxicity to control. On the other hand, Bassham suggests that the framers of the Constitution generally wanted their rich semantic intentions to control. See id. at 32, 80–82. But cf. id. at 51, 68–71 (preferring not to treat "interpretive intentions" as dispositive).

29 Id. at 51–56.

30 Id. at 68–71.

31 See generally Ralph Shain, "Mill, Quine, and Natural Kinds," 24 *Metaphilosophy* 275–92 (1993) (discussing problems with the concept of "natural kinds"). See also Marmor, supra note 16, at 144–45.

32 Bear in mind that we believe that exemplars, definitions, and referents ultimately are interrelated and cannot be neatly opposed.

For an analysis of how the various types and levels of generality of intentions should be reconciled that is similar to ours, see Whittington, supra note 2, at 184–87; Keith E. Whittington, "Dworkin's 'Originalism': The Role of Intentions in Constitutional Interpretation," 62 *Rev. of Pol.* 197, 215–25 (2000). And see Nicos Stavropoulos, *Objectivity in Law* 189–95 (1996) (dealing with conflicts of legislative intentions); M. B. W. Sinclair, "Legislative Intent: Fact or Fabrication?," 41 *N.Y.L. Sch. L. Rev.* 1329, 1363–64, 1370 (1997) (same); Michael W. McConnell, "The Importance of Humility in Judicial Review: A Comment on Ronald Dworkin's 'Moral Reading' of the Constitution," 65 *Fordham L. Rev.* 1269, 1280–84 (1997) (arguing that "[a] genuine commitment to the semantic intentions of the [lawmakers] requires the interpreter to seek the level of generality at which the particular language was understood by [them]"); Hirsch, supra note 9 (discussing speakers' dominant intentions); Greenawalt, supra note 2, at 131, 140–41 (arguing that legislator's dominant intention is what his rule means where his specific and general intentions conflict).

33 Note that because the role of authorities is to determine what ought to be done—to make moral principles concrete enough to guide citizens and officials—when the authorities intend the true nature of the referents of the terms they employ to dominate their own inconsistent definitions and exemplars, they

are in some sense defaulting on their role. In making binding effects of enactment turn on the true nature of moral terms, whatever that nature happens to be, the authorities have failed to give moral guidance; and in making those effects turn on the true nature of natural kinds, they have left a good deal to the unknown (which is why we believe that reference cannot completely take leave of sense).

34 The best discussion of why interpretation should not be tied to the true nature of the things to which the legal text's words refer is found in Stephen R. Munzer, "Realistic Limits on Realist Interpretation," 58 *S. Cal. L. Rev.* 459 (1985). Munzer, replying to Michael Moore's realist theory of legal interpretation, points out that many words do not name "kinds" of any type (461–62), that words that name "functional kinds" do not presuppose an underlying true nature of these kinds (466–68), that moral terms and natural-kind terms may not map on to reality in any neat way (462, 464), and finally, that for many legal texts, conventional understandings should dominate the true nature of terms' referents (468–70). In the latter category, Munzer places a statute limiting the harvest of "fish" written at a time when whales were thought to be fish. Given certain purposes for the statute, it should be read to include whales (468–70). And see Anthony Dardis, "How the Radically Interpreted Make Mistakes," 33 *Dialogue* 415, 423–25 (1994) (discussing malapropisms, classic instances where semantic intentions come apart, not in terms of referent versus definition, but in terms of word chosen versus word meant).

35 Lawrence Lessig, "Fidelity inTranslation," 71 *Tex. L. Rev.* 1165 (1993).

36 Id. at 1211.

37 Id. at 1211 et seq.

38 Id. at 1213–14.

39 Id. at 1234–36.

40 384 U.S. 436 (1966).

41 Lessig, supra note 35, at 1215–17.

42 U.S. Const. amend. X.

43 Lessig, supra note 35, 1224–28.

44 Id. at 1251.

45 Id. at 1176–77.

46 Id. at 1251 et seq.

47 Id. at 1252–61.

48 Id. at 1253–54.

49 Id.

50 Id. at 1254–55.

51 Id. at 1253.

52 Lessig could be read as endorsing a counterfactual test for determining the intentions of the authorities—for example, their intentions are what they should have enacted had they realized the conflict between their specific and their more general or abstract purposes. David Brink endorses just such a test, though he realizes that because authorities would always resolve such conflict between

levels of generality of purpose in favour of the more abstract level, the approach threatens to make all laws into an injunction, "do the right thing," which would not be an authoritative determination or in any way constrain interpreters. David O. Brink, "Legal Theory, Legal Interpretation, and Judicial Review," 17 *Phil. and Pub. Aff.* 105, 126–29 (1988). And see Michael J. Klarman, "Antifidelity," 70 *S. Cal. L. Rev.* 381 (1997) (arguing against Lessig's theory of translation on the ground that it reduces the meaning of the law to how the subjects would resolve the problem to which the law is addressed); Greenawalt, supra note 2, at 133 (same). But see Marmor, supra note 16, at 171–72 (advocating reliance on the highest level purposes of the authorities). Marmor believes that giving precedence to how legislators intend their law to apply in given circumstances over what they intend to accomplish through such applications is incoherent. It seems to us, however, that we can intend to ban the bomb in order to promote peace and without any incoherence maintain that banning the bomb is what we intended even when confronted with arguments that peace is better maintained through nuclear arms. See also Ronald Dworkin, *Life's Dominion* 136–37 (1993). The problem with such a counterfactual test is that it ultimately cannot distinguish two things that must be distinguished if authorities are to play their role: what the authorities *did* and what the authorities *would have done* (had they not made various mistakes). See Win-Chiat Lee, "Statutory Interpretation and the Counterfactual Test for Legislative Intention," 8 *Law and Phil.* 383, 397–401, 403–4 (1989).

With respect to factual and legal errors, Lessig's approach ultimately collapses the distinction between what is implied *in* a statute and what is implied *by* a statute. Many things about the world are implied by statutes but are not in them, in the sense that they are legally operative. A law criminalizing prostitution may imply that the legislature holds a view of the world such that refusing to enforce contracts entered into by prostitutes would be desirable. Nonetheless, it does not follow without more from this implication about the world that the law criminalizing prostitution itself renders prostitutes' contract unenforceable. Or a law imposing a duty regarding sex discrimination may imply that the legislature would view a private right of action to enforce that duty as a good idea, were it to consider the question. In order to find such a private right of action to be implied *in* the law imposing the duty, however, it has to be such a good idea that we can infer that the legislature actually determined that it existed.

For an excellent discussion of how changed circumstances can affect the meaning of a directive, see Greenawalt, supra note 2, at 1017–26.

53 Lessig, supra note 35, at 1253.

54 Id. at 1255.

55 See Coleman and Leiter, supra note 3, at 568–72. Kripke's interpretation of Wittgenstein is found in Kripke, supra note 3, at 55–113. The primary passages in Wittgenstein that serve as the basis for the skeptical argument are in Ludwig Wittgenstein, *Philosophical Investigations* sec. 203 (G. E. M. Abscombe trans., 1953).

56 Coleman and Leiter, supra note 3, at 569–70.

57 See John A. Humphrey, "Quine, Kripke's Wittgenstein, and Sceptical Solutions," 37 *S.J. Phil.* 43, 47 (1999) (denying the existence of "meaning facts"); Alex Byrne, "On Misinterpreting Kripke's Wittgenstein," 56 *Phil. and Phenomenological Res.* 339 (1996) (denying that any fact can determine meaning); Charles M. Yablon, "Law and Metaphysics," 96 *Yale L.J.* 613, 627 (1987) (same); Thomas Nagel, *The Last Word* 45–46 (1997) (same).

58 See Christian Zapf and Eben Moglen, "Linguistic Indeterminacy and the Rule of Law: On the Perils of Misunderstanding Wittgenstein," 84 *Georgetown L.J.* 485, 500–6 (1996) (correct application of a rule is the product of training rather than reflection); Arthur Ripstein, "Law, Language, and Interpretation," 46 *U. Toronto L.J.* 335, 338–39 (1996) (understanding rules is a matter of skill rather than an intellectual feat); Andrei Marmor, "The Separation Thesis and the Limits of Interpretation," 12 *Canadian J.L. and Jurisprudence* 135, 136–41 (1999) (understanding linguistic rules is learning how to engage in a complex practice); Yablon, supra note 57, at 631–32 (same).

59 See, e.g., Yablon, supra note 57, at 629–30 (rule-following is learned in a community); Lawrence B. Solum, "On the Indeterminacy Crisis: Critiquing Critical Dogma," 54 *U. Chi. L. Rev.* 462, 477–80 (1987) (same); Michael Robertson, "Picking Positivism Apart: Stanley Fish on Epistemology and Law," 8 *S. Cal. Interdisciplinary L.J.* 401, 437–41 (1999) (attributing to Stanley Fish the view that clear meanings of rules come from "seeing" them with eyes shaped by a common embeddedness in the training, practices, beliefs, goals, and categories of a community); Byrne, supra note 57, at 343 (arguing that the meaning of a rule is in its use in a form of life); Onora O'Neill, *Toward Justice and Virtue* 83–84 (1996) (same); Gary Ebbs, *Rule-Following and Realism* 296–98, 300–3 (1997) (arguing that the meaning of a rule is derived from social practices of rule-following); Anthony J. Sebok, "Finding Wittgenstein at the Core of the Rule of Recognition," 52 *S.M.U. L. Rev.* 75, 92 et seq. (same); Nagel, supra note 57, at 52–53 (same); Stavropoulos, supra note 32, at 147–55 (same).

60 See, e.g., Ripstein, supra note 58, at 338–39 (commenting on how we just "grasp" the meaning of many rules); Schauer, supra note 4, at 207–8 (asserting that in ordinary cases, we just "grasp" what a rule means).

61 See, e.g., Coleman and Leiter, supra note 3, at 571–72 (pointing out that the absence of "meaning facts" does not undermine the determinacy of rules); Endicott, supra note 9, at 690–91 (same); Kay, supra note 15, at 28–29 (noting that the claim that all rules are indeterminate is operationally self-refuting); Schauer, supra note 4, at 66–68 (noting how, despite the skepticism traceable to the interpretation of Wittgenstein under consideration, we *do* understand and follow rules); Yablon, supra note 57, at 628–33 (same); Kent Greenawalt, *Law and Objectivity* 72–73 (1992) (same). But see Shogenji, supra note 3 (expressing skepticism about whether the claim that we understand rules can be justified).

62 See, e.g., Frederick Schauer, "Formalism," 97 *Yale L.J.* 509, 526–28 (1988) (showing how a rule's meaning can be a function of its purpose without being re-

ducible to or necessarily consistent with that purpose); Kent Greenawalt, "The Nature of Rules and the Meaning of Meaning," 72 *Notre Dame L. Rev.* 1449, 1462–68 (1997) (arguing that having context and purpose supply meaning to rules does not undermine their ruleness); Greenawalt, supra note 2, at 40–43, 66, 69 (same); Campbell, supra note 15, at 141–42 (same). See also Goldsworthy, supra note 8, at 454–55 (giving examples of cases where purpose behind rule contributes to the rule's meaning).

63 For some other examples like this in the literature, see William N. Eskridge Jr., "Textualism, The Unknown Ideal?," 96 *Mich. L. Rev.* 1509, 1553 (1998) (arguing that the NBA rule forbidding players from leaving the bench during a fight should not be read to forbid a player's going to the restroom or coming to the aid of a player about to be killed); Bernard W. Bell, "'No Motor Vehicles in the Park': Reviving the Hart-Fuller Debate to Introduce Statutory Construction," 48 *J. Legal Educ.* 88, 97 (1998) (giving the example of a "No vehicles in the park" rule as applied to an ambulance that enters to pick up a heart attack victim); Alexander, supra note 2, at 376–77 (giving example of handing a friend your checkbook and asking him to purchase some curry powder for a dinner party you are giving, only to have him return with a bottle of curry powder and a $2,500 deduction from your checkbook occasioned by curry powder's being in short supply); Greenawalt, supra note 61, at 16–18 (discussing Sam's [a superior's] request to Beth [a subordinate] to shut Sam's office door, and suggesting that the request does not require shutting the door in the face of the company president, who, unbeknownst to Sam, is about to enter Sam's office); Goldsworthy, supra note 8, at 454–55 (discussing such cases as the ordering of a hamburger in a restaurant, in response to which the waiter brings a hamburger encased in a cube of hard plastic); id. at 456–57 (discussing how certain meanings are implied *in* statements on the basis of context and background assumptions, which meanings are different from the more general worldview implied *by* statements); Wittgenstein, supra note 55, at 33 ("Someone says to me: 'Shew the children a game.' I teach them gaming with dice, and the other says, 'I didn't mean that sort of game.' Must the exclusion of the game with dice have come before his mind when he gave me the order to make this last statement true?"); Greenawalt, supra note 2, at 998 (arguing that an order from a basketball coach to his team, which has a three-point lead with twenty-four seconds remaining, not to take a shot, but to try to run out the clock, does not mean that if a player finds herself unguarded under the basket, she cannot take a shot that she is virtually certain to make); Cass R. Sunstein, *One Case at a Time* 219–21 (1999) (discussing the case of Church of the Holy Trinity v. United States, 143 U.S. 457 (1892), in which the question was whether a ban on the importation of laborers included a ban on a church's hiring a minister from abroad, and concluding that there are times when the context of legislation reveals that some literal application was not intended).

64 See, e.g., Alexander, supra note 2, at 376 (arguing that a request for curry powder is not satisfied by alfalfa sprouts, even if cultivating a taste for alfalfa sprouts

will ultimately lead to more pleasure in life, which is the most general purpose behind the original request).

65 See Cass R. Sunstein, "Justice Scalia's Formalism," 107 *Yale L.J.* 529, 544 (1997) ("Because of the inevitable limitations of human foresight, even the most carefully chosen words can become unclear because and not in spite of their generality."). Sunstein cites H. L. A. Hart's famous passage in which Hart attributes penumbral uncertainty in the meaning of all rules to "relative indeterminacy of aim." H. L. A. Hart, *The Concept of Law* 125 (1961).

66 See Greenawalt, supra note 2, at 1015–17 (discussing how goal of coordination interacts with goal of expertise). See also Stavropoulos, supra note 32, at 192–93 (arguing that intent to enact a determinate rule affects understanding of rule's content).

67 See note 63 supra.

68 See Cernauskes v. Fletcher, 21 Ark. 678, 201 S.W.2d 999 (1947).

69 U.S. Const. amend. XVII.

70 See Smith, supra note 12, at 13–16. See also Hirsch, supra note 9, at 66–67 (discussing cases where someone utters "Friday" but can correctly claim "I meant Thursday," and those where someone must say "I meant Friday, but I was mistaken"). For another perspective on these matters, see P.M.S. Hacker, "Davidson on First-Person Authority," 47 *Phil. Q.* 285, 296–99, 302–3 (1997).

71 471 U.S. 84, 93–96 (1985).

72 See Whittington, supra note 2, at 193. We do not deny, of course, that collective bodies frequently possess *an* intended meaning that they successfully communicate to others. We think that as we move from individual Lexes to group Lexes, the range of indeterminacy will generally increase, but in a large number of cases, the rules will remain determinate. See Prakash, supra note 13, at 536 (pointing out that groups of people can meaningfully communicate); Raz, supra note 15, at 263 (same); Greenawalt, supra note 2, at 147–49 (deeming the intentions of the majority to be *the* intention that constitutes the rule). For different views of the intentions of multimember legislative bodies, see Bret Boyce, "Originalism and the Fourteenth Amendment," 33 *Wake Forest L. Rev.* 909, 954–55 (1998) (noting problems with aggregating intentions to construct a group intention); Jeremy Waldron, *Law and Disagreement,* chap. 6 (1999) (arguing against intentionalist interpretation of the rules enacted by multimember legislatures on the ground that it is undemocratic). But see Alexander, supra note 2, at 396–99 (discussing Waldron).

73 In chapter 3, we outlined a hierarchy of rules within our imaginary community, comprised of preconstitutional rules agreed to by all members of the community (including the rule "Let Lex decide"), constitutional rules adopted by a large segment of the community, and rules issued by Lex. Constitutional rules are not subject to the will of Lex and can only be adopted or changed by processes approved at the preconstitutional level. Preconstitutional rules are wholly dependent on the continuing endorsement of the community, but nevertheless tend to endure because of the strong common interest in settlement.

74 See Raz, supra note 15, at 285 n.25 (pointing out how "mindless" law can result from the process described); Steven D. Smith, "Law without Mind," 88 *Mich. L. Rev.* 104 (1989) (same).

75 See chapter 3. Interpretation of constitutional rules may differ if those rules are set in the form of standards rather than determinate rules.

76 See Lon L. Fuller, *The Morality of Law* (1969).

77 Lex will, of course, formulate his rules in light of such preconstitutional norms, so that there will be a convergence of Lex's intended meaning and the meaning forced by operation of the preconstitutional norms. See Campbell, supra note 15, at 140–41.

For an excellent discussion of the costs and benefits of a norm dictating that Lex's rules should be read as if Lex intended their "plain meaning" in a particular language, see David A. Strauss, "Why Plain Meaning?," 72 *Notre Dame L. Rev.* 1565, 1574–80 (1997). Strauss looks at a "plain meaning" norm in terms of how well it captures Lex's intent, including Lex's intent to make his rules determinate, and how well it achieves coordination. See also Cass R. Sunstein, *One Step at a Time* 222–24 (1999).

78 Of course, interpretation of preconstitutional rules follows the same basic principles as interpretation of Lex's rules, or of Super Lex's constitutional rules. Therefore, the community's intent may be inaccessible in some cases that call for application of preconstitutional rules such as a rule that prefers dictionary meaning to highly idiosyncratic intended meaning. At that point, how Michael proceeds depends on whether there is a preconstitutional norm assigning him authority to settle the matter.

79 If evidence of Lex's intent is accessible differentially, consulting it may achieve the goal (for some) of utilizing Lex's expertise but may raise the costs of decision-making and also fail to achieve coordination among those subject to Lex's rule. See Goldsworthy, supra note 8, at 453 n.66; Sunstein, supra note 77, at 224–25; Adrian Vermeule, "Legislative History and the Limits of Judicial Competence: The Untold Story of *Holy Trinity Church*," 50 Stan. L. Rev. 1833, 1862 (1998) (pointing out costs of consulting legislative history). An important factor in the calculus regarding when it is advisable to have a norm excluding from consideration types of evidence of Lex's intent is to whom the rules in question are primarily addressed. If they are addressed to ordinary citizens, then exclusion of some kinds of evidence of Lex's intent may be more warranted than if the rules are primarily addressed to expert bodies, such as courts and administrators.

80 This is not to deny that if there is a high degree of consensus on what counts as moral absurdity and serious injustice, the community might agree, either constitutionally or preconstitutionally, to limit Lex's authority through such standards, or through rules implementing such standards. But the process should not be confused with the process of interpreting Lex's rules. Moreover, it is important to distinguish *rules* that might be absurd or seriously unjust from *applications* (of otherwise good rules) that might be absurd or seriously unjust,

even though the rules Lex promulgates are in a sense only applications of "Let Lex decide." If each application of a rule can be overridden by a norm against serious injustice or absurdity, the costs to coordination and decision-making efficiency will rise relative to the costs of overall assessments of rules under such norms.

81 See Whittington, supra note 2, at 40.

Chapter 6. Reasoning by Analogy

1 For more on this point, see Larry Alexander, "The Banality of Legal Reasoning," 73 *Notre Dame L. Rev.* 517, 518–19 (1998).

2 See John Rawls, *A Theory of Justice* 46–53 (1971) (explaining the method of "reflective equilibrium"); Scott Brewer, "Exemplary Reasoning: Semantics, Pragmatics, and the Rational Force of Legal Argument by Analogy," 109 *Harv. L. Rev.* 923, 938–39, 963, 1023 (1996) (discussing analogical reasoning and characterizing it as a form of reflective equilibrium); Norman Daniels, "Wide Reflective Equilibrium and Theory Acceptance in Ethics," 76 *J. Phil.* 256, 256–61 (1979) (discussing the role of background theories in reflective equilibrium); Howard Klepper, "Justification and Methodology in Practical Ethics," 226 *Metaphilosophy* 201, 205–6 (1995) (discussing the force of reflective equilibrium and the role of intermediate rules).

3 This example is based on the case of Bridges v. Hawkesworth, 21 L.J.Q.B. 75, [1843–60] All Eng. Rpts. 122 (1851), with minor adjustments in the facts.

4 See Alexander, supra note 1, at 519–22. Of course, as we pointed out in chapter 2, "rules" that refer to moral principles—that is, standards—fail to fulfill the function of rules to settle authoritatively what morally ought to be done. And as we pointed out in chapter 5, any interpretive methodology that made "interpretation" of a posited rule turn on the morality of its prescription would similarly undermine the function of rules.

5 E.g., Anthony Kronman, *The Lost Lawyer* 170–85 (1993); Cass R. Sunstein, *Legal Reasoning and Political Conflict* 62–100 (1996); Brewer, supra note 2.

6 Our discussion of analogical reasoning refers to analogy as a method by which judges develop common law in the absence of rules. It has been suggested that analogical reasoning also plays a role in the interpretation of statutes, particularly when courts apply the maxim "ejusdem generis," which calls for interpretation of general language by reference to specific examples given in the statute. See Brewer, supra note 2, at 937–38.

We think this is a misunderstanding, or at least a very different use of the analogical method. If the enterprise of interpretation is understood as an effort to ascertain the authors' intent or the audiences' understanding, the method of reasoning is empirical. Analogical reasoning may provide evidence of intent if there is reason to think it tracks what was intended or what was understood. But the object is to determine what was intended or understood, not what is correct, and the examples are important only insofar as they may bear on intent or understanding.

If interpretation is understood as an effort to reach the best moral outcome in light of the enactment of the text, the method involved is ordinary moral reasoning. Textual examples may be relevant to gauging the effects the text has had, such as reliance, and a judge might employ analogical reasoning as one way to discover what expectations the text is likely to have produced. But because the process of interpretation is ultimately independent of the text on this view, there is no reason why textual examples should be treated as unalterable starting points for reflective equilibrium. See Larry Alexander, "Bad Beginnings," 145 *U. Pa. L. Rev.* 57, 77–78 (1996).

7 See Kronman, supra note 5; Charles Fried, "The Artificial Reason of the Law or : What Lawyers Know," 60 *Text. L. Rev.* 35, 57 (1981).

8 See Henry M. Hart Jr. and Albert M. Sacks, *The Legal Process: Basic Problems in the Making and Application of Law* 398 (1958).

9 See Edward Levi, *An Introduction to Legal Reasoning* 2–4 (1949).

10 See Ronald Dworkin, *Law's Empire* 95–96, 225–75.

11 See Sunstein, supra note 5, at 65–69.

12 See Kronman, supra note 5; Fried, supra note 7, at 57. See also Brewer, supra note 2, at 952 (discussing the "mystical" view of analogical reasoning). Brian Leiter also appears to endorse this "judges' special know-how" view of analogical reasoning in "Heidegger and the Theory of Adjudication," 106 *Yale L.J.* 253 (1996).

13 Here we agree with Richard Posner. See Richard A. Posner, *The Problems of Jurisprudence* 89 (1990) (suggesting that one form of analogical reasoning is in fact enthymematic).

14 Brewer, supra note 2, at 938–39.

15 Id. at 954–55, 966.

16 This example is based on the facts of Foster v. Fidelity Safe Deposit, 174 S.W. 376 (Mo. 1915).

17 This example is based on the facts of MacAvoy v. Medina, 11 Allen 548 (Mass. 1866).

18 See Foster v. Fidelity Safe Deposit, supra note 16, at 378.

19 This is the view of analogical reasoning suggested by Fred Schauer and Peter Westen. See Frederick Schauer, *Playing by the Rules* 183–87 (1991); Peter Westen, "On 'Confusing Ideas': Reply," 91 *Yale L.J.* 1153 (1982).

20 See Brewer, supra note 2, at 947–48.

21 Id. at 954.

22 See Alexander, supra note 6, at 73–75 (1996); Alexander, supra note 1, at 526–28.

There are really three critical ways in which analogical reasoning from prior judicial decisions differs from the method of reflective equilibrium. First, a judge employing analogical reasoning looks only to the judgments of other judges as starting points. A reasoner employing reflective equilibrium may consider anyone's judgment. Second, a judge employing analogical reasoning must accept the judgments of other judges as correct, even if they are not. Those judgments are unalterable. That is not so in the method of reflective equilibrium, where all judgments about particular cases can be revised. Third, a judge employing analogical reasoning must deal with only those aspects of prior cases that the earlier judges deemed sufficiently relevant to note. In other words, the actual cases are not perceived by later judges in all their particularity but only in a rationale-filtered, stylized form. The method of reflective equilibrium, however, allows and encourages the moral reasoner to add and subtract facts from imaginary situations in order to discern how her moral judgments are affected and to identify the governing moral principles. See Alexander, supra note 6, at 73–75.

23 See Alexander, supra note 6, at 80–83; Alexander, supra note 1, at 530–31. The situation of the judge employing analogical reasoning is therefore like that of a zoologist asked to continue a project of sorting animals into "fish" and "mammals" begun by another zoologist whose classifications must be accepted as correct. The first zoologist has classified whales and porpoises as "fish" and bats and kangaroos as "mammals." The current zoologist must now decide analogically how to classify seals—in other words, decide whether seals are more like whales and porpoises or more like bats. He will, of course, find it impossible to do so nonarbitrarily. In effect, the question he must answer is "What would seals be in a world in which whales and porpoises were fish?" We doubt that such a question is meaningful.

24 See Alexander, supra note 6, at 86–87 n.96. Conceived this way, reasoning by analogy is closely related to Ronald Dworkin's "legal principles"—principles he describes as the morally best principles that can be made to "fit" with past decisions. See Ronald Dworkin, *Law's Empire* 238–50 (1986) (describing the process by which judges discover legal principles); Ronald Dworkin, *Taking Rights Seriously* 22–39 (1977) (describing legal principles). We take up Dworkin's legal principles and their relation to reasoning by analogy and to following precedent in chapter 8. See also the discussion of the result model of precedent in chapter 7.

25 See Emily Sherwin, "A Defense of Analogical Reasoning in Law," 66 *U. Chi. L. Rev.* 1179 (1999).

26 Cognitive studies provide strong evidence that our reasoning is affected by a bias in favor of facts that are particularly salient or "available." Our attention is drawn to information of this kind, at the expense of more remote or abstract information bearing on the same problem. See, e.g. Amos Tversky and Daniel Kahneman, "Availability: A Heuristic for Judging Frequency and Probability," in *Judgment under Uncertainty: Heuristics and Biases* 163, 163–65, 174–78 (Daniel Kahneman, Paul Slovic, and Amos Tversky eds., 1982).

27 The hindsight bias is discussed in an interesting article by Jeffrey Rachlinski. Rachlinski argues that the law has developed a number of effective second-best strategies for coping with hindsight bias. Jeffrey J. Rachlinski, "A Positive Psychological Theory of Judging in Hindsight," 65 *U. Chi. L. Rev.* 571, 619–23 (1998).

28 See text at note 26 supra.

29 We have deemed the incorporation of past error to be analogical reasoning's

chief defect. We do not mean, however, to minimize the fact that when analogical reasoning incorporates past error, it also becomes indeterminate. For analogizing from past error amounts to asking what would justify unjustifiable decisions. And no answer to that question can be rationally supportable. We are assuming, therefore, that judges *do* answer that question even though their answers will of necessity lack rational force.

30 See, e.g., Edmund Burke, *Reflections on the Revolution in France, and on the Proceedings in Certain Societies in London Relative to that Event* (1790), reprinted in Edmund Burke, *Selected Writings and Speeches* 424, 469–70 (Peter Stanlis ed., 1963). Lord Coke said that "if all the reason that is dispersed into so many sevarall heads, were united into one, yet could he not make such a law as the law of *England* is; because by many successions of ages it hath beene fined and refined by an infinite number of grave and learned men, and by long experience growne to such a perfection." So. Lit. 97b (1621).

Chapter 7. Reasoning in Light of Precedent

1 Larry Alexander first described these three models of precedent in Larry Alexander, "Constrained by Precedent," 63 *S. Cal. L. Rev.* 1 (1989). A more recent version of the three models appears in Larry Alexander, "Precedent," in *A Companion to Philosophy of Law and Legal Theory* 503 (Dennis Patterson ed., 1996).

2 See Alexander, "Constrained by Precedent," supra note 1, at 5–7; see also Michael S. Moore, "Precedent, Induction, and Ethical Generalization," in *Precedent in Law* 183 (Laurence Goldstein ed., 1987).

3 On the expectations generated by prior decisions, see, e.g., Stephen R. Perry, "Judicial Obligations, Precedent and the Common Law," 7 *Oxford J. Legal Stud.* 215, 248–50 (1987).

4 Throughout this discussion, we have in mind "horizontal" precedents—that is, cases decided by the same court or a court of equal rank in the adjudicative hierarchy. When the prior cases were decided by a court of superior rank, there are additional and often conclusive reasons for the lower court to conform to the prior decisions, which are derivative from the reasons of judicial coordination that led Lex to establish the hierarchy. See Alexander, "Precedent," supra note 1, at 512.

5 See, e.g., Annot., "Liability for Loss of Automobile Left at Parking Lot or Garage," 13 A.L.R. 4th 362, 407–13 (1982) (collecting cases in which lot owner was not liable).

6 See, e.g., Kent Greenawalt, "How Empty Is the Idea of Equality?," 83 *Colum. L. Rev.* 1167, 1170–72 (1983); Moore, supra note 2, at 204.

7 A prior decision that was correctly decided is of no moment here. Moral correctness is a sufficient reason for a similar decision in the present case, without reference to equality.

8 See Peter Westen, *Speaking of Equality: An Analysis of the Rhetorical Force of "Equality" in Moral and Legal Discourse* 119–23 (1990) (people and things can only be "alike" by reference to some criterion of relevant likeness, and the criterion

of relevant likeness must depend on an underlying conclusion about proper treatment).

9 See Alexander, "Constrained by Precedent," supra note 1, at 12–13.

10 See, e.g., Allen v. Hyatt Regency-Nashville Hotel, 661 S.W.2d 286, 289 (1984).

11 See John E. Coons, "Consistency," 75 *Cal. L. Rev.* 59, 102–7 (1987) (doubting "that repetition is a good in itself").

12 Alexander, "Constrained by Precedent," supra note 1, at 10.

13 See Larry Alexander and Ken Kress, "Replies to Our Critics," 82 *Iowa L. Rev.* 923, 937–38 (1997) (responding to a similar self-effacing view of moral principles held by Postema).

14 Put differently, it requires the judge to ask whether Browns are relevantly similar to Blacks or are relevantly similar to Whites, which reduces to the incoherent question "What treatment would Browns deserve in a world in which Blacks deserved worse treatment than Whites?" See id. at 930 n.41.

15 See, e.g., Westen, supra note 8, at 119–23; Christopher J. Peters, "Equality Revisited," 110 *Harv. L. Rev.* 1210 (1997); Peter Westen, "The Empty Idea of Equality," 95 *Harv. L. Rev.* 537 (1982).

16 See Ronald Dworkin, *Taking Rights Seriously* 266–78 (1978) (identifying a basic right to equal concern and respect as the source of more concrete rights and liberties).

17 We take up this topic again in chapter 8 in our critique of Ronald Dworkin's notion of legal principles. See also Larry Alexander and Ken Kress, "Against Legal Principles," 82 *Iowa L. Rev.* 739, 754–55, 778–85 (1997); Alexander, "Constrained by Precedent," supra note 1, at 9–13.

18 See Alexander, "Constrained by Precedent," supra note 1, at 17–19. See also Frederick Schauer, *Playing by the Rules: A Philosophical Examination of Rule-Based Decision-Making in Law and Life* 185–87 (1991) (adopting a rule model).

19 See Alexander, "Precedent," supra note 1, at 506.

20 See Schauer, supra note 18, at 185–87 (discussing the implicit constraint of prior decisions).

21 See, e.g., Hannah v. Peel, (1945) 1 K.B. 509, 517–19 (1945) (distinguishing a prior case on the basis of facts not relied on in the prior opinion); Edward Levy, *An Introduction to Legal Reasoning* 1–4 (1949) (endorsing the method).

22 We pointed out in chapter 4 that rule-sensitive particularism depends on rules having value, which in turn requires that most people not be rule-sensitive particularists. Rule-sensitive particularism cannot be generally publicized as the correct approach to rules.

23 See Alexander, "Constrained by Precedent," supra note 1, at 28–34. And see, e.g., Ronald Dworkin, *Law's Empire* 240–50, 254–58 (1986); Levy, supra note 21, at 1–27; Joseph Raz, *The Authority of Law* 183–89 (1979).

24 See, e.g., Levy, supra note 21, at 2 (judges are not bound by the statements of prior judges).

25 See Alexander, "Constrained by Precedent," supra note 1, at 29–30.

26 See id. at 34–37.

Confusion increases because case 1 has a fortiori force for the opposite result as well—a decision for the finder, which would yield four more utiles than a decision for the owner of the garage. In fact, at this level of generality, all cases, whether decided correctly or incorrectly, will qualify as precedents for all other cases, with correct cases and incorrect cases pulling in opposite directions. See id. at 35–36.

Larry Alexander illustrates the problem with a fortiori decision-making with this example:

> Criminal cases upholding a privilege against self-incrimination where the threat against defendants for remaining silent is loss of employment appear to make administrative cases involving threats of criminal prosecution for failures to file incriminating reports *a fortiori* cases in favor of defendants. Yet the decisions in the latter case were decided against those invoking the privilege. Thus, they make the criminal cases *a fortiori* cases in favor of the state.
>
> The upshot of these examples is that we cannot use a correct metric of weight for determining what is an *a fortiori* case relative to a precedent case that was incorrectly decided (by that same metric). Either the incorrectly decided precedent case is like a misshaped piece of a jigsaw puzzle that cannot be pieced together with correctly decided precedents, or, alternatively, correct decisions will always dominate incorrect decisions on the *a fortiori* analysis, producing no precedential constraint.
>
> Alexander, "Precedent," supra note 1, at 508.

27 Dworkin, supra note 23, at 230–32, 254–58.

28 Id. at 255.

29 Id. at 95–96, 225–54.

30 We are taking some liberty in interpreting Dworkin this way. It is not entirely clear whether Dworkin would confine judges to consideration of past results, or would have them consider rules and rationales announced in past cases as well. It is possible, in other words, that Dworkin has in mind a hybrid of the rule and result models, in which judges construct principles in the absence of canonical judicial rules. Our reading of Dworkin's remarks, however, is that he would limit the authoritative effect of past cases to their results and would give announced rules only their natural weight in the construction of principles. Compare Dworkin, supra note 16, at 110–15 (referring to the "enactment force" of precedents) with Dworkin, supra note 23, at 284 (fit with "past judicial rhetoric and opinion" is only "one desideratum that might be outweighed by others in deciding whether an interpretation fits"). We shall briefly consider the possibility of a hybrid model later in this chapter.

31 See Dworkin, supra note 23, at 255–56 (discussing "hard cases").

32 See, e.g., Schauer, supra note 18, at 31–34, 47–52.

33 See Alexander, "Constrained by Precedent," supra note 1, at 27–28; Moore, supra note 2, at 186–87.

34 See Amos Tversky and Daniel Kahneman, "Availability: A Heuristic for Judg-

ing Frequency and Predictability," in *Judgment under Uncertainty: Heuristics and Biases* 163, 163–65, 174–76 (Daniel Kahneman, Paul Slovic, and Amos Tversky eds., 1982); Jeffrey J. Rachlinski, "A Positive Psychological Theory of Judging in Hindsight," 65 *U. Chi. L. Rev.* 571, 576–81 (1998).

35 Levy is explicit that rules and rationales should be ignored. Levy, supra note 21, at 2. Dworkin is ambiguous but strongly suggests prior rules are not authoritative. See note 30 supra.

36 See Dworkin, supra note 16, at 14–45 (discussing legal principles as sources of preexisting obligation, prior to the announcement of rules).

37 See Alexander, "Precedent," supra note 1, at 509.

38 See Edmund Burke, "Reflections on the Revolution in France," (1798), reprinted in Edmund Burke, *Selected Writings and Speeches* 424, 469–70 (Peter J. Stanlis, ed. 1963); Robert C. Clark, "Contracts, Elites, and Traditions in the Making of Corporate Law," 89 *Colum. L. Rev.* 1730–37 (1989); Isaac Erlich and Richard A. Posner, "An Economic Analysis of Legal Rulemaking." 3 *J. Legal Stud.* 257, 266–67 (1974).

39 See Alexander, "Constrained by Precedent," supra note 1, at 50.

40 See Heidi M. Hurd, "Challenging Authority," 100 *Yale L.J.* 1611, 1620, 1625–28 (1991); Michael S. Moore, "Authority, Law, and Razian Reasons," 62 *S. Cal. L. Rev.* 827, 873–83 (1989); Donald H. Regan, "Authority and Value: Reflections on Raz's *Morality of Freedom*," 62 *S. Cal. L. Rev.* 995, 1006–18, 1028–31 (1989).

41 For an argument in support of this practice, see Beryl Harold Levy, "Realist Jurisprudence and Prospective Overruling," 109 *U. Pa. L. Rev.* 1, 2 (1960) (prospective overruling "sharpen[s] the appellate process as an implement of legal change"). The United States Supreme Court has disapproved the practice of prospective overruling in a series of cases. See, e.g., Harper v. Virginia Dept. of Taxation, 509 U.S. 86 (1993); James B. Beam Distilling Co. v. Georgia, 501 U.S. 529 (1991); Griffith v. Kentucky, 479 U.S. 314 (1987).

42 See Harper v. Virginia Dept. of Taxation, supra note 41, at 102–10 (Scalia, J., concurring); James B. Beam Distilling Co. v. Georgia, supra note 41, at 549 (Scalia, J., concurring) (judges should "at least act as if they were 'finding' law").

43 A judge concerned about reliance might warn in one opinion that she intends to disregard a certain precedent rule in a future opinion, but statements of this kind would have no performative effect as overrulings. They too would be given their natural weight in future decision-making.

44 This is something like the "peek" at rules that Frederick Schauer recommends in his defense of "presumptive positivism." See Schauer, supra note 18, at 677. In chapter 4, we discussed some of the difficulties of "presumptive positivism" as an approach to decision-making by rule-subjects. Particularly in the case of coordination rules, the presumptive threshold will be highly unstable because the value any decision-maker assigns to following the rule depends on the value other fallible decision-makers assign to following the rule. A presumptive overruling standard, while likely to be understood differently by different judges, does not suffer from the same weakness. Judges applying such a standard are

assessing the net effect of the rule, assuming it is universally followed. Because this analysis is not dependent on the decisions of others, there is not the same danger that the standard will erode.

Chapter 8. Reasoning from Legal Principles

1 See chapter 7 supra.

2 See chapter 6 supra.

3 See note 1 supra.

4 See the discussion of rules and standards in chapter 2.

5 Ronald Dworkin, *Taking Rights Seriously* 22 (1978).

6 115 N.Y. 506, 22 N.E. 188 (1889).

7 32 N.J. 358, 161 A.2d 69 (1960).

8 Id. at 387, 161 A.2d at 85.

9 Id. at 389, 161 A.2d at 86.

10 Dworkin, supra note 5, at 24–25.

11 Id. at 26.

12 Id.

13 See id. at 110–23, 340–41.

14 See id. at 340–41, 360; Ronald Dworkin, *Law's Empire* chaps. 6, 7 (1986); Larry Alexander and Ken Kress, "Against Legal Principles," 82 *Iowa L. Rev.* 739, 744 (1997); Larry Alexander, "Striking Back at the Empire: A Brief Survey of Problems in Dworkin's 'Theory of Law,'" 6 *Law and Philosophy* 419, 420–21 (1987).

15 See esp. Dworkin, supra note 5, at chaps. 4 (118–19), 6–7.

16 See id. at 37–38. Dworkin is not completely clear whether legal principles are constructed solely from past legal decisions, including decisions under legal rules, or whether they are constructed from both decisions and legal rules qua rules.

17 See Ken Kress, "Legal Indeterminacy," 77 *Cal. L. Rev.* 283, 299–301 (1989).

18 Another way of understanding Dworkin's account of legal principles is to view them as counterfactual moral principles. Thus, we might say that legal principles are principles that would be correct moral principles in a world in which most of the extant legal rules and decisions, including those that are morally incorrect, were morally correct. Such a counterfactual approach is in fact the best description of the dominant methodology for dealing with precedential constraint, what we have called the result model of precedent. See chapter 7 supra; Larry Alexander, "Constrained by Precedent," 63 *S. Cal. L. Rev.* 1, 28–34, 38 (1989). As we said, according to the result model, an incorrectly decided precedent case binds the court in a subsequent case to the extent that, relative to the subsequent case, the precedent case is an a fortiori case in favor of a particular result, even if in the absence of the precedent neither case should be decided that way. And what makes a precedent case an *a fortiori* case is that, *in a world in which its incorrect decisions were correct,* the analogous decision in the subsequent case would also be correct and even more strongly supported. The counterfactual test for employing the result model of precedential constraint is identical

to Dworkin's account of legal principles, the principles that would be morally correct in a world in which certain morally incorrect decisions and rules were morally correct. See Alexander, id. at 28–39.

19 217 N.Y. 382, 111 N.E. 1050 (1916).

20 Melvin Aron Eisenberg, *The Nature of the Common Law* 58–61 (1988); Edward H. Levi, *An Introduction to Legal Reasoning* 7–18 (1948); Henry Hart and Albert Sacks, "The Legal Process" (mimeographed materials published by the *Harv. L. R.,* 1958), 574–77.

21 6 N.Y. 397 (1852).

22 217 N.Y. at 385; 111 N.E. at 1051.

23 217 N.Y. at 385–86; 111 N.E. at 1051–52.

24 10 Meeson and Welsby 109 (1842).

25 217 N.Y. at 394; 111 N.E. at 1054.

26 1 KB 509 (King's Bench, 1945).

27 2 QB 44 (Court of Queen's Bench, 1896).

28 1 KB at 517–18.

29 21 L.J., N.S., 75 (Court of Queen's Bench, 1851).

30 Another case illustrating the reconstructive method is the treatment of Christensen v. Thornby, 255 N.W. 620 (1934), in Sherlock v. Stillwater Clinic, 260 N.W.2d 169 (1977). For an illuminating discussion of these cases, see Eisenberg, supra note 20, at 56–58.

31 Samuel D. Warren and Louis D. Brandeis, "The Right of Privacy," 4 *Harv. L. Rev.* 193 (1890).

32 Id. at 195, 205.

33 Id. at 205.

34 See Dworkin, supra note 5, at 119 (discussing Warren and Brandeis's analysis of privacy as an example of Dworkin's reconstructive method); Kress, supra note 17, at 304.

35 W. Page Keeton, et al., *Prosser and Keeton on the Law of Torts* (5th ed. 1984).

36 Kellogg v. Village of Viola, 67 Wis. 2d 345, 349, 227 N.W.2d 55, 58 (1975).

37 Prosser and Keeton, supra note 35, at 635.

38 Lawrence Alexander and Michael Bayles, "Hercules or Proteus? The Many Theses of Ronald Dworkin," 5 *Soc. Theory and Prac.* 267, 271–78 (1980).

39 Id. at 277.

40 Id. at 272.

41 See also Alexander, supra note 18, at 48–51; Alexander, supra note 14, at 432–33; Larry Alexander, "Pursuing the Good—Indirectly," 95 *Ethics* 315, 317–30 (1985); Larry Alexander, "Modern Equal Protection Theory: A Meta-theoretical Taxonomy and Critique," 42 *Ohio St. L.J.* 3, 12–14 (1981).

42 See Larry Alexander, "The Constitution as Law," 6 *Const. Comment* 103, 107–9 (1989). See also chapter 3 supra.

43 Alexander and Bayles, supra note 38, at 277–78.

44 Ronald Dworkin, supra note 14, chaps. 6, 7. In *Taking Rights Seriously,* the case for principles was grounded in the duty of political officials to act on the basis of an

articulated, consistent justification applying to past, present, and hypothetical governmental actions. Dworkin, supra note 5, at 162–63.

45 Ken Kress, "Coherence and Formalism," 16 *Harv. J.L. Pub. Pol'y* 639, 652–53 n.46 (1993); Dworkin, supra note 5, at 134.

46 Alexander, supra note 14, at 426–31.

47 For a fuller elaboration of Dworkin's conception of Integrity and its difficulties, see Alexander and Kress, supra note 14, at 768–85.

48 See Dworkin, supra note 5, at 30, 44, 84.

49 See Alexander and Bayles, supra note 38, at 284–85.

50 Reliance values, like equality, are theory-dependent, that is, internal to whatever moral theory is correct. No set of incorrect decisions, no matter how numerous, can ever give one reason to depart from applying correct moral principles. Incorrect decisions are, of course, part of the furniture of the world to which correct moral principles apply, and they can and certainly do affect how those principles apply (and whether the principles should be directly or indirectly applied). That is, incorrect decisions in the past can alter what are correct outcomes in the present. But incorrect decisions can never alter the principles by which correctness is gauged. See Alexander, supra note 14, at 430; Alexander and Bayles, supra note 38, at 272.

51 See Kenneth J. Kress, "Legal Reasoning and Coherence Theories: Dworkin's Rights Thesis, Retroactivity, and the Linear Order of Decisions," 72 CAL. L. REV. 369 (1984).

52 The main exceptions are when courts apply law prospectively only, in any of a number of variations—see sources cited in Kress, supra note 51, at 386 n.77; Linda Meyer, "'Nothing We Say Matters': *Teague* and New Rules," 61 *U. Chi. L. Rev.* 423 (1994)—and when courts attempt to avoid retroactive effects on property rights.

53 T. R. S. Allan shares our intuitions about incorrect principles. He, too, argues that principles cannot exist without weight, and that Dworkin's legal principles, being morally incorrect, are always outweighed by correct principles:

> It is important to see that the weight of a principle is a function of the relevant facts. It is the nature of a principle to argue in favour of certain result, but not conclusively: it does not dictate a decision in the manner of a rule, which applies absolutely (subject only to stated or acknowledged exceptions). The weight of a principle can only be determined by the court seised of the particular case and acquainted with the proven facts. . . . A rule may be applied, at least in the case of statutes, by a process of definition. Where a set of circumstances fall within the ambit of the rule, as determined by its enacted terms, no further deliberation is required: the rule dictates a particular result. It is precisely the function of rules to foreclose such deliberation in advance of particular cases arising for decision. By contrast, a principle makes an appeal directly to reason. It follows that [the Dworkinian judge] can only apply a principle he understands and shares and therefore values. Since the weight

of a principle inevitably depends on all the circumstances of the case, its application is always a matter of judgement—necessarily personal judgement.

It is hard to see how [the Dworkinian judge] could determine the weight of a principle whose results he thought unfortunate, perhaps pernicious. If he applied the principle to the extent he thought truly appropriate—ascertaining its weight—he would inevitably reject it altogether. He could not, then, discriminate between particular cases, distinguishing or following precedents in all their complexity, on the basis of a popular conception of principle he himself rejected. It follows that it makes no sense to attempt to compare principles one accepts with those one rejects, even if the latter are popular. The comparison would be wholly theoretical: it could gain no purchase on the particular facts of concrete cases.

T. R. S. Allan, "Justice and Fairness in *Law's Empire*," 52 *Cambridge L.J.* 64, 69–71 (1993) (footnotes omitted). See also M.J. Detmold, *The Unity of Law and Morality* 83–93 (1984); Alexander, supra note 14, at 431–32 n.20.

54 See Peter Westen, "The Empty Idea of Equality," 95 *Harv. L. Rev.* 537 (1982).

55 We cannot do better in terms of morally significant equal treatment than to treat everyone in accordance with our current best view of justice. A past injustice creates no reason, not even a very weak one, to commit a present injustice. See chapter 7 supra; Alexander, supra note 18, at 9–13; Alexander, supra note 14, at 426–31.

56 See John Rawls, "Outline of a Decision Procedure for Ethics," 60 *Phil. Rev.* 177 (1951); John Rawls, *A Theory of Justice* 14–21 (esp. 19–21), 43–53, 578–82 (1971); Norman Daniels, "Wide Reflective Equilibrium and Theory Acceptance," 76 *J. Phil.* 256 (1979).

57 See Dworkin, supra note 5, at 159–66.

58 See chapter 6 supra.

59 See Daniels, supra note 56.

60 See chapter 6 supra.

61 Owen Fiss, "Objectivity and Interpretation," 34 *Stan. L. Rev.* 739 (1982); Dworkin, supra note 14, at chap. 3 (discussing conventionalism).

62 Dworkin would agree with us on this point. See Dworkin, supra note 14, at 120–39.

Chapter 9. Legal Positivism and Natural Law

1 See chapter 3 supra.

2 See Stewart J. Schwab, "Limited-Domain Positivism as an Empirical Proposition," 82 *Corn. L. Rev.* 1111 (1997).

3 See Jules L. Coleman, "Incorporationism, Conventionalism, and the Practical Difference Thesis," 4 *Legal Theory* 381, 391, 399 (1998); Richard Holton, "Positivism and the Internal Point of View," 17 *Law and Phil.* 597 (1998); Michael Moore, "Hart's Concluding Scientific Postscript," 4 *Legal Theory* 301, 307–8 (1998); Philip Soper, "Two Puzzles from the Postscript," 4 *Legal Theory* 329, 333–35 (1998); Brian

Bix, "Jules Coleman, Legal Positivism, and Legal Authority," 16 *QLR* 241, 252 (1996); Joseph Raz, "The Purity of the Pure Theory," 35 *Revue internationale de philosophie* 441, 455 (1981).

4 See Larry Alexander, "Law and Exclusionary Reasons," 18 *Phil. Topics* 5, 10 (1990).

5 See chapter 10 infra.

6 Both natural lawyers and positivists attribute moral functions to law. See, e.g., Moore, supra note 3, at 313 n.51, 327 (attributing a moral function to law from a natural lawyer's perspective); Joseph Raz, "Authority, Law and Morality," 68 *Monist* 295, 315 (1985) (attributing a moral function to law from a positivist's perspective).

Although both natural lawyers and positivists attribute a moral function to law, some natural lawyers assert, and positivists deny, that this attribution undermines positivism. See, e.g., Gerald J. Postema, "Jurisprudence as Practical Philosophy," 4 *Legal Theory* 329, 333–35, 355–56 (1998); Stephen R. Perry, "Hart's Methodological Positivism," 4 *Legal Theory* 427, 457–58, 464–66 (1998); Holton, supra note 3; Joseph Raz, "Intention in Interpretation," in *The Autonomy of Law* 249, 261 (Robert P. George, ed., 1996).

7 See chapter 10 infra.

8 See id.

9 Joseph Raz, *The Authority of Law* (1979).

10 Id. at 42–43.

11 Id. at 43–45.

12 Id. at 47–49.

13 Id. at 50–51.

14 Joseph Raz, "Authority, Law and Morality," supra note 6.

15 Id. at 296.

16 Id. at 296–97.

17 Id. at 297–98.

18 Id. at 299.

19 Id. at 300.

20 Id. at 301–2.

21 Id. at 303.

22 Id.

23 Id. at 304.

24 Id. at 303–4.

25 Id. at 304.

26 Id. at 304–5.

27 Id. at 305–6.

28 Id. at 315–16.

29 See chapter 2 supra.

30 As we also pointed out, Raz could say that what makes the evaluative matters determinate is the "social fact" of agreement on their application.

31 See note 30 supra.

32 Jules Coleman is a leading inclusive legal positivist who accepts the principal

inclusivist thesis, namely, that morality can be a condition of legality. See Coleman, supra note 3, at 382–83. Coleman is a positivist in that he rejects the natural lawyer's contention that morality can be a sufficient condition of legality and deems the existence of a social convention regarding what shall count as practically authoritative to be a necessary condition. Id. at 385. H. L. A. Hart is also widely interpreted to have accepted the inclusive legal positivist position. See H. L. A. Hart, *The Concept of Law* 250–54 (P. Bullock and J. Raz eds., 2d ed. 1994); Coleman, supra note 3, at 382 n.5.

33 The same point applies to rules directing judges to apply moral principles to cases not governed by preexisting rules, or to resolve interpretive difficulties by recourse to moral principles. The inclusive legal positivist would deem moral principles to be "law" in such cases because they are made binding by rules that are unquestionably law.

34 See Scott J. Shapiro, "On Hart's Way Out," 4 *Legal Theory* 469, 495, 504 (1998).

35 There are several more arrows in the exclusive legal positivist's quiver. First, there is Raz's argument from the nature of authority, that the mediating role of authority entails that an authoritative directive must be identifiable without consulting the reasons on which the directive is based. See Raz, supra note 5, at 303. See also Coleman, supra note 3, at 413–14.

Raz's argument has been countered by Jules Coleman. Coleman rejects both that law must be a practical authority in Raz's sense and also more generally that law need serve an epistemic (identification) function with respect to what ought to be done. Id. at 415–20. See also Jules L. Coleman, "Second Thoughts and Other First Impressions," in *Analyzing Law* 257, 270–75 (B. Bix ed., 1998).

Coleman accepts a strong inclusivist positivist position that would encompass as "law" "Do what is morally required" if there were a social rule to that effect. The fact that "what is morally required" is controversial does not concern Coleman because he denies that law necessarily serves an epistemic function and that it must meet the Razian test of authoritativeness. (Raz, too, denies that the controversiality of morality is what undermines inclusive legal positivism. For him, morality cannot function as a test of legality because moral reasons are the reasons on which legal rules and decisions are dependent, and authoritative rules and decisions must be identifiable apart from such dependent reasons. See text at note 24 supra. We, on the other hand, in stressing the settlement function of Lex and his rules, are concerned precisely with controversiality and only secondarily with whether the terms of rules are factual or evaluative. See text at notes 29–30 supra. Others have asserted the primacy of law's epistemic function. See, e.g., Brian Leiter, "Realism, Moral Positivism, and Conceptual Analysis," 4 *Legal Theory* 533, 537–39 (1998); Eleni Mitrophanous, "Soft Positivism," 17 *Oxford J. Legal Stud.* 621, 628, 634 (1997).)

Coleman's position has been attacked, however, on the ground that no social rule such as "Do what is morally required" can be said to exist if there is disagreement over what is morally required. Coleman distinguishes between the content of such a rule and its application. See Coleman, supra note 3, at

410–11; Coleman, "Second Thoughts and Other First Impressions," supra, at 264; Jules L. Coleman, "Negative and Positive Positivism," 11 *J. Legal Stud.* 139, 159–60 (1982). Will Waluchow argues, however, that if the basic rule incorporates controversial moral matters, then those who accept "it" will actually be accepting different rules corresponding to their different moral views. See W. J. Waluchow, "The Many Faces of Legal Positivism," 48 *U. Toronto L.J.* 387, 427 (1998). The same criticism has been leveled by Eleni Mitrophanous supra, at 640–41.

Because Coleman accepts a strong version of inclusive legal positivism that would make morality a sufficient condition of legality so long as there existed a social rule to that effect, he also accepts weaker versions, such as those that would make morality a necessary condition of legality or that would make some part of morality a necessary condition of legality. With respect to the latter, Coleman claims that such a condition would be consistent with the Razian conception of authority because the moral principles that limit the law might be different from those on which the law is based. See Jules L. Coleman, "Authority and Reason," in *The Autonomy of Law* 287, 306 (Robert P. George ed., 1996). See also Jules L. Coleman and Brian Leiter, "Legal Positivism," in *A Companion to Philosophy of Law and Legal Theory* 241, 255–57 (D. Patterson ed., 1996). Others have argued, however, that Coleman's picture assumes that the moral principles that underlie the law can be cabined off from those that limit it, a picture that would be inaccurate if moral principles either were seamless or did not fissure along the lines the law assumes. See Anthony J. Sebok, *Legal Positivism in American Jurisprudence* 295–314 (1998); Mitrophanous, supra, at 637–39.

The weaker version of positivism, namely, that morality can be a necessary condition for law, has been attacked by Scott Shapiro on the ground that if law's existence were conditioned on its morality, law would not guide conduct, either epistemically or motivationally, in the way the rules guide conduct—peremptorily, without regard to their merits. Shapiro, supra note 34, at 501–2. Shapiro's argument is subtle; he distinguishes between moral conditions that are part of a rule and limit its application and those that are a test for its legality. Only the latter moral conditions deprive law of its capacity to guide behavior. But they do so irrespective of whether they are the moral conditions on which the rules are dependent in a Razian sense. In other words, for Shapiro, *any* evaluative conditions that operate as a test for whether a rule is a "law" are ruled out, not only because they are inconsistent with the Razian conception of authority, which Raz asserts that all law claims, but because they undermine law's capacity to guide conduct through rules. Id. at 476, 494–96, 507. Law must make a practical difference, and morality as a condition of law's existence—as opposed to a limitation on application built into every individual legal rule—renders law incapable of making a practical difference. Id. at 504. For a later refinement of Shapiro's position, see Scott J. Shapiro, "Law, Morality, and the Guidance of Conduct," 6 *Legal Theory* 127 (2000) (responding to various defenses of inclusive legal positivism).

Shapiro makes a related argument against those forms of inclusive legal positivism that allow morality to be a *sufficient* condition of legality: if morality were sufficient for legality, then no rules validated by the basic rule could make a practical difference; the basic rule itself would provide all the guidance of conduct. Shapiro, supra note 34, at 499–500; Scott J. Shapiro, "The Difference That Rules Make," in *Analyzing Law* 53, 57–59 (B. Bix ed., 1998).

36 Exclusive legal positivists like Raz and Shapiro are concerned with guidance, identification, and authority—law's practical function. Inclusive legal positivists like Hart, Coleman, and Waluchow are concerned with ontology—law's existence. See note 35 supra.

37 See, e.g., Coleman, supra note 35, at 280–85; Brian Leiter, "Rethinking Legal Realism: Toward A Naturalized Jurisprudence," 76 *Texas L. Rev.* 267 (1997).

38 See Brian Leiter, "Legal Realism," in *A Companion to the Philosophy of Law and Legal Theory* 261, 268–69 (D. Patterson ed., 1996).

39 M. J. Detmold, *The Unity of Law and Morality* (1984).

40 Id. at 21–72, 123–29.

41 Id. at 37–38.

42 Id. at 58–60.

43 See chapter 3 supra.

44 Dworkin is not a pure natural lawyer because for him a proper interpretation of the law must "fit" with a certain quantity of the legal materials, which if sufficiently at odds with morality, will result in immoral law. See chapter 8, supra. However, because Dworkin regards integrity—the principle that compels the requirement of "fit"—as itself a moral principle, one can view him as a pure natural lawyer who, because of integrity, regards morality as potentially self-effacing. See Larry Alexander and Kenneth Kress, "Replies to Our Critics," 82 *Iowa L. Rev.* 923, 937–38 (1997).

45 H. L. A. Hart, supra note 32, at 97–107.

46 Id. at 105–06.

47 Ronald Dworkin, *Taking Rights Seriously* 53–58 (1977).

48 Id. at 53.

49 Id. at 58, 62.

50 Id.

51 See chapter 3 supra.

52 See Dworkin, supra note 47, at 53.

53 See chapter 3 supra.

54 See Waluchow, supra note 35, at 429.

55 See Dworkin, supra note 47, at 63–64.

56 See chapter 5 supra.

57 Dworkin, supra note 47, at 64.

58 Roger A. Shiner, *Norm and Nature* 13 (1992).

59 Id. at 326.

60 See chapter 4 supra.

61 See chapter 4 supra.

Of course, this dilemmatic relationship can result in diachronic movements in law from rules to standards to rules ad infinitum. It can result in synchronic rules-standards divisions within courts and legislatures. And it can result in tensions between law and equity, procedure and substance, finality and correctness. These could perhaps be characterized as "dialectical" relationships, though we think "dilemmatic" is a more accurate characterization.

62 One of us has made such a claim elsewhere. See Larry Alexander, "'With Me, It's All er Nuthin': Formalism in Law and Morality," 66 *U. Chi. L. Rev.* 530 (1999); Larry Alexander, "Can Law Survive the Asymmetry of Authority?," in *Rules and Reasoning* 39 (L. Meyer ed., 1999).

63 See Joseph Raz, *The Authority of Law* (1979). See also Shapiro, supra note 34 (defending exclusive legal positivism from the standpoint of law's function of guidance by rules).

64 See Frederick Schauer, *Playing by the Rules: A Philosophical Examination of Rule-Based Decision-Making in Law and Life* (1991).

65 See Thomas Campbell, *The Legal Theory of Ethical Positivism* (1996).

66 John Austin, *The Province of Jurisprudence Determined* (1832).

67 Hans Kelsen, *General Theory of Law and State* (1949).

68 See Hart, supra note 32.

69 Stephen R. Perry, "Hart's Methodological Positivism," 4 *Legal Theory* 427, 457–58 (1998) (emphasis in original).

70 Id. at 466.

71 Gerald J. Postema, "Jurisprudence as Practical Philosophy," 4 *Legal Theory* 329, 355–56 (1998) (emphasis in original; footnote omitted).

Jules Coleman describes the views of Perry and Postema thus:

> The aim of jurisprudence is to shed light on actual legal practice. There are many ways of shedding light, but the distinctive philosophical method is to do so by analyzing the concepts that figure prominently within it. In analyzing the concept of law, the theorist specifies the features of law one deems especially important or central. A theory of law is a contestable conception of law, reflecting, as it must, an account of law's function or purpose. Disputes between or among conflicting legal theories are ultimately normative disputes, resolvable by substantive moral and political argument.
>
> In evaluating a jurisprudence, one, therefore, has to assess not only the explanation it provides of the "data"—the law—but also the plausibility of its conception of the person presupposed by the theory as well as its account of the purpose or function of law. Legal theory is thus a branch of normative philosophy in two senses: a jurisprudential theory is itself a normative theory; disputes between or among theories are resolvable by recourse to moral or political theory.

Jules L. Coleman, "Incorporationism, Conventionality, and the Practical Difference Thesis," 4 *Legal Theory* 381, 387 (1998). Coleman himself rejects the Perry/Postema position he characterizes, at least insofar as it implies that the normative elements of legal theory make a general, descriptive jurisprudence impossible. See id. at 388, 392 n.23, 412 n.47. In Coleman's view, the positivist enterprise, as exemplified by Hart, is to identify the essential features a social practice must have in order to qualify as law, and those features do not depend on a controversial view of law's purpose. They are the features that all theories of law must have in common. See id. at 391–94.

72 See, e.g., Coleman, supra note 71, at 392.

73 See Joseph Raz, "Authority, Law and Morality," 68 *Monist* 295, 320 (1985).

74 See Shapiro, supra note 34.

75 See Larry Alexander and Frederick Schauer,"On Extrajudicial Constitutional Interpretation," 110 *Harv. L. Rev.* 1359 (1997).

76 This is the assumption that we are making in this section.

77 See Michael Moore, "Hart's Concluding Scientific Postscript," 4 *Legal Theory* 301, 327 (1998).

78 See Brian Leiter, "Realism, Hard Positivism, and Conceptual Analysis," 4 *Legal Theory* 533, 544–46 (1988) (disputing Perry's position that attributing a function to law in order to do conceptual analysis of it requires a normative argument).

79 See Joseph Raz, "Intention in Interpretation," in *The Autonomy of Law* 249, 260 (Robert P. George ed., 1996).

80 Id. at 261.

81 We did, however, raise the possibility that authoritative rules, in attempting to achieve moral improvement by reducing the sum of moral errors, might violate deontological side-constraints. See chapter 4 supra.

82 See id.

83 See Thomas C. Schelling, *The Strategy of Conflict* 18 (1980).

84 See Brian Z. Tamanaha, *Realistic Socio-Legal Theory* 183 (1997). And see Coleman, supra note 71, at 387–88 (rejecting Ronald Dworkin's conception of jurisprudential methodology, namely, that jurisprudence should aim at making law the best that it can be and that the line between committed and detached legal statements is untenable—see Ronald Dworkin, *Law's Empire* 13–14, 45–86 (1986)).

85 On this point we disagree with Anthony Sebok. See Anthony J. Sebok, "Is the Rule of Recognition a Rule?," 76 *Notre Dame L. Rev.* 1539 (1997).

86 See text at notes 23–24 supra; note 35 supra.

87 See Jules L. Coleman, "Rules and Social Facts," 14 *Harv. J.L. and Pub. Pol'y* 703, 720 (1991).

88 Nor do we believe Shapiro's arguments on behalf of exclusive legal positivism are conclusive. See note 35 supra.

Chapter 10. Lex, Rules, and Some Miscellaneous Problems of Jurisprudence

1 See chapter 3 supra.

2 This position has probably now attained the status of an orthodoxy. See. e.g., Frederick Schauer, "Amending the Presuppositions of the Constitution," in *Re-*

sponding to Imperfection: The Theory and Practice of Constitutional Amendment 145 (Sanford Levinson ed., 1995); Richard S. Kay, "American Constitutionalism," in *Constitutionalism: Philosophical Foundations* 16, 58 n.108 (Larry Alexander ed., 1998). See also Larry Alexander, "Introduction," in Alexander, *Constitutionalism,* supra at 1, 3.

3 "This Constitution . . . shall be the Supreme Law of the Land." U.S. Const., art. I, sec. 2.

4 See chapter 3 supra.

5 See chapter 4 supra.

6 See id. See chapter 7 supra.

7 See pp. 213–14. Note that Lex's inability to bring about a tolerable level of obedience to his rules will create a moral reason, based on the benefits of coordination, for Lex's adherents to switch their allegiance to someone else who is more powerful vis-à-vis miscreants and dissenters and/or more widely acceptable.

8 H. L. A. Hart, *The Concept of Law* 113 (1961). (Hart does not require the officials to accept the basic rule on moral grounds—see id. at 198–99; Philip Soper, *A Theory of Law* 174–75 n.38 (1984); Joseph Raz, *The Authority of Law* 154–55 (1979); Stephen R. Perry, "Hart's Methodological Positivism," 4 *Legal Theory* 427, 454–55 (1998)—but many positivists believe that Hart should have required moral acceptance. See, e.g., Soper, supra, at 38–51.)

9 See, e.g., Kent Greenawalt, *Conflicts of Law and Morality* (1987); John Finnis, *Natural Law and Natural Rights* 354–62 (1980); Michael S. Moore, "Law as a Functional Kind," in *Natural Law Theory* 188, 198–200, 213–15 (Robert P. George ed., 1992).

10 See Raz, supra note 8, at 233–49; M. B. E. Smith, "Is There a Prima Facie Obligation to Obey the Law?," 82 *Yale L.J.* 950 (1973).

11 Philip Soper has argued that respect for those who are in good faith attempting to achieve morally proper results through law should result in a *prima facie* obligation to obey it. See Soper, supra note 8, at 57–90. Most positivists do not accept Soper's conclusion that an obligation to obey immoral laws is the proper way to show respect for lawmakers who act in good faith but are morally misguided.

12 As we have pointed out repeatedly, a nonideal rule may be but an "application" of an ideal more basic rule—e.g., "Let Lex decide"—and a basic rule that is non-ideal may be ideal in the sense that it is the morally best rule that all will accept, where acceptance by all is morally preferable to its absence.

13 The moral theory of what to criminalize and what justifies criminal punishment is, of course, a well-established department of moral theory. Somewhat less well-established is the moral theory of adjudicative procedures. But that does not mean moral theorizing about such procedures is unheard of. See, e.g., Larry Alexander, "Are Procedural Rights Derivative Substantive Rights?," 17 *Law and Phil.* 19 (1998).

14 See Gregory S. Kavka, "Why Even Morally Perfect People Would Need Government," 12 *Soc. Phil. and Pol'y* 1 (1995).

15 See Jules L. Coleman, "Second Thoughts and Other First Impressions," in *Analyzing Law* 257, 290 (B. Bix ed., 1998); Jules L. Coleman and Brian Leiter, "Determinateness, Objectivity, and Authority," 142 *U. Pa. L. Rev.* 549, 608–9 (1993).

16 See Coleman, supra note 15, at 289–90.

17 See id. at 291; Coleman and Leiter, supra note 15, at 608, 616–20.

18 Obviously, it is possible to have an elite's or even one person's beliefs fix the standards for fashion. Nonetheless, fashion would be minimally objective for everyone else.

19 See Coleman, supra note 15, at 292.

20 See Coleman, supra note 15, at 291–92; Coleman and Leiter, supra note 15, at 621–25.

21 See Coleman and Leiter, supra note 15, at 627. Leiter characterizes legal facts as minimally objective. Id. We are somewhat skeptical about the notion of modest objectivity, because we suspect that full specification of ideal conditions of observations may eliminate the element of judgment that separates modest objectivity from strong objectivity. In any event, we are skeptical about the application of modest objectivity to law. For our position, see text accompanying note 27 infra.

22 See Coleman and Leiter, supra note 15, at 630.

23 See Coleman, supra note 15, at 285; Coleman and Leiter, supra note 15, at 587.

24 See Coleman, supra note 15, at 287 n.46.

25 Given what we said in chapter 9, we do not mean by labeling this question "the legal question" to be taking a jurisprudential stand in favor of positivism in general or exclusive legal positivism in particular.

26 See Coleman and Leiter, supra note 15, at 626–27.

27 As we said in chapter 5, we agree with Coleman and Leiter that the "Kripkenstein" analysis of rules and rule-following does not undermine the possibility of rules' determinateness or objectivity. See chapter 5 supra; Coleman and Leiter, supra note 15, at 568–73.

INDEX

Larry Alexander is Warren Distinguished Professor of Law at the University of San Diego. He is the author of various works, including *Legal Rules and Legal Reasoning* (2000) and (with Paul Horton) *Whom Does the Constitution Command?: A Conceptual Analysis with Practical Implications* (1998). Emily Sherwin is Professor of Law at the University of San Diego.

Library of Congress Cataloging-in-Publication Data
Alexander, Larry
The rule of rules : morality, rules, and the dilemmas of law / Larry Alexander and Emily Sherwin.
p. cm. Includes index.
ISBN 0-8223-2736-8 (cloth : alk. paper)
1. Jurisprudence. 2. Law and ethics. 3. Law—Philosophy. I. Sherwin, Emily. II. Title.
K247.6 .A43 2001 340'.1—dc21 2001025091